Denmark and EC Membership Evaluated

EC Membership Evaluated Series
Series Editor: Carl-Christoph Schweitzer, The University of Bonn

The Netherlands and EC Membership Evaluated
ed. Menno Wolters and Peter Coffey

Federal Republic of Germany and EC Membership Evaluated
ed. Carl-Christoph Schweitzer and Detlev Karsten

Ireland and EC Membership Evaluated
ed. Patrick Keatinge

The United Kingdom and EC Membership Evaluated
ed. Simon Bulmer, Stephen George and Andrew Scott

Denmark and EC Membership Evaluated
ed. Lise Lyck

Italy and EC Membership Evaluated
ed. Francesco Francioni

Belgium and EC Membership Evaluated
ed. M.A.G. van Meerhaeghe

Denmark and EC Membership Evaluated

Edited by Lise Lyck

Pinter Publishers
London
St. Martin's Press
New York

Pinter Publishers
25 Floral Street, Covent Garden, London, WC2E 9DS, United Kingdom
and **St. Martins Press**
175 Fifth Avenue, New York, NY 10010

First published in 1992

British Library Cataloguing in Publication Data

A CIP catalogue record for this book is available from the British Library.

ISBN 0 86187 898 1 (Pinter)
ISBN 0 312 09081 1 (St. Martin's)

Library of Congress Cataloging in Publication Data

Denmark and EC membership evaluated/edited by Lise Lyck.
p. cm.
Includes index.
ISBN 0–86187–898–1. – ISBN 0–312–09081–1 (St. Martin's Press)
1. Denmark – Relations – European Economic Community countries.
2. European Economic Community countries – Relations – Denmark.
I. Lyck, Lise.
DL261.D46 1993
948.905'9–dc20 92–30749
CIP

Typeset by Mayhew Typesetting, Rhayader, Powys
Printed and bound in Great Britain by Biddles Ltd., Guildford and King's Lynn

Contents

List of contributors

Bislev, Sven, Copenhagen Business School, Center for International Business Administration and Modern Languages, Dalgas Have 15, DK-2000 Frederiksberg; Phone 45 31 19 19 19; Fax 45 - 31 86 11 88.

Bregnsbo, Henning, University of Copenhagen, Institute of Political Studies, St. Kannikestræde 13, DK-1169 Copenhagen K; Phone 45 - 33 91 08 28; Fax 45 - 33 32 27 28.

Duelund, Peter, University of Copenhagen, Department of Cultural Sociology, Linnésgade 22, DK-1361 Copenhagen K; Phone 45 - 33 15 05 20.

Friis, Peter, Roskilde University Centre, Postbox 260, DK-4000 Roskilde; Phone 45 - 46 75 77 11; Fax 45 46 75 74 01.

Hansen, Per Vejrup, Copenhagen Business School, Institute of Industrial Research and Social Development, Nansensgade 19, 6, DK-1366 Copenhagen K; Phone 45 - 38 15 25 35; Fax 45 - 38 15 25 40.

Hoffmann, Peter, Department of Energy, Slotsholmsgade 1, DK-1216 Copenhagen K; Phone 45 - 33 92 75 00; Fax 45 - 33 12 87 07.

Jensen, Hans Rask, Business School South, Grundtvigs Allé 150, DK-6400 Sønderborg; Phone 45 - 74 43 42 25; Fax 45 - 74 43 01 93.

Lyck, Lise, Copenhagen Business School, Institute of Economics, Nansensgade 19, 5, DK-1366 Copenhagen K; Phone 45 - 38 15 25 75; Fax 45 - 38 15 25 76.

Nedergaard, Peter, Copenhagen Business School, Institute of International Economics and Management, Nansensgade 19, 7, DK-1366 Copenhagen K; Phone 45 - 38 15 25 15; Fax 45 - 38 15 25 00.

Nehring, Niels Jørgen, The Prime Minister's Department, Prins Jørgens Gaard 11, DK-1218 Copenhagen K; Phone 45 - 33 92 33 00; Fax 45 - 33 11 16 65.

Nielsen, Ruth, Copenhagen Business School, Departmente Law, Nansensgade 19, 2, DK-1366 Copenhagen K; Phone 45 - 38 15 26 26; Fax 45 - 38 15 26 10.

Nørgaard, Gert, Copenhagen Business School, The Management Research Institute, Rosenørns Allé 31, 1970 Frederiksberg C; Phone 45 - 38 15 36 30; Fax 45 - 38 15 36 15.

Sauerberg, Steen, University of Copenhagen, Institute of Political Studies, St. Kannikestræde 13, DK-1169 Copenhagen K; Phone 45 - 33 91 08 28; Fax 45 - 33 32 27 28.

Schou, Tove Lise, University of Copenhagen, Institute of Political Studies, St. Kannikestræde 13, DK-1169 Copenhagen K; Phone 45 - 33 91 08 28; Fax 45 - 33 32 27 28.

Sørensen, Henning, University of Copenhagen, Centre for Peace and Conflict Research, Vandkunsten 5, DK-1467 Copenhagen K; Phone 45 - 33 32 64 32; Fax 45 - 33 91 18 283.

Sølvkjær, Evan, Competition Council, EC/International Secretariat, Nørregade 49, DK-1165 Copenhagen K; Phone 45 - 33 93 90 00; Fax 45 - 33 32 61 44.

Væver, Ole, University of Copenhagen, Centre for Peace and Conflict Research, Vandkunsten 5, DK-1467 Copenhagen K; Phone 45 - 33 32 64 32; Fax 45 - 33 91 18 28.

Waagstein, Eigil, Teledanmark, Telegade 2, DK-2630 Tåstrup; Phone 45 - 42 52 91 11; Fax 45 - 42 52 93 31.

Østergaard, Uffe, University of Aarhus, Centre for Cultural Research, Finlandsgade 26, DK-8200 Aarhus N; Phone 45 - 86 16 36 11; Fax 45 - 86 10 82 28.

Series introduction

This volume is one in a series entitled *European Community Membership Evaluated*. The series examines the gains and losses of European Community (EC) membership for a number of the twelve states.

Over the entire period since the first steps in European integration were taken, with the formation of the European Coal and Steel Community, the impact of membership upon the individual states has been both a matter of importance to, and an issue for evaluation by, the political parties, interest groups, government elites, researchers and, increasingly, the public at large. The renewed dynamism of the EC in the period following the signing of the Single European Act in 1986, and the approach of the completed internal market by the end of 1992, have raised awareness of EC membership to new heights.

It is against this backdrop that the project leading to this series was undertaken. Policy-makers and the European electorate alike require the information to make informed judgements about national gains and losses (or costs and benefits) arising from EC membership.

- How far have the EC's economic policies brought gains?
- Does EC membership impose constraints on the powers of national and regional/local government, or on the legal system?
- What have been the effects of the hitherto somewhat disparate EC activities in the social, cultural and educational policy areas?
- What are the gains and losses of foreign policy co-operation among the member states?
- How pronounced are the specific national interests of the individual member states?

In order to answer questions such as these, each volume brings together a team of specialists from various disciplines. Although the national teams are composed predominantly of academics, the series is aimed at a readership beyond the confines of the education world. Thus each volume seeks to present its findings in a manner accessible to *all* those affected by, or interested in, the EC. Extensive footnoting of academic literature is avoided, although some guidance is offered on the legal bases of EC policies; a bibliography at the end of each study gives guidance on narrower sectoral impact studies and on further reading.

A distinctive feature of the series as a whole is that a common framework has been followed for all eleven studies. This is aimed at facilitating comparison between the national studies. No systematic international comparative study of this kind has been attempted before. Indeed, for some member states there exists no study of the impact of EC membership. The absence of such a series of studies initially seemed rather surprising. However, as the project progressed, the reasons for this became clearer. It is by no means easy to find a common framework acceptable to the academic traditions of all the member states *and* all the policy areas and academic disciplines involved.

The project co-ordinators experienced these tensions in a striking way. Their international 'summit meetings' meant reaching compromises acceptable to all the diverse academic traditions of the countries involved. Then the individual national contributors had to be convinced of the merits of the international compromises. These negotiations brought many insights into precisely the type of problem faced by EC policy-makers themselves. Hence academic perfectionism has been subordinated to some extent to pragmatism and the wish to address a wider readership.

In some countries, for instance the Netherlands, Great Britain, Portugal and Germany, up to thirty scholars of various disciplines make up the national team. In other countries, such as Ireland, a team numbers less than ten authors. In the latter, *one* author deals with several parts of a subject-group or even with the whole of a subject-group. In either case, however, authors have assured comparability by making cross-references to subsections of policies.

The basic principle of the project has been to assess the gains and losses of EC membership for the individual state, with the hypothetical alternative in mind of that state leaving the EC. This alternative may be deemed to be somewhat simplistic but it is far more manageable than making assumptions about where individual states would be, had they not joined the EC in the first place. Such speculation is virtually impossible scientifically and would undermine efforts to make the findings accessible to a wider readership. The terms 'benefits', 'gains' and 'positive effects', and 'costs', 'losses' and 'negative effects', respectively, are used synonymously.

The activities of the EC, together with the foreign policy co-operation process EPC (European Political Co-operation), are grouped under four broad headings in the project (see Table A at the end of this Introduction). *Economic policy* covers a range of EC policies: from the internal market to the Common Agricultural Policy but also including environmental policy. *Foreign relations* comprise not only European Political Co-operation but also the EC's external trade policy and security policy. *Social and educational policy* brings together the rather disparate measures taken in a range of areas, some of which are now coming to be regarded as forming the 'social dimension' of the EC. Finally, the subject area *political and legal system* refers not to EC policies but rather to the EC's impact upon the principles and practices of government.

Each of the EC policy headings is assessed following a common approach. The objectives of the EC policy, and the accomplishments thus far, are assessed against the equivalent set of national policy goals and legislation, many of them common to all countries, some of them obviously specific national ones. The idea, then, is to arrive at a 'balance sheet', both at the level of the individual policy area or sector and, at the macro level, for the member state as a whole. Drawing up the individual sectoral balance sheets has to involve a rather flexible approach. The 'mix' of quantitative and qualitative assessments varies according to the subject matter. There can be no quantitative data on how far foreign policy co-operation has brought gains to national foreign policy; figures may be available, however, on the impact of EC trade policy on national trade patterns. In the case of quantitative data it is important to note that very little, if any, primary statistical research was involved in the project. In consequence, quantitative assessments generally present available evidence from previous studies; they follow no consistent methodological approach while qualitative assessments are often arrived at for the first time. One further point must be made with regard to the common approach of the project: it is clear that the importance of individual EC policy areas varies from one member state to another.

It follows, therefore, that the weighting, and in some cases the categorization, of EC policy areas will vary between the national studies. To assign the same weight to fisheries policy in the British and Luxembourg cases, for instance, would be irrational. Some national policy goals and national interests are related to specific interests of some member countries; for instance, the German question and the problem of Northern Ireland are specific to the Federal Republic, Ireland and the United Kingdom respectively.

The whole project has been brought to fruition under the auspices of 'Europe-12 – Research and Action Committee on the EC'. Created in 1986, Europe-12 brings together academics of all disciplines and from all member states, as well as policy-makers and senior politicians. It aims to inform the policy debate through collaborative research and to raise public awareness of the important issues raised by European integration.

As with any such project, a large number of acknowledgements must be made. A number of the participants took on the additional task of horizontal co-ordination, i.e. seeking to ensure consistency of approach across the national studies. For *economic policy* this was undertaken by Detlev Karsten, Bonn, and Peter Coffey, Amsterdam; for *foreign relations* by Carl-Christoph Schweitzer, Bonn, and Rudolf Hrbek, Tübingen; for contributions on *the political and legal system* by Francesco Francioni, Siena, and K. Kellermann, The Hague; finally, for *social and educational policies* by Bernard Henningsen, Munich and Brigitte Mohr, Bonn. Sadly, Guenther Kloss, a co-ordinator of the British volume, died during the preparation of the series.

Last but by no means least, we are indebted to the Commission of the EC and to those bodies supporting the project: the German foundations, Stifterverband für die Deutsche Wissenschaft, Essen; Bosch GmbH, Stuttgart; Ernst Poensgen-Stiftung, Düsseldorf; as well as the Government of the Saarland and the Federal Ministry for Science and Technology, Bonn. The British and German Studies were made possible by the support of the Anglo-German Foundation for the Study of Industrial Society, London.

Carl-Christoph Schweitzer
Bonn

Table A: Project's categorization of EC policies and structures

I	**Economic policy**	
	Internal market policy	Agricultural policy
	Competition policy	Environmental policy
	Industrial policy	Fiscal/taxation policy
	Technology policy	Monetary policy
	Transport and communications policy	Regional policy
	Energy policy	
II	**Foreign relations**	
	Foreign policy co-operation	Development policy
	Security policy	External trade policy
III	**Political and legal system**	
	Sovereignty	National legal system
	Parliamentary control of the executive	Judicial procedures
	Electoral system	Maintenance of public order
	Political parties	Protection of fundamental rights
	Regional and local government	State organization
	Policy-making process	
IV	**Social, educational and cultural policies**	
	Manpower (employment/unemployment)	Consumer protection
	Movement of labour and migrant workers	Education and training
	Industrial relations	European identity and cultural policies
	Social security and health	
	Equal treatment of men and women	Media policy

Note: This list was a schematic guideline for the project; not every subsection will be dealt with individually and the sequence is purely illustrative.

Europe-12: Action and Research Committee on the EC

Hon. President:
Lord Jenkins of Hillhead
Chancellor of the University of Oxford
H.E. Emilio Colombo,
Minister Rome

Board:
Chairman: Former Minister Dr Ottokar Hahn
Senior Advisor, EC Commission, Brussels

Vice-Chairmen:
Prof Dr Hélène Ahrweiler
Rector and Chancellor, University of Paris
Enrico Baron Crespo, MEP,
President European Parliament Brussels, Madrid
Piet Dankert
Undersecretary, Foreign Office, den Haag
Dr Garret FitzGerald
former Prime Minister, Dublin
Niels Anker Kofoed, MP
former Minister, Copenhagen
Dr Hans Stercken, MP
Chairman Bundestag Foreign Affairs Committee, Bonn
Franz Ludwig Graf von Stauffenberg, MEP
Representative of the President of the European Parliament

Senior Economic Advisor:
Dr Otto Graf Lambsdorff, MP
former Minister of Economics, National Chairman FDP, Bundestag, Bonn

Co-ordinator of Committees:
Prof Dr C. C. Schweitzer
University of Bonn, Political Science

Steering Committee:
Spokesman: Dr Renate Hellwig, MP
Bundestag, Bonn, Chairman Sub-Committee on Europe
Dr Peter Baehr
Netherlands Scientific Council, The Hague
Prof Dr P. D. Dagtoglou
University of Athens, Law
W. Dondelinger, MP
Chairman Foreign Affairs Committee, Luxembourg
Prof. Dr Francesco Francioni
University of Siena, Law
Fernand Herman, MEP
Chairman Institutional Committee, EP, Brussels
Dr J. de Silva Lopes
Caixa General de Depositos, Lisbon, Economics
Anthony J. Nicholls
Senior Fellow, St Antony's College, Oxford
Dr Hans-J. Seeler
Chairman FVS Foundation, Hamburg
Georges Sutra de Germa, MEP
former Vice-Chairman, Institutional Committee, EP, Pezenas, France
Prof Count L. Ferraris
Council of State, Rome
Jacques Maison Rouge
ex Vice President IBM, Paris
Dr Claude Treyer
Director, European Affairs, IGS, Paris

Research Committee:
Dr Simon Bulmer
University of Manchester, Dept of Government
Gerry Danaher
Secretary, Irish National Economic and Social Council, Dublin
Prof Alfonso Ortega
Political Science, University Pontifica Salamanca, Spain
Prof Dr Grotanelli de Santi
University of Siena, Law and Political Science
Prof Dr R Hrbek
University of Tübingen, Political Science
Prof Dr Detlev Karsten
University of Bonn, Economics
Prof Dr M. A. G. van Meerhaeghe
University of Ghent, Economics
Prof Dr Stavros Theofanides
Panteios School of Pol. Science, Athens
Prof Dr Christian Tomuschat
University of Bonn, International Law

Media Advisers:
Rolf Goll
Chairman, Communications and Marketing, Ansin-Goll, Frankfurt
Prof Dr E. G. Wedell
Chairman, European Media Centre, University of Manchester

Hon. Secretary:
Dr Hartmut Schweitzer, Bonn

Preface

Since the project 'EEC Membership Evaluated' started, major events have changed the formerly stable framework into a dynamic and difficult unforeseen world development.

At the time the project started the world regime was dominated by the cold war regime, with the main goal for the EC being to develop efficiently enough to compete with the US and Japan. The internal market was seen as an economic means to achieve economic growth and competitiveness. It was considered worth trying to give an overview of the gains and losses related to EC membership and EC development. This project has become historic in the way that it sums up what has been achieved in economic cooperation.

The breakdown of the two superpowers scenario broke down the military framework. It gave rise to the question: should the EC be not only a mainly economic but also a military and a political cooperation? And, related to this, how should the Western European Union develop and what positions should it have in relation to NATO?

The Iraqi war and the Yugoslavian civil war became, in a sense, the first pilot tests of the EC as a political force and a political unity. They did not prove extremely successful.

The unification of Germany gave rise to the fear of Germany becoming too powerful and to thinking back to World War II. At the same time it was an enormous challenge especially of economic character to transform an old-fashioned radical socialist economic system of 18 million people into a high-level, highly capitalistic world of West German standard. This challenge caused economic troubles inside Germany and also in the other EC economies and it effectively demonstrates the overwhelming problems of the transition to the capitalistic system in Eastern Europe and in the former Soviet Union.

Furthermore, the endless negotiations — with small results — to form a European Space including the EC and the EFTA countries have given rise to applications for EC membership by EFTA countries and also to applications from the new East European countries longing for a higher materialistic standard and for closer relations with the Western world.

As this project started our concerns were the consequences of free market economic cooperation. Now we are examining the enlarging of the EC with new members and with new areas of economic, military and political character while also looking at the deepening cooperation and loss of dimensions of national sovereignty.

Lise Lyck

Introduction

For hundreds of years Denmark was a middle-sized European kingdom. The South of Sweden was lost in wars in the mid-17th century, Norway in 1814 and the North of Germany in 1864; in fact in 1864 the country was reduced to two-thirds. In 1920 the South of Jutland again became part of Denmark.

Today the Danish realm includes Greenland and the Faroe Islands – both with homerule and a population of less than 100,000 persons – and the Danish realm itself has a total population of 5.2 million.

In the last twenty-five years heavy traffic investments have been undertaken. At the end of the 1960s and in the 1970s most of the old bridges from the 1930s were replaced. In 1986 it was decided to build a bridge over the Great Belt (17.5 km) which should be completed by 1997, and in 1991 it was decided to construct a 17-km bridge from Malmø in Sweden to Copenhagen (Amager) and furthermore a bridge from the Danish island of Lolland to Germany was beginning to be discussed seriously. These constructions are essential for the increased traffic to EC countries.

The Danish economy is a small open economy with a GDP per capita in 1990 of 159.100 DKr; 52 per cent of the imports and the exports being trade with EC countries. Taxes and charges as a percentage of GDP amounted to 48.2 per cent, down from its maximum in 1988 at 51.3 per cent. More than half of tax revenue is raised from personal income tax. It has been officially calculated by the Tax Department that adjustment to the EC duty level would cost a loss of 40 billion DKr.

It is common that both men and women are in the labour force (84.6 per cent men and 75.9 per cent women in 1989). In 1990 the unemployment rate among men was 9.4 per cent, with 12.6 per cent among women.

During the last ten years inflation has gone down to the present level of 2–3 per cent. Also the economic growth rate has decreased to one per cent. The balance of payments has changed from deficit to surplus.

The Danish adjustment problems to the EC are confined to 1) a relatively large part of the trade with non-EC countries; 2) the Danish tax structure being different from the tax structure of the EC countries and, 3) labour market problems and structural differences.

Furthermore, the Danish attitudes to the EC are also different from the attitudes in most of the other EC member states. A large part of the Danish population has a sceptical attitude to the EC and an even larger part only tolerates the EC because of the lack of alternatives. A large part of the voters in most political parties are critical of EC activities. The EC debate tended to split the political parties, and threats of all kinds have been common when ballots were taken. For example, Danish Prime Minister Poul Schlüter argued: 'If you vote for the internal market, the European Union will be stone dead'. In addition, as the only member country Denmark has a grassroots movement against EC membership which holds four of the sixteen Danish seats in the European Parliament.

Denmark is also the only member country that has a special EC Committee under the Danish Parliament from which the Danish ministers have to have a mandate for decisions concerning the EC. At the same time Denmark is the member state which has incorporated most of the EC directives into national laws.

It has to be admitted that the Danish attitude and behaviour concerning EC matters are of a very special and not always easily understandable character.

Lise Lyck

PART I: FOREIGN RELATIONS

Chapter 1

State, society and democracy and the effect of the EC

Henning Sørensen and Ole Væver

Introduction

The question of the effect of the EC on the Danish form of state and state organization is divided into parts: what are the effects of the EC on:

1. *the four state organizations* – the Government, the Parliament, especially its EC Committee, the Central Administration and the High Court of Justice, and on their way of functioning.
2. *Danish Society*, or more precisely its population measured by Danish *public opinion*, and its political life measured by the activity of Danish *interest groups*, and the economy measured by the freedom of manoevring for the *public and private economy*. This chapter therefore takes a psychological, logical and economical approach.
3. *Danish democracy*, or more precisely an interpretation of how the EC will in the future influence the interplay of state and society.

There will be no distinction in the type of influence exercized by the EC, for instance as an institution or as a policy decision-making organization. In short, the EC is an independent variable, a black box with its effect only reflected in Danish reactions/changes.

The state organizations

A main characteristic of the functioning of the four Danish State institutions – Government, Parliament, Central Administration and High Court of Justice – is their cooperation. A visible sign of this cooperative norm may be found in the concentration of all four state institutions in the same building complex. Moreover, you can walk from one part to another without leaving the building. Only between the Court and the other State organizations is there a wall.

The tradition of close cooperation between Government and Parliament probably rests on the fact that in this century only from 1901 to 1910 has one party, the Liberals, enjoyed absolute majority in Parliament. Since then, all Danish Governments have comprised two or more political parties, ruling either as a majority coalition or, more often, as a minority Government, which has had to look continuously (from issue to issue) for a majority in the Parliament. In either case, it has been necessary for the Government to cooperate closely with Parliament. This principle of cooperation has been labelled 'the cooperative democracy' and it is such a generally accepted norm that almost every political party and Government feel obliged to find a compromise when they are negotiating.

Even the High Court of Justice seems to be influenced by this principle. Of course it has stated its *rights* to evaluate and even contradict the laws passed by Parliament, but it has never done so, probably out of respect for the 'cooperative democracy'.

Another way of describing the influence of the cooperative principle is to point out the voting consensus in Parliament at the last stage of the legislative process. Here, about 90 per cent of all bills are passed by a broad majority of more than two-thirds of all MPs.

Many other examples of the 'cooperative democracy', which stands in contrast to the division of power according to Montesquieu, can underline the presence of the 'cooperative spirit'. For instance, MPs are nominated for administrative bodies, Government is expected to fill the framework laws passed by the Parliament and therefore functions as a legislator, and ministers and all civil servants, even officers, can be elected to Parliament.

In short, there is no sharp distinction between legislative and executive power in Denmark. Together they form a strong 'cooperative power'.

This cooperative principle is also formulated in our constitution. The Parliament's power base in relation to Government is given in paragraph 15 (the principle Parliamentarism): 'No minister can continue in his office if the Parliament has expressed its mistrust in him'.

The power base of the Government, or more specifically the Prime Minister, is stated in paragraph 32: 'The King (i.e. the Prime Minister) can call an election at any time'. So, if the PM (or one of his ministers) has been defeated by an 'unwilling' Parliament and therefore has (chosen) to resign, the PM can punish the Parliament by calling an election on the issue. And from experience we know that about one fifth or even more of the MPs will not be re-elected.

This tradition of close cooperation between the four state organizations – Government, Parliament, Administration and the High Court of Justice – is also reflected in 'the Danish EC decision making process . . . which builds on the principle of centralization and consensus' (Tygesen, 1986) and it is the influence of the EC on each of the four powers that will be described below.

Government

Danish membership of the EC in January 1973 undoubtedly increased the power of Government at the expense of the Parliament, for two reasons. First, the Danish Parliament delegated some of its sovereignty to the EC. It was a move from national to international decision-making.

Second, according to the EC Treaty, each national government (not the Parliament, which originally exercised a monopoly in decision making) was given a right to legislate in the EC council. So, at the international level, EC governments make decisions with consequences for their own and other EC countries.

The effect and reaction of the other Danish State organizations to the improved decision-making position of the Danish Government is the theme for analysis in the rest of this chapter.

Parliament

So, a major effect of our EC membership was the creation of the standing Parliamentary EC Committee (Markedsudvalget) with the purpose of out-balancing the improved power-situation of the Parliament.

At the beginning of Danish EC membership, the Parliament burdened the Government with two obligations: to *inform* the Parliament and, more precisely, its EC Committee, on the agenda and policy of the EC Council; and, in specific cases, to follow the instructions of the EC Committee on *how to vote* in the EC Council before essential decisions were made. Therefore, in contrast to the negotiation position of other EC Ministers, the Danish Minister may be given a limited mandate of bargaining compared with that of his collegues.

The two original tasks have, during almost twenty years of Danish EC experience, become more qualified and explicit.

In 1983, the general duty of the Government to inform was qualified in that the Government was required to inform the EC Committee only on those issues with an expected degree of political conflict. This reduction of information to the EC Committee might be seen as a reduction of its influence. But a minority Government will always prefer to over-inform rather than to withhold information, in order to avoid confrontations in Parliament and accusations of keeping back essential information.

In 1986, another controlling procedure was introduced. Møller explains: 'At the beginning of each new period of Chairmanship [the Government is asked] to produce a working programme on the Internal Market' on the basis of which 'the Committee decides which proposals from the EC Committee it wants to pass in the Parliament . . .' and thereby 'introduces a normal reading of selected directive-proposals in the Parliament' (Møller, 1982).

Two other methods of Parliamentary control have been proposed. One suggests public hearing of the debate in the Danish EC Committee, which will be a new praxis. The other is the extension of Danish Administrative Law (which allows every person to look at the correspondence of almost any case handled by public authorities) to cover EC matters.

The reason why the Danish Parliament (which is said already to be the most controlling EC country) wishes to increase its control may be best understood as a reaction to the nature of the EC system compared with the cooperative Danish State system; it is therefore based upon two motives.

First, the Danish Parliament wants to be the 'watchdog for democracy' on behalf of the *population*. Therefore, at the national level, it wants to create a basis for debate and thereby protect minority groups inside and outside Parliament, and on the whole make the work of the EC institutions more open. Second, Parliament sees itself as a 'watchdog for democracy' at the international or EC level on behalf of the *national interest*. It feels obliged to take care of a 'proper representation' of the Danish interest by the Government at the EC Council meetings, as if the Government would do the opposite. This has actually been the dominant argument, however disloyal it might appear. In both cases, the control of the Parliament can be seen as a reaction against a legislative competitor, the Government, which has challenged the 'cooperative democracy'.

Therefore, 'the Danish EC policy has been extremely restrictive with respect to the development of the EC institutions' except for the '"European Political Co-operation", EPC, which since the 70s developed considerably, when the Danish attitude towards this tendency was surprisingly positive compared with earlier Danish reservations' (Schou, 1989).

However, as already indicated, the wish of the Parliament to exercise control over the Parliament and its Central Administration is not only based on the EC experience. For a long time and before Danish EC membership, the 'cooperative reality' meant that Parliamentary control was seen as insufficient. This was partly because it mostly concentrated on single political issues, not on broader political planning committing the Government to action, and partly because the number of framework laws has increased leaving their fulfilment to the Executive Authorities.

So it is not only at the EC level that the Danish Parliament has experienced a 'democratic deficit': it has done so even at the national level. The effect of the EC on the Danish Parliament has only underlined these problems, not caused them.

Therefore, as a positive effect of the EC, Parliament has urged the Government to act more openly in EC matters than is normally the case in foreign policy. In the future, the pressure from Parliament to let the EC and the Government open their doors will not diminish, because after the Single Act it will be possible to overrule the Danish Ministers in Brussels on matters which no longer require unanimity.

Table 1.1 The development in types of work of the Danish EC Committee (EC-C) compared to all committees of the Parliament (all) 1972–73 to 1988–89

	1972–73			1978–79	1984–85	1988–89		
	EC-C	All	%	%	%	EC-C	All	%
1. Meetings	44	835	5	5	7	52	748	7
2. Consultations *with* the minister	90	499	18	18	21	158	492	32
3. Deputations	0	962	–	1	2	0	488	–
4. Written enquiries to the EC-C	3	867	–	–	2	20	2253	1
5. Questions from the EC-C	14	2939	–	1	1	158	7784	2
6. Consultative questions *from* EC-C	0	709	–	1	2	26	478	5
7 Enclosures to the EC-C	119	5307	2	2	3	746	12954	6
TOTAL	270	11418	2			1260	25167	5

Source: compiled from Folketingsårbogen, respective years

A closer look at the development in the working conditions of the Danish EC Committee (see Table 1.1) may give us an impression of the effects of the EC. However, the figures in the table should be interpreted with some reservation, because they do not give a complete picture of the number of papers presented for the EC Committee.

For instance, only those papers given a number are counted in this registration. Moreover, papers from the EC Parliament presented for the EC Committee are not counted. Finally, many papers have the same number even if their contents have changed.

However, even if the figures can be critized, they still are the official ones and the best we have. And they do give us some impression of the working conditions of the Committee, which have become worse – especially since the EC Committee decided to use only a few more meetings to accomplish twice the amount of work. This can be seen by comparing all seven types of work performed by the EC Committee with the work of all Parliamentary committees. Here, the EC Committee has increased its share from 2 to 5 per cent.

The absolute growth of these figures reveals, of course, the general bureaucratic trend of most Parliamentary Committee work, where verbal communication has changed to written information.

But in this case, the Danish EC Committee has itself to blame too, as can be seen from the growth of the three types of self-requested works: '2. Consultations with the Minister'; '3. Questions from the EC Committee' and '6. Consultative Questions to the Minister'.

One reason for this growth is, as mentioned, that the EC Committee has felt its control of the Government's EC policy insufficient. However, the EC Committee is today no better off with the new procedures of control than it once was (Grove, 1989).

The negotiations in the Committee seem to follow two main principles. One is the respect for minority groups. The other is the will to reduce confrontations between Government and Parliament. Each principle is reflected in a number of regulations decided by Parliament. For instance, two-fifths of the MPs of the EC Committee have the right to pass proposed directives in Parliament for debate. Another illustration is the establishment of a Sub-Committee for the EC Committee. This Sub-Committee consists of a representative from each party, and they can prepare the negotiation of the EC Committee or give information on the problems in the EC Committee to get a feedback impulse. A third example is found in the Chairman of the EC Committee asking 'Who is against the directive . . .', and thereby securing a higher degree of unanimity than otherwise obtained.

Consequently, the staff of the EC Committee has gradually been increased. One of the unique tasks of the staff is to write down the negotiations in the EC Committee, and not only its decisions. It is in itself a resource-demanding task. The protocol from each year consists of 1,000–1,500 pages, and they have to be accepted by each representative of the EC Committee.

Moreover, the staff writes 'Background-notes' for the Committee. Then, of course, it takes care of all the papers and paperwork, as can be seen from Table 1.1. A quick calculation shows that the staff copies and distributes more than 100,000 sheets a year.

In order to carry out its task, the EC Committee is now the best staffed of all the Committees in Parliament, including the staff of the Finance Committee. It is one effect of the EC.

The losses incurred by the Parliament as a whole include its reduced influence as a legislator within the economics area. Another loss is the perceived inability to exercise proper control of the Government and the EC. Further, the work of the Parliament, especially its EC Committee, has been more bureaucratized (see Table 1.1).

Finally, 'the possibility of each country to influence decisions made in the EC rests first and foremost on the shoulders of civil servants, who have taken part in forming the directives' (Espersen, 1989). This means that experts gain a stronger position compared to that of politicians and that they may play a more crucial role in foreign policy than before (Due-Nielsen, 1986).

The gains take the form of increased influence for Parliament in two ways and areas. Directly, Parliament, and especially its EC Committee, participates in the Danish *Foreign* Policy Process, for example the consultations with Danish Ministers in the EC Committee and, of course, the restrictive mandate the Committee can give to any Danish Minister before decisions are made in the EC Council.

Indirectly, it participates in the formulation of the *National* Policy of all the EC countries, because the EC Committee functions as a rather effective sparring-partner for the Danish Minister. The many discussions between Committee and Minister give the latter a high degree of preparedness and insight at the EC Council meetings.

As a concluding remark, it can be mentioned that the EC Committee, formerly much criticized as an obstacle to an effective decision-making process in the ERC Council, has now been praised by Jacques Delors, Chairman of the EC Commission, as an example for other EC countries to follow (Delors, 1990).

Administration

The administration of foreign policy is normally a centralized matter, which gives the Ministry of Foreign Affairs a rather decisive position. Thus, the EC issues are centralized too, to the extent that they are treated as foreign policy. This is even the case 'in France, Denmark and the Netherlands, [where] the Ministry of Foreign Affairs . . . coordinates relations with the EC', for which reason 'the Danish decision making process can be classified as centralized and based upon consensus' (Møller, 1989).

However, it has been noticed that the position of the Ministry of Foreign Affairs has been weakened. Its 'centralization has . . . been eroded during the last decades, especially after the Danish EC membership' due to 'decentralization of foreign policy from the Foreign Ministry to each of the involved Resort-Ministries' (Buksti and Martens, 1983).

This argument is based upon a zero-sum consideration and does not include the overall extended influence of the Foreign Administration, as such. For instance, the Foreign Ministry is represented on the Government's EC Committee. It forms part of the Danish representation to the EC in Brussels. It decides what material from Brussels the Danish Government and Parliament are going to receive. It is present when the Foreign Minister has consultations with the EC Committee, etc.

So the participation of Danish Resort Ministries in the EC process does not exclude the influence of the Foreign Ministry, mainly because it coordinates the combined relations between Denmark and EC institutions.

Another positive effect of the EC is its contribution to international thinking in the Administration. Today, almost all ministries have an EC department staffed with many experts, all of whom have an EC perspective in common.

On the other hand, the increase in numbers of experts and staff members may be regarded as a loss. This is felt not only by the Parliament, because of its bureaucratization, but also by the Foreign Office, in particular, and the Administration, in general, since it costs money and time and results in lack of efficiency. However, it forms 'on the bottom line', the conditions necessary for democracy.

The High Court of Justice

The Danish High Court of Justice has in principle only one task: to regulate the behaviour of the population in *society* and of the representatives/civil servants in the *state organizations*. The EC Court in Luxembourg actually has the same task: to control the behaviour of populations, state organizations and *EC institutions*.

However, only in some matters of *economic behaviours* of persons and private companies and state organizations, such as competition, technical obstacles, etc., do they overlap. Here, 'the EC Court has declared that the EC's competence of the Trade-Policy excludes an equivalent national competence' and that 'the citizens can advance the legal rules for the national courts or the EC Court' (Gulmann, 1983). But the two court systems will very seldom be combatants for a number of reasons. For instance, the EC Commission will interfere if 'illegal' economic behaviour is observed.

Perhaps more decisive are three factors that show how much the EC has influenced the Danish juridical system. First, the Danish High Court will in its verdicts look at what the EC Court decided. Second, from the beginning of Danish EC membership, we adapted our legal system to that of the EC (Gulmann, 1983). Third, for political and ethnic reasons we have normally avoided legislating/administering against the EC law complex.

Besides, much of the EC law complex (on products and their passage over the borders) has to do with agriculture and fishing. In Denmark, they do not represent central juridical areas in which lawyers and courts are mostly involved.

So an evaluation of the direct influence of the EC on the High Court of Justice is difficult due to the anticipated reaction of the Danish state organizations. However, this adaptive policy shows maybe even more convincingly the high degree of effect of the EC on the Danish state organizations.

The direct influence can be measured in two areas: in the conflict between the EC and the Danish state organizations and in the EC influence on Danish legislation.

There have been some cases of conflict: the Snapse case, the Border case, the recycling of empty bottles case and latest the Storebælts case (the Great Belt case). The Danish reaction in almost all cases is to negotiate with the Commission, then if disagreement still exists to wait for the EC Court's decision and follow it no matter what.

This adaptive pattern is also reflected by the high proportion of directives from the EC Commission (77 per cent by April 1990) we have so far implemented into Danish laws and regulations. This proportion is the highest for any EC country.

The direct influence on Danish laws of the EC is, of course, more difficult to trace. However, it is widely recognized that some laws – on Cooperations, on Consumer-Protection and on the Finance Sector – have been improved in substance and clarity thanks to EC influence. Positive aspects of the adaptive policy by the Court system and other state organisations are perhaps less relevant if regarded in only a legal perspective.

Of course, a major gain is the high degree of preparedness of the Danish legal system for the Internal Market. But even more decisive may be the moral right Denmark gains from this behaviour, when we negotiate other matters in the EC. As the 'good guy' in the EC, we may exercise a higher degree of influence than our small country is entitled to.

The losses are that, sometimes, the EC legal system sets standards that do not fit in with the Danish legal system – for instance, the Snapse case.

To conclude, the most prominent effect of Danish EC membership is the fact that the High Court of Justice is no longer the final court in Denmark: the EC Court at Luxembourg, in some economic cases, holds that position. An evaluation of the gains and losses is, due to the adaptive policy, more difficult to formulate. It has to be based more on speculation than on observation. But the effect on the daily life of the Danish legal system has, in short, not been very noticeable.

Society

From the evaluation of the effects of the EC on the Danish state organizations we shall focus more widely on the gains and losses for the Danish society, *psycologically* with respect to the Danish public opinion of the EC on Danish interest groups, and *economically* with respect to the consequences for the private and the public economy. In short, we shall try to pin down the Danish understanding of what the EC means to them.

Danish public opinion of the EC

In this part we shall try to answer three questions.

First, has the EC contributed to political apathy in Denmark? This apathy is measured here by comparing the voting percentages of the three EC Parliamentary elections in 1979, 1984 and 1989 with the two referenda in 1972 on the Danish membership of the EC and in 1986 on the European Single Act.

Second, what aspects of the EC make the Danes so sceptical about the EC? This scepticism is measured by comparing Danish public opinion of our EC membership with the EC Commission's survey of Denmark and other EC countries as contributors or beneficiaries of the EC.

Third, within which areas is it then possible to indicate the major losses and gains of the EC in the Danish opinion?

The proportion of Danes participating in the two referenda was 90 per cent in 1972 and 75 per cent in 1986. The voting percentage for the three EC Parliamentary elections was respectively 48 in 1979, 52 in 1984 and 46 in 1989.

So the interest of the Danes in EC Parliamentary elections is not only lower than that in the decision on EC membership in 1972 and on the extent of the future EC cooperation in 1986; it is also lower than the average of all EC countries and of the voting percentage for the national Parliamentary elections. Therefore it might be argued that the EC election has not inspired the Danes to participate in a political democratic process, but has actually contributed to political apathy among the Danes.

However, this is not the case. First, the acceptance of Danish EC membership has become stabilized in the long run (see Table 1.2). Five out of ten Danes are now EC supporters, whereas from 1976 to 1985 it was only three out of ten.

Second, it is not a negative EC attitude that lies behind the low voting

Table 1.2 Danish public opinion on the acceptance of Danish EC membership, 1961–89 (percentage)

'How will you vote today on membership of the European Community?' (Iversen)

	For	Against	Don't know
1961	53	9	38
1964	50	9	41
1968 (Dec)	60	15	33
1970 (Oct)	54	15	31
1971	37	30	33
1972 (Referendum)	57	33	10
1976	40	43	17
1981	35	46	19
1983	31	43	26
1985	39	40	21
1986 (Single Act)	56	44	0
1989	53	35	12

percentage. This is better explained by referring to the fact that Danes who disagree with their preferred political party have a lower voting percentage than those who agree. The same is true for undecided people, who more often refrain from voting than do the conscious EC supporters or EC opponents.

On this basis it is possible to argue that the Danish population has a more differentiated EC attitude than may normally be believed. It is without any doubt, however, that the Danes are rather sceptical about the EC (see Table 1.2). The table shows that scepticism, i.e. the proportion of EC opponents, increased before Danish membership from below 10 per cent in the 1960s to over 30 per cent from the beginning of the 1970s. The proportion of EC supporters has changed as drastically as that of the EC opponents, from 31 to 60 per cent. The number of 'Don't knows' has been reduced, from about one-third in the 1960s to one-fifth or even lower for the last twenty years.

As the EC is an economic community, the reason for the Danish scepticism could be a feeling of 'economic exploitation'. This is, however, not the case. In a series of surveys administered by the EC Commission voters were asked: 'Taking everything into account would you say that Denmark has on balance benefited or not from being a member of the European Community?' (Commission of the EC).

Respectively 51, 44, 56 and 63 per cent of Danes in 1984, 1985, 1986 and 1990 answered that Denmark 'has benefited', while for the same three years only 31, 27 and 32 per cent replied 'has not'. So the relatively low acceptance of Danish EC membership is not caused by a feeling of being a contributing country. On the contrary: the two public polls, combined, show that the Danish population feels it is a beneficiary of the EC and that it has gained from the EC membership.

The three types of data on the Danish population – its political activity, acceptance of EC membership and evaluation of being a contributor to or beneficiary of the EC – allow us some conclusions.

First, the higher voting percentages on the referenda than for those on the EC Parliamentary elections show a political consciousness among the Danes. When important matters are 'at stake' they want to vote. So the EC is not alone to blame for an (increased) political apathy, which, of course, must be characterized as a loss.

Second, the higher proportion of Danes voting for increased economic integration at the two referenda than the numbers of EC opponents in public polls indicates that it is within the economic area that a major gain of the EC may be perceived, even if it will cost us a reduced sovereignty. Moreover, as the number of Danes acknowledging that it is beneficial to be a member of the EC is higher than the proportion of EC opponents, it is confirmed that increased economic integration is regarded a gain.

Third, as neither political apathy nor economic exploitation are the cause of discontent, and since increased economic integration is more positively than negatively evaluated by most Danes, it is possible to see the perceived negative effects of the EC in another light.

It is in the psychological field of society that we find the Danes' sense of loss on joining the EC. The feeling of losing something immaterial – such as national identity, cultural significance, solidarity – deserves attention.

Danish interest groups

Denmark, as a small state, presents a paradox. On the one hand, we as a minor state have limited possibilities of influencing the international system – but why should we be content to adapt to greater nations' decisions?

On the other hand, Denmark and its strong interest groups at national level has a clear will to influence international organizations and we feel that size is less crucial than the argument.

According to this, 'research has shown that the established Danish interest groups (for agriculture, industry and employees) as a whole have been rather cautious in their activities at the EC level. They participate in order to gain advantages, but having a strong position in the Danish political process, they are not all that happy to displace power to the EC institutions .... However, a weakness at the national level can intensify their activity at the EC level ...' and this development means that 'The problems are displaced from the technical to the political ....' (Buksti and Martens, 1983).

For the less-established interest groups and the grass roots, the situation may be the same. However, they will often be denied at the national level and will therefore try to challenge the Danish system at the EC level. This displacement has to do with the fact that 'national Parliaments are about to delegate their competence to . . . local political bodies . . . and to the EC institutions' (Christophersen, Henning).

At the public political level, the gains of the EC can be summed up into three factors.

First, the EC is another actor for the interest groups' attempt to influence and thereby 'take independent foreign policy initiatives' (Buksti and Martens, 1983).

Second, the EC can in specific political areas – such as environment protection, or employee questions – set standards and see them kept, because otherwise the EC through the Commission and the Court can punish non-obedient countries.

Third, the EC has shown its ability to take dynamic steps and thereby overcome national political deadlock situations, which are often the mark of modern states (Janowitz, 1978).

This deadlock position of the state organization is a result of the high degree of consideration from the political parties to the interest groups. The state organization has been described as a Gulliver tied up by each political party's concern for specific interest organizations.

Another explanation of the deadlock situation is a high degree of agreement in most political questions. For instance, the welfare state in the Western World has been introduced and elaborated irrespective of the governments' colour, whether socialist, liberal or conservative.

Finally, the political deadlock can be caused by the state organization, voluntarily. For instance, Denmark has a tradition of leaving the regulation of the labour market to its main interest groups: the Danish TUP, LO (Lands Organisation – Danish Confederation of Trade Unions) and the Employers Association, DA.

In all three cases, the EC has become a new actor for national politicians and interest groups. Not only because the EC can serve as an opponent or inspirator, but also because some of the most complex problems of today's world – for instance pollution and debt crises, where the national interest groups have blocked a solution – are now being addressed through the initiatives of the EC institutions.

The negative aspects of EC membership lies, of course, in the same area as its strengths. The many standards and initiatives stop Denmark forming national solutions. However, as stated above, many political problems call for international solutions: national actions would be insufficient.

Private and public economy

The capitalist system is characterized by its markets, lack of ideology and right to decide on production and consumption, assuming you have money.

The Danish capitalist system is more concrete, marked by a *heavy public sector* (the public sector accounts for more than 50 per cent of the Gross National Product and two out of three persons are employed in the public sector); *small business* (75 per cent of all private companies have a trade per year of less than 2.5 million DKK, the equivalent of 0.5 million GDP, and 80 per cent of all employees are in companies with less than 500 persons); a *well-organized labour market* (more than 80 per cent of all employees are members of a union) and *few export cooperations* (of 6,000 companies, only 500 firms constantly export, whereas companies with less than 200 persons state that they have an unused export potential of 70 per cent; Udenrigsministeriet og Danske Erhvervschefers Fællesråd, 1988).

Moreover, we know that our trade is not with countries or in lines of business different from our own. We export and import goods to countries we resemble, (Germany, Great Britain, Sweden and Norway) and we have much trade with the same type of products, called Intra-Industry Trade, ITT (Pultz, 1985).

In general, the major economic gain of the EC is in the psychological field, and in the *predictability* of foreign trade within the EC society. As has been stated with respect to the EMC (Economic Monetary Community), 'The most essential gain from EMC for Denmark is the removal of some uncertainties for the action of the business and working life community' (Økonomiministeriet).

This predictability is, however, based on the view that 'in a historical perspective – perhaps the most epoch-making [consequence of the EC] . . . is the introduction of a whole new form of international *jurisdictional* cooperation [where] the decision making [of the EC] commits each EC member' (Pultz, 1985).

In order to enforce its decision, the EC therefore established itself as a 'police force', which in some situations has been regarded as a loss in the sense that it contradicted national laws and regulations.

On the other hand, this 'EC police force' not only provides us with predictability, it also guarantees the efficiency of the market (Wolf, 1988).

However, the predictability, the jurisdictional cooperation and the EC police force are only tools, not aims. In the long run, the present control system of the EC has only accomplished its fundamental business if its task is so generally accepted that no hindrances are made for EC trade. Therefore, on the bottom line the present big EC control-system is expected to be reduced. As we in Denmark do not need a control system to secure the free passage from Jutland to Copenhagen, we ought not to need any controlling system for the exchange of goods from Copenhagen and Paris.

In a more specific evaluation of the effect of the EC on the public and private economy, we shall focus on the freedom of manoeuvring, as other chapters in this book deal with the economic consequences such as wealth, growth, etc.

With respect to *public economy*, it is evident that Danish sovereignty in the money – and currency – areas is rather tied up. It has been said that Danish sovereignty takes only fifteen minutes: the time-lag we in Denmark have before adapting to the money policy decided in Frankfurt.

However, this development has more to do with the internationalization of finance and currency than with the initiatives of the EC.

Danish finance policy has per definition been outside the influence of the EC. However, it is clear that the decisions of the great EC countries and other great nations do influence Denmark. 'The combined effect of a certain [finance-political] action in the US, Great Britain and Germany has the same effect as an equivalent Danish action. Hereby is illustrated the vulnerability of the Danish economy' . . . . 'It is the greater industrial countries that have a dominating influence on the Danish economy [not] the other Nordic countries . . . in spite of the rather great influence these countries [have] on the Danish foreign trade . . .' (Madsen, 1989).

So, on one hand, Denmark need not to worry about its state deficit, or its high coverage for unemployment, because its finance policy and social benefit policy, etc., are out of the reach of the EC.

On the other hand, there is no doubt that in the long run the EC will influence the Danish tax policy, because we cannot continue to have budget deficits. Therefore, we will be forced to reduce the level of the DOEs (Danish welfare services) – so indirectly the EC has, and will have, influence on Danish tax policy.

The effect of the EC on the *private economy* is more complicated to grasp. On the one hand, the direct influence seems to be rather confined. For instance, Denmark pays only 1.3 per cent of its Gross National Product towards the *financing of the EC*.

'Danish foreign investment has increased five times to almost 1 billion USD [and] . . . foreign investment in Denmark has increased four times to ¾ of a billion USD (from 1979 to 1989). However, while half the Danish investments goes to the EC countries, almost half the sovereign investments to Denmark comes from Sweden' (Wiberg).

Moreover, with respect to the composition of Danish foreign trade for EC and Nordic countries, '. . . there is no significant support for the theory that Denmark should move away from the Nordic countries' (Wiberg).

However, this result is based on *all* EC and Nordic countries taken together. If we concentrate, for instance, on Sweden and Germany, we find that our exports to Sweden from 1977 to 1987 only grew from 8 billion DKK to 22 billion DKK, and our imports from 11 billion DKK to 22 billion DKK. The equivalent figures for Germany are that exports increased from 9 billion to 30 billion and imports grew from 15 billion to 42 billion.

Finally, the Danish foreign trade with EC countries has only levelled 50 per cent, far from the high level of other EC countries.

On the other hand, in a number of areas of the market we find an influence of the EC. For instance, the mere debate of the coming 'Internal Market', more than *the* 'Internal Market' has sharpened the international perspective of businessmen and women.

As an example we can take the financial sector in Denmark. Here we have almost witnessed two revolutions. The one is the former system – divided into banks, savings banks, real estate institutes, stockbroker offices and assurance – now *melting* together: former distinctions are now blurred. The other is the *merging* of banks, etc. But in either case this integration is probably based more on the internationalization of the business world than on the initiative from the EC.

The combined effect of the EC, i.e. the direct regulations and the indirect harmonization, on the Danish economy can be summed up as follows.

In contrast to the often held position that the EC primarily and directly regulates our private economy through common standards, etc., this is in fact only a minor aspect of the EC effect.

The indirect influence of the EC is probably more decisive. The EC has, no doubt, influenced the awareness of Danish business people, and their preparedness for competition and thereby the will to merge together.

Even more decisive, however, is the effect of the EC on our social welfare system. Here, the EC does not need to take any regulating steps, because the harmonization of trade provides an incentive to adapt to the tax level of the other EC countries. Denmark has yet to do so, but it will, because the internationalization of the economy will gradually force us to adapt to common standards.

If the direct EC influence on our high welfare standard can be critized as a loss, we in Denmark would regard it as a gain if the EC could equal the environmental standards at the high level we want, and thereby create more equal competition between the Danish and multinational corporations.

At this point, it should be admitted that the arguments are no longer bound to economic theory, but to political wishful thinking. This development reflects the evolution of the EC from an economic to a political community.

Our democracy and the EC

In the previous two sections we have analysed the influence of the EC on state and the society. In this section we bring them together under the heading of democracy.

Historically, 'the meaning of democracy' can be reduced to three categories: method of decision-making, state formation and concepts like freedom, equality etc. (Christophersen, J.A., 1968). So here democracy means a state formation, the organization of a nation.

This is an interesting approach for at least two reasons. It focuses on the interplay between state/elite and society/public and gives us a point of reference, the consideration of the people, from which we can evaluate not only the type of democracy we are talking about here, but also what the effect of the EC will be for this democracy.

State and society

However, before doing that, the identity and difference between state and society and the effect of the EC placed in between will be examined.

A state is normally defined by three characteristics: an elite, citizens and a territory. A society – i.e. a population, an interest group or a cooperation – is based upon individuals having feelings for each other and economic cooperation. Of course, the actors of a state and society are the same, comprising a population and probably an elite, too.

If so, both units, state and society, have the power to coerce their participants. Therefore equality, efficiency, justice etc. are not more safe in a society than in a state.

The difference between state and society lies in the significance each of them gives to different aspects of life. The unity of society seemed no longer to depend on political factors, but rather on economics, labour and communications operating within a wide social system designed to meet human needs' while the state will feel it necessary to argue for rules and institutions and therefore grow into a political system. So, the political state will have to justify its institutions, laws and especially its independence of each individual citizen after the rule 'all is equal' (Luhmann).

From this perspective, the EC is both society and state. It has some of the characteristics of a state, i.e. institutions and laws, and the EC is looked upon as a problem solver. But the EC lacks some of the characteristics of a modern state, especially with respect to democracy. For instance, the Parliament has almost no legislative power.

On the other hand, the EC has a state ideology or a purpose, to secure the free transport of man, money and manufacturing goods across the borders. But even if the EC has been given institutions and laws to function as a police-force of a state, it is not obliged to accept public pressure unless it comes from EC representatives such as ministers or, to a much lesser degree, EC MPs.

This lack of democratic aspects may have to do with the different time of introduction of state and democracy. States have existed for centuries, but it is only at the beginning of this century that 'Democracy arrived on the scene where it had to come to terms with [the State, Bureaucracy, Capitalism etc.'] (Bealey, 1988). Democracy, the newcomer, has forced itself upon the state.

The reason for the state's acceptance of democracy may lie in the former's obligation to solve problems (Dyson, 1980). And citizens have for the same reason renounced the use of violence in order to get their way. They have, as civilized citizens, accepted the state's monopoly on violence and taxation. In exchange the state protects each of us from attack by other citizens (Elias, 1939).

So today the main question concerning the introduction of more democracy into EC institutions is not that the EC is against that type of state formation, but that democracy, not the state, respects public pressure as legislator. So, even if the EC implements democracy, it at the same time values public pressure higher than the Community as such. Then the EC, as mentioned above, is entitled to work in accordance with public opinion, whatever it might be, and not for the purpose of integration.

The ideal democracy

According to Ross, the ideal topographic democracy is charactarized by:

- *Extensity*: i.e. how many of the state institutions do the citizens influence;
- *Intensity*: i.e. how many citizens participate; and
- *Efficiency*: i.e. the effect of the people on the state.

Figure 1 gives an illustration of the three aspects of Ross' democracy model.

Extensity

Transferred to Denmark and the EC influence, it is clear that the area of the Danish State affected by the EC has been reduced, partly because the Danish Parliament has agreed to delegate its sovereignty to the EC. And partly because all the information sent from the EC over Danish Representation in Brussels and the Foreign Ministry to the EC Committee makes its control somewhat insufficient. On the other hand, the Danish Government, based upon a minority of MPs in the Parliament, is more sensitive to criticism and therefore more prepared to inform than a majority-based government.

Besides, there are suggestions from the EC on 'more opened doors'

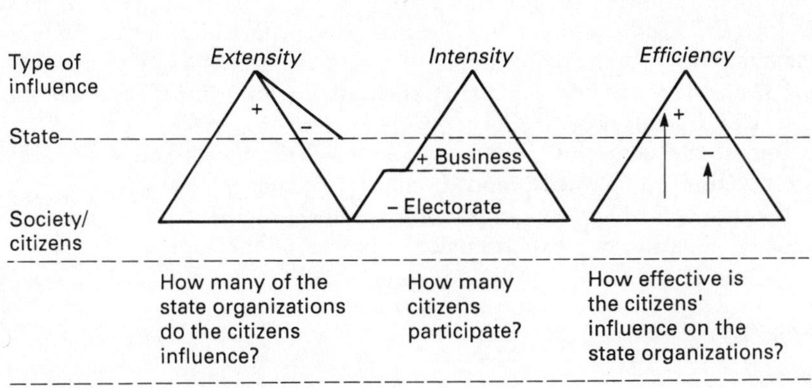

Figure 1.1 Illustration of the three aspects of democracy

(Ersbøll, 1990), which again can be interpreted as if up till now this has not been fully the case.

So, the EC has caused a reduced democratic extensity, but is prepared to improve the situation. Besides, the EC has never – as far as we know – tried to limit the extent and the degree of information to the Danish Foreign Minister although the EC Committee's ability to withhold sensitive information from the EC has been criticized.

Intensity

It is obvious that many Danes have not participated in the EC Parliamentary election. In Denmark, only one out of two now votes while in Great Britain it is as low as one out of three.

So those elections have not reduced political apathy concerning the EC. However, in more essential decisions (referenda), the Danes have shown a much higher degree of political activity.

From this perspective, it is rather obvious that the business world is better off than the consumers. However, a well functioning 'Internal Market' is a condition for the EC to turn to consumer and labour issues. After the implementation of the Internal Market, the more interesting aspects of EC cooperation can begin – the work for a European Social Dimension, as has been said.

Another aspect of EC influence on democratic intensity is that it has been more difficult for political groups to be represented at EC bodies.

In Denmark, we are witnessing a development where the small political parties have to join forces in order to get (more) representatives to the EC Parliament.

Here, through a harmonization from the EC, we may expect a reduction in the number of political parties in the Danish Parliament, as the Danish EC Commissioner has already argued, in the name of 'stability'. He suggests a higher percentage of voters required for representation in the Danish Parliament, a majority instead of proportional representation, and a bicameral system (Christophersen, Jens A., 1968).

But, at the same time, there is a very high degree of consensus on the preservation of national identity, cultural distinctiveness, etc.

In the area between improving political stability and preserving national identity, we expect major ruptures in the future.

Efficiency

As mentioned above in connection with the problems for the EC in implementing democracy, the main characteristic of the latter is that it allows its members to take initiatives that can even overcome the inertia of the state and the EC itself.

However, the political process of increased integration will, of course, reduce the democratic efficiency of the Danish citizens. And even if, as Jacques Delors has argued, 'each EC country will independently decide on at least 95 per cent of its own public spending, and the EC Commission only will decide on 5 per cent . . .', he has also stated that '80 per cent of all laws [of each EC country] will be decided in the EC (Delors, 1989).

Besides, making decisions in the EC Council, by majority vote, will even further reduce the Danish population's possibilities for efficient democratic control. An indirect admission by a high ranking Civil Servant of the Danish Foreign Ministry claims that the Danish Government has not always involved the Danish interest groups 'properly' in the political proces (Ørstrøm).

This direct effect of the EC on democratic efficiency in Denmark is a loss. The gain is, however, that our influence in the EC on the other EC countries is greater than this loss. Another gain is that in the model we do not look at the substance of each issue, only at the decision-making method. Therefore, it is possible that our losses in one area are much smaller than our gains in another.

Other aspects of democracy

As just illustrated, this model of democracy omits the substance or contents of each political issue that is going to be decided upon. The model of democratic extensity, intensity and efficiency describes only the *relation* between two institutions, state and society, and how the decisions of the former may be influenced by the latter.

Another democratic element left out in the model is that it does not take into account the size of each institution, state and society. And here we do not doubt that the EC will influence the size of the state apparatus in this country, where one out of three employees is a civil servant, while in the rest of the EC the average is about one in six.

This expected reduction can be argued as a reasonable change, but it is obvious that one source of this change is the harmonization from the EC and that thereby the EC has influenced an area we have been told lies outside its reach: the size and content of the Danish welfare state.

The other aspect omitted from the democratic model follows from this harmonization of state and society by the EC. If the harmonization is to be really successful, it raises a fundamental question: what will be left for each EC country to influence? This is not a rhetorical question, but has been asked in connection with the NATO integration (Chrismas Møller, 1983).

It would be 'the irony of the EC' if the introduction and success of the Community as a way for Europe to survive competition from the US and Japan led us to a position where all individual/national European distinctiveness was eroded, and – in the name of harmonization – left us with an American-Japanese 'nightcap' with a little European dash on the top of it.

Then the influence of the EC would become the victim of its own success.

References

Bealey, Frank (1988), *Democracy in the contemporary state*, New York: Oxford University Press, p. 291.

Buksti, Jacob and Martens (1983), 'Interesseorganisationer i EF', ('The Interest Organizations in the EC'), in *DUÅ 1983*, (Danish Foreign Policy Yearbook), Copenhagen: Dansk Udenrigspolitisk Institut, pp. 89–9, 91–2.

Chrismas Møller, W. (1983), 'Krisen omkrings Danmarks sikkerhedspolitik med særligt henblik på en bestemmelse af de borgerlige partiers positioner' ('The crisis of Denmarks's security policy especially with reference to a determination of the position of the Bourgeois Parties'), pp. 34–60 in *DUÅ 1983*. 'One may formulate it in the following way, that the intention of the NATO organization has succeeded so well, that it *de facto* has eliminated the effect of the individual member countries' independent policy'.

Christophersen, Henning (1989), *Tanker om Danmark i det nye Europa*, Copenhagen: Børsen, pp. 108, 116, 174.

Christophersen, Jens A. (1968), *The meaning of democracy as used in European ideologies from the French to the Russian Revolution*, Oslo.

Commission of the EC (1986), *Euro-barometre*, Brussels, p. 128, here pp. 88–90,

Table 44 for the 1984–1986 figures and *Europæsisk Nyhedsbrev* no. 10 af 25–5. 1990, ('European Newsletter').

Delors, Jacques, in Berlingske Tidende, 4 May 1990. Delors, Jacques, Brügge speech of September 1989, here quoted from Jørn Damgård Hansen, Europa-Parlamentet skal udfylde det 'demokratiske tomrum, ('The European Parliament shall fill the 'democratic deficit').

Due-Nielsen, Carsten (1986), '*Folketinget og udenrigspolitikken*' ('The Parliament and the Foreign Policy'), pp. 75–86 in Haagerup and Thune, 1986, p. 83.

Dyson, Kenneth (1980), *The state tradition in Western Europe*, Oxford: Robertson, p. 310, Chapter 9, 'The idea of State and Democracy', pp. 252–81.

Elias, Norbert, *Über den Prozess der zivilisation Sociogenetische Untersuchingen*, (Bern, München 1939, reprinted 1969), vol. 1 p. 320 and vol. 2. pp. 320 and 492.

Ersbøll, Niels, Danish EC Secretary for EC Council in *Weekendavisen*, April 6, 1990, 'Let the EC open its doors'.

Espersen, Ole, in *Børsen* 21 February 1989, 'The competence disappears from the Parliament to the EC'.

Grove, Henning, chairman of the EC Committee, in *Helsingør Dagblad* 7 April 1989, 'Danish Politicians cannot control consequences of the EC directives'.

Gulmann, Claus (1983), 'Danmarks og EF's sanktioner mod Sovjetunionen og Argentina', ('Denmarks's and the EC's Sanction Against the USSR and Argentina'), pp. 117–134, in *DUÅ 1983*, pp. 129 and 133.

Iversen, John (1984), *Om EF* (On the EC), Copenhagen: Reitzel, here p. 26 (for 1961–1972 figures) and *DUÅ, 1988*, (Danish Foreign Policy Yearbook), p. 468 (for 1972–1985 figures) and Worre, Torben, 'Danskerne og EF', pp. 335–49 in *Presse og politik. Festskrift til Niels Thomsen*, Copenhagen 1990: Odense Universitets Press, p. 347, Table 12.

Janowitz, Morris (1978), *The last half century: Societal change and politics in America*, Chicago: University of Chicago Press, p. 538, p. 546.

Luhmann, Thomas, 'Society', in C.D. Kernig *Marxism, Communism and Western Society*, 8 vols., here vol. 7. p. 22.

Madsen, Per Kongshøj, '*Men hvad der i London, Paris og Bonn*?' ('What happens in London, Paris and Bonn?'), pp. 165–186 in Heurlin and Thune, 1989, op. cit., p. 176.

Møller, J. Ørstrøm, 'Den danske EF-beslutningsproces i praxis, ('The Danish EC-Decision Making Process in Praxis'), pp. 258–279 in *Nordisk Adminstrativt Tidsskrift*, 1982.3, p. 259 and p. 260.

Møller, J. Ørstrøm, 'Danmark og EF's indre marked' ('Denmark and the Internal Market of the EC') pp. 78–93, in *Dansk Udenrigspolitisk Årbog (DUÅ), 1988* (Danish Foreign Policy Yearbook), (Copenhagen 1989: Dansk Udenrigspolitisk Institut), p. 83.

Pultz, Niels, 'Om international økonomisk integration og økonomisk union', ('On the International Economic Integration and Economic Union'), pp. 96–110 in *DUÅ 1985*, pp. 100 and 103.

Ross, Alf (1967), *Hvorfor demokrati*?, ('Why democracy?'), København: Gads Forlag p.115.

Schou, Tove Lise (1989), 'Danmarks politik over for internationale organisationer – i et regimeteoretisk perspektiv' ('Danish Policy towards International Organisations'), pp. 151–164 in Bertel Heurlin and Christian Tune, (eds), *Danmark og det internationale system. Festskrift til Ole Karup Pedersen*', (Copenhagen: Politiske studier), pp. 158 and 159.

Tygesen, K.E. (1986), 'Den Danske EF-beslutningsproces', ('The Danish EC decision making process'), pp. 55–67, in Haagerup, Niels Jørgen and Christian Tune, *Folketinget og Udenrigspolitikken*, (Copenhagen: DJØF's Forlag), p. 56.

Udenrigsministeriet og Danske Erhvervschefers Fællesråd, *Eksportreserve-undersøgelsen 1988*, ('The Export-Reserve-Research'), (Copenhagen 1988) and Danmarks Sparekasseforeing, *Eksporten under omvurdering – en erhvervsøkonomisk analyse af dansk erhvervslivs internationalisering*, ('The Export under Reevaluation . . .'), (Copenhagen 1988).

Wiberg, Håkan, '*Danmark mellem Norden og Europa*', ('Denmark between the Nordic Countries and Europe'), pp. 135–150 in Heurlin and Thune op. cit. p. 176, p. 140.

Wolf, Charles Jr. (1988), *Markets or Governments: Choosing between imperfect alternatives*, Cambridge: MIT Press, p. 220.

Økonomiministeriet, *Økonomisk Monetær Union*, ('Economic Monetary Union'), (Copenhagen 1989: Økonomiministeriet).

Ørstrøm, in *DUÅ 1988*, op. cit. p. 84 '. . . the Government has agreed to strengthen and improve the hearing procedure for interest groups . . . [because it has] . . . too late and sometimes too carelessly involved [them] in the Danish decision making process'.

Chapter 2

Denmark and the overlapping international institutions in Europe in the post-cold war period

Tove Lise Schou

Introduction

The period 1985 to 1990 has been one of international change on the global as well as the European level. How do small European states try to safeguard their interests? It is the object of this chapter to try to demonstrate how Denmark, through a foreign policy of balanced adaptation, has formulated a conception of a European political governing process for the internationalization and integration process in Europe. The states and international organizations of this region, experiencing fundamental changes resulting from the post-cold war dialogue between the United States and the Soviet Union as well as from internal societal factors, are now facing problems that challenge their political creativity regarding regime building and institutional development. The two processes currently in focus in the European development are EC integration towards a European Union and the bringing together of the two German states into a common institutional framework. These two processes might hamper each other, but they might also enforce each other. No doubt there are strong forces in the EC attempting to consolidate the EC role of the Federal Republic of Germany as a basis for establishment of new institutional ties between the two German countries. These actors are trying to speed up the integration process in the EC. A European Union with a Germany including the five former East German 'länder' in a development of ever closer cooperation will have to solve the problem of new conditions for the European security order.

For a small state such as Denmark, which has based its security policy on avoiding being caught in a two-sided relationship with a Great Power by means of multilateral negotiations within international organizations, the development of an enlarged and more integrated EC seems to be the answer. However, there has not so far been a majority in the Folketinget (the Danish Parliament) in favour of a development beyond the first stage of the Delors plan of an economic and monetary union to the second stage, which demands decision-making on national budgets at the community level. Institutional development in the direction of more supranationality was not what the voters gave as a mandate to their representatives in the Folketinget – not at the referendum in 1972, and certainly not in the referendum on the Single European Act in 1986, when the doubts of the Social Democratic party's parliamentary group about the consequences of the new procedure for the hearing of the European Parliament made this group urge voters to turn down the European Single Act.

Since then developments in expectations – within and outside the EC – of the Internal Market and the issues of the social dimensions and environmental problems have however, apparently changed the attitude of the Social Democrats to decision-making at the EC Community level on these issues. What will happen now that the German issue has revealed that the EC is not just an instrument to create more welfare is also seen from Denmark – a 'Pluralistic Security Community', as Deutsch defined it: a community of states that would never use force as a means of solving conflicts among themselves. The 'Amalgamated Security Community', the Federation, (Deutsch, 1968) has, however, had very few proponents in Denmark in comparison with other small members of the community such as the Netherlands and Belgium. The Danish conception of the EC is a functionalist one of an integrated EC organization, creating regimes for specific policy areas in order to have a collective political governing process and thus avoid the negative consequences of interdependence.

The post-war period is over

This is how the present situation in Europe is described by Danish officials. A new epoch has begun. The development in Eastern Europe has changed the agenda of the EC. Europe's Domestic Market, relations with EFTA and the Mediterranian countries and the Third World are still important items, but at present the relationship with the eastern countries is given highest priority.

The workload from the problems related to future EC membership of the Eastern German area and the speed of the changes in all the eastern countries have moved the attention of the decision-makers of the EC countries from these other important issues to the east. Every one will admit that these developments have come as a surprise. The economic problems of the eastern countries have been underestimated and the legitimacy of the eastern regimes overestimated.

The question is whether this new epoch will be one that will demand fundamental changes in the Danish foreign policy of 'balanced adaptation' or one that will make it easier to continue what has been Danish foreign policy so far.

Will the EPC be diluted as regards security matters to make it easier to enlarge the EC with new members? It looks as if this could be the case. How will a development like that affect the WEU?

Will the development towards an Economic and Monetary Union slow down because of the problems of adapting an Eastern German population of eighteen million to the conditions of a market economy?

More than a regime, less than a federation

This is how the development in the EC has been characterized, seen from a theoretical perspective by William Wallace in 'Policy-making in the European Community' (1983).

Regime theory is a useful framework for the analysis of Denmark's policy in the EC. The positive attitude of small states to the development of international organizations and regimes with abilities to facilitate the making of agreements will depend on their expectations regarding the consequences for their sphere of action in the international system and in relation to their internal societal development. If the regime will extend the sphere of action of the small state in relation to the great power structure of the international system, the attitude will be positive. If the regime will make it possible for the small state to make decisions in relation to structural changes of society, and to secure the balance of societal structures acceptable to the majority of the population, the attitude will be positive.

In Denmark in 1972 it was considered a threat to the structural balance of society if Denmark stayed outside the EC. A majority of the voters expected a serious decline for the agricultural sector if it was cut off from the common market. It was also expected that EC membership would mean gains for Danish industry. The EC issue was debated in Denmark as an obligation to economic cooperation, and the voters did not give a mandate to institutional development towards a political union. The conception of integration in the EC that has broad support is the functionalist idea of regimes in various policy areas with abilities to facilitate agreements regarding these areas and without more and less automatic spillover to other policy areas. It is supposed that regimes defined as norms and principles, rules and decision-making procedures regarding a specific international policy area, can be established without an institutional development imposing constraints on the national governments apart from the obligations of the agreements established by the regimes in the specific policy areas.

The long-term goal of a functionalist integration strategy is more peaceful relations among the states. The attitude in Denmark to the European Political cooperation has changed from the original avoidance of the subject in the EC debates to positive expectations from the left as well as the right wing of the party system. It seems that the regimes created within the EC have abilities to facilitate agreements about economic issues and the economic aspects and other non-military aspects of security.

What would happen if military and defence issues were put on the agenda of the EPC? With a neutral member, Ireland, in the EPC the situation will probably not arise very soon. An acceptance of the neutral applicant for membership, Austria, will make it still less likely.

A re-unified Germany as a member of the EC and the EPC will probably narrow down the EPC agenda regarding security issues. This will be in accordance with Danish EC/EPC policy.

Security questions as such have not been excluded from the EPC in the past. The EC members have acted in close cooperation in the CSCE (Conference on Security and Cooperation in Europe) on security matters (Haagerup and Thune, 1988). On several occasions the position of the EC countries on issues raised in NATO has been coordinated before the meeting, so that they acted as a bloc. Norway has reacted to these situations and others of importance to Norwegian interests by asking for an arrangement with the EPC giving the Government of Norway a right to be heard on issues involving the interests of Norway, and such an arrangement has been established.

The single European Act of January 1986 states that the provisions of the Treaty are no obstacle to closer cooperation in the field of security among certain of the EC members, within the WEU and the NATO. Military cooperation will continue to be dealt with outside the EC/EPC. The EC/EPC is still perceived mainly as a 'civilian power'.

The WEU should not be considered a substructure of the EC/EPC. From a Danish point of view it is an alternative international security structure. Its members are the original six EC members: France, the FRG, Italy, the Netherlands, Belgium and Luxembourg plus the United Kingdom. In 1988 Spain and Portugal became members of WEU, which since then has included all members of the EC/EPC except Denmark, Greece and Ireland. The European Parliament has during recent years referred to the WEU as an expression of the security policy dimension of the Community, but seen from the three Community members outside the WEU this model, 'Europe with two rates of speed', is not acceptable, and they will probably use a lot of energy in attempts to bring all the members into line again (Nehring, 1989).

Danish foreign policy as a 'fragmented' area

Denmark has a long tradition of multilateralization of foreign policy. The

League of Nations was judged by the Danish Foreign Minister P. Munch to be well-suited for safeguarding Denmark's 'normative interests' – i.e. the interests in influencing the remodelling of international norms in accordance with the viewpoints and rights of small states, as well as ensuring that the Great Powers uphold their declared norms. The Danish foreign minister was aware that it would be a very lengthy process (Karup Pedersen, 1970).

There is a link between this theory of small powers in international politics and regime theory. All states have normative interests, interests in influencing the creation of regimes, but it is supposed that the small states that are in a weak position in international politics regarding military and economic means have a special need for a regime in various issue areas in international politics. A regime might extend the scope for action of small states conditioned by the Great Power structure of the international system. The Danish foreign minister took initiatives towards cooperation among the small Nordic states and Belgium, the Netherlands and Luxembourg in the League of Nations with the long-term goal of establishing an international legal system. The normative interests are, of course, closely connected with security and trade interests. Taking part in the creation of norms and principles, rules and decision-making procedures in these policy areas are of great importance for all states.

In the post-war period Danish governments have stressed the importance of participation in international organizations as well as of continuing cooperation among the Nordic countries. There is a strong positive attitude in Denmark to Nordic cooperation, but it has been most successful in what could be called normative or value-promoting politics in Nordisk Råd among the Nordic Countries themselves. This kind of integration has been called 'cobweb integration', a pragmatic step-by-step integration with a lot of network contacts on many levels (Andren, 1967). In the United Nations system of international organizations the Nordic Countries have cooperated on their long-term goal, the establishment of an international legal order in many international policy fields.

It has been maintained that EC membership has drawn Denmark in a direction away from the common Nordic standpoints in the United Nations. However, studies of voting patterns have shown that this is not correct. Only in a very small number of decisions has Denmark been isolated in the Nordic voting (Schou, 1987). So Nordic cooperation in the United Nations, especially in the normative policy area and in relation to development policy in Third World countries, can still be called successful.

The plan for Nordic security cooperation in 1948 and the NORDEK plan for extended economic cooperation among the Nordic countries, which were negotiated during the years 1968 to 1970, both failed. Denmark became a member of NATO together with Norway, and Denmark got a unique position as the only member of both the Nordic system and the EC in 1972.

During the rest of the post-war period Danish Governments tried to avoid problems caused by these overlapping memberships by fragmentation of Denmark's foreign policy. Danish governments stressed that Danish security interests should be safeguarded in NATO, and not in the EC. The EC has been debated in Denmark as an organization for safeguarding Denmark's trade interests, and as regards Nordisk Råd and the United Nations, these organizations have been called the most important arenas for a value-promoting Danish foreign policy with a long-term goal.

It can be said that the fragmentation of Danish foreign policy corroborates the assumption put forward in small state theory: that small state foreign policy will stress the value of a complex balance among Great Powers in the environment of the small state. Negotiating different parts of Danish foreign policy in different international organizations might reduce the influence of Great Powers in the western international organizations.

As mentioned above, some changes in Danish attitudes to this functional division among the international organizations of the western countries can be seen now that the post-war period is over. Regarding the EC/EPC and the question of military and defence issues on the agenda in these fora, the political changes in the eastern European countries may have had the effect that Denmark will not have to adapt to new institutional development in relation to defence policy in these fora.

The former United Kingdom Prime Minister Mrs Thatcher has declared that the process of bringing together the two German states within the EC/EPC as well as creating close institutional links between the EC and other Eastern European countries might slow down the process towards a European Union, which would not be bad in the opinion of the British Government. The intergovernmental model for the EC/EPC development has British support.

Furthermore, Mrs Thatcher declared that the relationship between the United States and Great Britain is stronger than ever before now during the presidency of George Bush. 'The best way to characterize this relationship is that it is special', she is reported to have said (Danish Broadcasting 25 March 1990.)

The dilemma of the western European members of NATO is that on the one hand they feel the need of safeguarding specific Western European security interests when these seem to be in conflict with the policies of the United States, but on the other hand they fear that attempts to develop a separate European defence institution may result in a diminished US commitment to the defence of Western Europe.

The 'special relationship' between the United States and the United Kingdom – which was used by President de Gaulle as one of the arguments against British membership of the EC in 1963 – is still a factor of importance for the development of the security dimension of the Western European cooperation.

Denmark has consistently stressed the Atlantic cooperation in security policy and also the political aspect of NATO as formulated in the Harmel report in 1967. Denmark has also, as regards the europeanization of the security debate, been in favour of broad solutions. Denmark has been fully committed to the Helsinki Process, particularly to the 'third basket' dealing with 'human aspects' (Karup Pedersen, 1989). Now the CSCE process has been proposed as the framework for negotiations about future security arrangements in Europe with solutions to the problems of adaptation in connection with the reunification of the two German states. Establishing institutions in relation to the CSCE has also been proposed. It could be assumed that a development of All-European institutions in cooperation with both Superpowers will be preferred by the Danish Government and opposition to a narrow solution in the form of building up a stronger Eurogroup within NATO.

It seems unlikely that Denmark will become a member of the WEU in its present form. This Western European security regime has a set of rules that come into force automatically on the outbreak of war.

A broad agreement behind the foreign policy of Denmark

The constraints imposed on Denmark's foreign policy by membership of NATO and the EC has resulted in protests from a minority within the opposition in the Folketinget. There has, however, been a long tradition in Denmark of consensus on foreign policy issues and apart from a small minority the consensus about Denmark's membership of NATO and of the EC survived the period from 1982 to 1988, when a coalition of four bourgeois parties, the Conservatives, the Agrarian Liberals, the Centre Democrats and the Christian People's Party formed the Government, and an alternative majority on security policy was formed in the Folketing.

The unique situation during this period was that the Government did not resign when there was a majority in the Folketinget against the standpoints of the Government on a specific security policy issue. The Government must resign if there is a vote of no confidence against it, but it may stay in office when there is a majority against a Government proposal. This had never happened before in relation to foreign policy issues, but this Government did not find the specific foreign policy issues so important that they should be given higher priorities than Denmark's economic policy. They therefore chose the unexpected strategy of staying in office and implementing the decisions of the alternative security policy majority. Prime Minister Schlüter issued writs for the last election (in 1988), however, when a Social Democratic security policy proposal won a majority against the Government. The proposal called upon the Government to deliver a letter to the captains of foreign naval vessels visiting Danish harbours and territorial waters. The letter should impress on the captains Denmark's long-standing policy of refusing to allow nuclear weapons on its territory in time of peace.

Various explanations of the disappearance of Danish foreign policy consensus have been given. One explanation could be the attempt of the opposition to profile their parties by means of foreign policy standpoints in a situation when very few essential alternatives to the economic policies of the Government could be presented. Another possible explanation could be changes in the international situation that opened opportunities for action for a foreign policy line that the opposition had had for some time.

The multilateralization of Denmark's foreign policy could be a third explanation. On the one hand it has pushed the participation of the small power in the international policy process forward to the initiative stage; on the other the institutional development may create constraints on Denmark's sphere of action, so that the opposition now needs to control in detail the policies in the international organizations (Schou, 1989).

The election in 1988 did not give any clear mandate. After protracted negotiations about the composition of the government a three-party coalition was formed under Prime Minister Schlüter. The coalition this time included the Radikal Liberals, who had been part of the majority which had voted the Government down. The formation of this coalition put an end to open disagreement between Government and majority in Parliament. A number of parliamentary commissions have been established to deal with disagreements, and the opposition parties seem to be satisfied with this opportunity to influence security policy issues. Under the previous arrangement with the many 'footnotes' from the alternative security policy majority it could in fact not control the Government's foreign policy. The line of the opposition was not advanced (Karup Pedersen, 1989).

The open debate between Government and opposition about security policy issues has, however, encouraged the Danish public to take an interest in European security questions. Denmark is still considered a low tension area (Heurlin, 1989).

A survey has recently shown that many Danish citizens are concerned about the problems in relation to the re-unification of the two German states, but the Danish Government and the Social Democratic opposition express their confidence in a solution within the EC, which Denmark in its own interest must take an active part in (Politiken, 3—4 February 1990).

The question is, then, what kind of development of the EC that is more than a regime will be supported by a broad agreement in the Folketinget. There have been changes in the attitudes to decision making at the Community level with majority voting. The social dimension of a European Union and environment issues are seen as areas where it would be in Denmark's interest to have decision making at the Community level with majority voting. It remains to be seen whether the dynamics of the integration will lead to a process with a higher rate of speed than it is possible for Denmark to keep up with.

The political government process in Europe

There are four values that the actors in the European development all express as the fundamental ones that motivate their policies: welfare, security, identity and democracy.

Maybe it is a better idea to focus on the process rather than on the end goal of an integration process, and to evaluate its direction in relation to the actors obtaining more or less of these values for the populations of the European countries.

With the new opening towards the EFTA and the Eastern European countries the All-European perspective is a political reality and not just a theoretical model, as formulated by Martin Sæter years ago (Sæter, 1984).

The present complex pattern of real processes of political and economic changes in Eastern Europe should be studied. They will produce an important part of the All-European process. The EC countries and among them Denmark have given the relationship with the Eastern countries highest priority on the agenda.

The establishment of rules of the game for the East-West interaction, a policy of détente and an increase in transnational European policy is, in the opinion of Ole Wæver, the real All-European project, when the constraints on the process set by security interests are taken into consideration. This policy is in form far from radical. It is a controlled reform process (Wæver, 1989).

The relationship EC/EFTA is the other important aspect of the All-European perspective. Denmark has welcomed the application for membership from Austria. As regards the Nordic countries, Denmark seems to be too eager to see them as EC members in the opinion of these countries themselves.

Denmark had the idea of being able to act as a bridge between the EC and the Nordic countries. It was, of course, in Denmark's own interest to try to obtain broad solutions that were in line with the EC as well as the Nordic countries. It appeared that such solutions were not so difficult to achieve. The other Nordic countries established close relations with the EC (Schou, 1982).

Conclusion

A 'fragmentation' of Denmark's foreign policy is no longer possible. The development in the Western European 'core area', the EC, must be considered in relation to the development in the All-European processes and the relationship between the United States and the Soviet Union.

The German question in European politics has revealed that the separation of international economy and the non-military aspects of security policy is artificial, and that the problems in relation to the military aspects must find their solution within an institutional framework including all the actors participating in the process of change in Europe (Kelstrup, 1989).

The EC is now considered by Government and opposition in Denmark 'a security community', and it is an important element in Denmark's security policy to have a solution to the German problem in the EC/EPC.

As regards Denmark and NATO, it can be supposed that NATO will adapt to the fundamental changes in the environment. Bertel Heurlin concludes in his analysis of NATO (1990) that the development in Europe in the post-cold war period means that Denmark has reached the most important objects of Danish foreign policy: detente and arms reduction.

As regards the fundamental value, security, the process in Europe has been very positive for Denmark.

Danish welfare in general will not be threatened by the Internal Market of the EC – on the contrary. But further institutional development in the direction of a European Union in the EC will be a new challenge for Denmark's policy of balanced adaptation. Will it be possible for Denmark to steer the economic development in the country in accordance with the distribution of wealth and the level of public service that in Denmark is considered to be the object of a welfare state?

The identity values of Denmark can be expected to be preserved in an All-European development: Denmark as both a Nordic country and a member of a more integrated EC/EPC. Developments in an All-European process leading to closer cooperation among the EFTA countries and the EC will make it easier for Denmark to keep this double identity.

Democracy is a focus of the All-European process and this is an instrument for cooperation among the European countries and for a creativity necessary for establishing new international institutions and regimes in the region, so that the political government process in Europe can continue in directions that are positive in relation to the fundamental values of the actors on the European scene.

References

Andren, Nils (1967), Nordic Integration, *Cooperation and Conflict*, 1.

Bisgaard, Thomas (1989), *Balanceret tilpasning i et interdependent internationalt system. Norge og EF fra 1972 til 1987*, Speciale. Institut for Samfundsfag og Forvaltning. Københavns Universitet.

Deutsch, Karl W. (1968), *The Analysis of International Relations*, Prentice Hall, Inc, New Jersey.

Federspiel, Ulrik (1985), *Integration i teori og praksis*, Jurist- og Økonomforbundets forlag, Denmark.

Haagerup, N.J. and Thune, C., (1988), Problems of Transition, in Alford, J. and Hunt, K. (eds), *Europe in the Western Alliance*, MacMillan Press Ltd, London.

Heurlin, Bertel (1989), Er Danmark et lavspændingsområde?, Heurlin, B. & Thune, C. (eds), *Danmark og det internationale system*, Politiske Studier, København.

Heurlin, Bertel (1990), *NATO, Europa, Denmark. Perspektiver for 90'erne*, Det sikkerheds- og nedrustningspolitiske Udvalg, København.

Jensen, Frede P. (1989), *WEU Den vesteuropæiske Union*, Det sikkerheds- og nedrustningspolitiske Udvalg, København.

Karup Pedersen, Ole (1970), *Udenrigsminister P. Munchs opfattelse af Danmarks stilling i international politik*, English Summary, pp. 634–642, København.

Karup Pedersen, Ole (1989), The Debate on European Security in Denmark, Wæver, Ole *et al.* (eds), *European Polyphony: Perspectives Beyond East-West Confrontation*, MacMillan Press Ltd, London.

Kelstrup, Morten (1989), Sikkerhedsbegrebet og Dansk sikkerhedspolitik, in Heurlin, B. and Thune, C. (eds), *Danmark og det internationale system*, Politiske Studier, København.

Lodge, Juliet (ed.), (1989), *The European Community and the Challenge of the Future*, Pinter Publishers, London.

Nehring, N.-J. (1989), *EF, det indre marked og sikkerhedspolitikken*, Det sikkerheds- og nedrustningspolitiske Udvalg, København.

Nørgaard, Ole (1989), *Gorbatjov og Vesteuropa*, Det sikkerheds- og nedrustningspolitiske Udvalg, København.

Pedersen, Thomas (1989), *Bonn-Paris-London: Partnere eller rivaler?*, Det sikkerheds- og nedrustningspolitiske Udvalg, København.

Sæter, Martin (1984), *Europa mellem Supermagterne*, Universitetsforlaget, Oslo.

Schou, Tove Lise (1982), Danmark mellem Norden of EF, *Økonomi og politik*, 56 (3), pp. 34–55.

Schou, Tove Lise (1989), Danmarks politik over for internationale organisationer – i et regimeteoretisk perspektiv, in Heurlin, B. and Thune, C. (eds), *Danmark og det internationale system*, Politiske Studier, København.

Wallace, W. (1983), 'Less than a Federation, More than a regime: the Community as a Political System', in Wallace, W. and Webb (eds), *Policy-making in the European Community*, John Wiley and Sons, London.

Wæver, Ole (1989), *Hele Europa projekter, Kontraster*, Det sikkerheds og nedrustningspolitiske udvalg.

Chapter 3

Protection of fundamental rights

Ruth Nielsen

Introduction

Denmark offers – like the other Nordic countries – a weak legal protection of fundamental rights, including the right not to be discriminated against on grounds of race, colour or ethnic origin. The question addressed in this chapter is whether Community law provides a legal basis for a stronger protection of human rights in Denmark than that offered by the Danish tradition.

Legal basis for protection of fundamental rights in Community law

Unlike a number of continental European constitutions, the EEC Treaty contains no catalogue of fundamental rights. The right not to be discriminated against on grounds of nationality (within the EEC) and the right to equal pay are, however, expressly provided for in the Treaty; see in particular articles 7, 48–66 and 119. These provisions have been complemented by secondary legislation (Nielsen, 1988).

The European Court of Justice has, since the early 1970s, developed a Community law protection of fundamental rights, in particular as regards individual rights. In addition, a number of declarations express Community support for fundamental rights. In 1977 the European Parliament, the Council and the Commission adopted a joint declaration on fundamental rights (OJ 1977 C 103). In 1978, the Member States adopted a declaration on democracy (EC Bulletin). Race discrimination has been the subject of a special declaration (OJ 1986 C 158) and the Council is currently considering a proposal for a resolution on racism.

When the EEC Treaty was amended in 1986, a general acknowledgement of fundamental rights as laid down in the constitutions and laws of the Member States and in the European Convention on Human Rights and the European Council's Social Charter was included in the preamble of the Single European Act.

Some of the provisions mentioned above are binding (e.g. articles 48, 119 and the preamble of the Single European Act) while others (the various declarations on fundamental rights) are non-binding. Even non-binding EEC rules have, however, some legal effect.

Impact on Danish Law

Human rights conventions

Denmark has ratified a number of international conventions on human rights, but they are not transformed into national labour law and are usually not considered binding upon individuals. It is, for example, a widespread view among Danish labour law practitioners that a private Danish employer is free to make racist recruitment decisions.

As another example, the following conclusion concerning the Danish implementation of the European Council Social Charter may be mentioned:

> . . . it is evident that the Danish governments have at no time had any intention of adhering strictly to those principles, if this would mean a necessity to abolish traditional principles of the Danish labour market. . . . This means that the Charter cannot get a strong profile in the national state of law, and it must also necessarily mean that the national state of law on certain points may be in violation of the principles of the Charter (Jacobsen)

Denmark ratified ILO convention no. 100 on equal pay in 1960 and ILO convention no. 111 on equal treatment in 1961, as well as the UN convention of 1979 on the elimination of all forms of discrimination against women in 1982. None of these conventions have been incorporated into Danish law by special legislation.

Following the ratification of ILO convention no. 100 in 1960, the question of whether or not to adopt legislation was raised in the Danish Parliament. The answer was in the negative (Nielsen, 1979a) until in 1976 Denmark felt forced to adopt legislation on the issue in order to comply with the Equal Pay Directive (see below).

Denmark has a strong tradition of not providing special protection for women and has consequently not ratified the ILO conventions prohibiting night work, etc., for women (Nielsen, 1980).

In respect of international law, Denmark has traditionally adhered to the so-called dualistic theory. International conventions ratified by Denmark are not regarded as part of Danish law unless they are in some way incorporated into it. The dualistic theory has, however, been contested during recent years (Espersen, 1970) and it is possible to reconstruct Danish law so that it becomes compatible with international standards.

After the adoption of the Single European Act, which as mentioned above refers to fundamental rights in the preamble, human rights conventions are to some degree incorporated into Community law. This provides a further argument for taking them into account in Danish Law.

Labour law

Community law on fundamental rights has so far had most impact on labour law, where the express provisions on free movement of workers and equality between the sexes are of direct relevance.

Changes in the general pattern of sources of law

Originally, the Danish Equal Pay Act did not mention work to which equal value is attributed. In 1983, the Commission took infringement proceedings against Denmark under article 169 on this ground (CASE 143/83).

The Danish Government asserted that Danish law conformed entirely with the directive. In that regard the Danish Government stated that the Equal Pay Act was only a subsidiary guarantee of the principle of equal pay, in cases where observance of that principle was not already ensured under collective agreements. Collective agreements, which govern most employment relationships in Denmark, are, according to the Danish government, based on the principle of equal pay as applying also to work of equal value. All Danish collective agreements on wages provide for equal pay rates for men and women unless the opposite is expressly stated. Respect of the equal pay principle is regarded as an implied term.

The EC Court found that Member States may leave the implementation of the principle of equal pay to collective agreement. That possibility does not, however, discharge them from the obligation of ensuring that all workers in the Community are afforded the full protection provided for in the directive. That State guarantee must cover all cases where effective protection is not ensured by other means, for whatever reason, and in particular cases where the workers in question are not union members, where the sector in question is not covered by a collective agreement or where such an agreement does not fully guarantee the principle of equal pay.

In that respect the Danish Equal Pay Act did not exhibit the clarity and precision necessary for the protection of the workers concerned. Even accepting the assertions of the Danish Government that the principle of equal pay for men and women, in the broad sense required by the directive, was implemented in collective agreements, it had not been shown that the same implementation of that principle was guaranteed for workers whose rights were not defined in such agreements. The principles of legal certainty and the protection of individuals require an unequivocal wording which would give the persons concerned a clear and precise understanding of their rights and obligations and would enable the courts to ensure that those rights and obligations are observed.

The wording of the Danish law did not fulfil those conditions inasmuch as it set out the principle of equal pay without speaking of work of equal value, thus restricting the scope of the principle. The fact that the Danish government in the explanatory remarks to the draft Equal Treatment Act stated that the expression 'same work' was intended to cover 'work to which equal value is attributed' was not sufficient to ensure that the persons concerned are adequately informed.

Industrial arbitration

Judicial process within the meaning of article 2 of the Equal Pay Directive and article 6 of the Equal Treatment Directive must be interpreted within the context of article 6 of the European Convention of Human Rights by which all Member States of the EC are bound. This article provides that in the determination of his civil rights and obligations . . . everyone is entitled to a fair and public hearing within a reasonable time by an independent and impartial tribunal established by law.

Industrial arbitration in Denmark is governed by the procedural rules the parties law down by collective agreement. The hearing and the arbitral award is not usually public. One can therefore put a question mark on whether Denmark fulfils its obligation under the Directives by leaving equal pay cases to be handled by industrial arbitration (Nielsen, 1989).

Indirect sex discrimination

It has been the general opinion in Denmark until recently that Danish law on equality was sufficiently developed to cover at least the full scope of directly applicable community provisions so that there was no room for Danish cases based directly on article 119.

After the ruling of the European Court of Justice in the Rinner-Kühn case (CASE 171/88), it has been argued (Nielsen, 1979b) that the Danish Salaried Employees' Act section 5 on sick pay (which limits the entitlement to sick pay to employees with at least fifteen hours' work per week) is a violation of article 119 as interpreted by the Rinner-Kühn judgement. A Danish female salaried employee working less than fifteen hours a week should therefore be able to claim pay during sickness under article 119 before a Danish court.

It follows from the judgement in the Marshall case (CASE 152/84) that the Equal Treatment Directive has no direct effect on private employers.

Some of its provisions, e.g. article 5, are directly applicable against a public employer. It is the prevailing opinion in Denmark that it also follows from the Marshall case that the Equal Pay Directive has no direct effect on private employers (Gulmann and Hagel-Sørensen, 1989).

The ECJ ruled in the Borrie Clarke case (CASE 384/85) and the Ruzius-Wilbrink case (CASE C-102/88) that article 4 of directive 79/7 is directly applicable.

The Danish Labour Market Supplementary Pension (ATP) and the Danish Unemployment Act, which only accord limited rights to part-time workers, are probably in contravention of article 4 of directive 79/7 as interpreted in the Ruzius-Wilbrink case.

The ruling of the European Court in the Danfoss case (CASE 109/88) shows that the burden of proof on an employer to justify indirectly discriminatory pay criteria is much more rigorous than it has been regarded hitherto by Danish courts and tribunals.

Conclusion

As seen from the above-mentioned cases on indirect sex discrimination and burden of proof, it seems obvious that Community law provides a stronger protection than traditional Danish law in the areas covered by these cases. Community law also, as seen from the infringement case against Denmark on the Equal Pay Act, puts a stronger emphasis on the principle of legal certainty than has been usual in Denmark. Whether there is sufficient legal basis in Community law to claim respect for all kinds of fundamental rights in Denmark is more doubtful. In my view, the fundamental rights declaration in the preamble of the Single European Act and the non-binding Community provisions on fundamental rights must be taken into consideration when interpreting any Danish piece of law, including unwritten principles of law.

References

CASE C-102/88, L. Ruzius-Willbrink versus Bustuur van de Bedrijfsverenining voor Overheidsdiensten, judgement of 13.12.89.

CASE 109/88, Handels- og Kontorfunktionærernes Forbund i Danmark versus Dansk Arbejdsgiverforening for Danfoss A/S, judgement of 17.10.89.

CASE 171/43, Commission versus Denmark, *ECR*, 1985, p. 427.

CASE 152/84, M.H. Marshall versus Southampton and South West Hampshire Area Health Authority (Teaching), *ECR*, 1986, p. 273.

CASE 171/88, Ingrid Rinner-Kühn versus FWW Spezial Gebäudereinigung GmbH und CO KG, judgement of 13.7.89.

CASE 384/85, Borrie Clark versus the Chief Adjudication Officer, *ECR*, 1987, p. 2865.

Espersen, Ole (1970), *Indgåelse og opfyldelse af traktater*, Copenhagen, p. 163.

Gulmann and Hagel-Sørensen (1989), *EF-ret*, Copenhagen.

Jacobsen, Per (1986), in Jaspers and Betten (eds), *25 years European Social Charter*, Kluwer, p. 81.

Nielsen, Ruth (1979a), *Kvindearbydsret (Women Labour Right)*, Copenhagen, p. 222.

Nielsen, Ruth (1979b), Judiciel aktivisme i EF-Arbejdsretten, *Retfærd*,

Nielsen, Ruth (1980), Special protective legislation for women in the Nordic countries, *International Labour Review*, vol. 119 no. 1 Geneva.

Nielsen, Ruth (1988), *EF -arbejdsret*, Copenhagen.

Nielsen, Ruth (1989), *EF-arbejdsret*, Copenhagen, pp. 45–48.

PART II: ORGANIZATIONAL AND POLITICAL SYSTEM

m

grated part of Danish
egrated part of modern
c pluralism incident to

hrough of industrialism
vestern industrial coun-
mained the dominant
al' industry in a small
e century) two million
ther preconditions for
een pushed back by –
t still plays a major role
rrency-earning industry
facturing industry.
n inhabitants and a total
hom are women. There
ity of which are 'small'
the Danish debate one
y large firms, so-called
siness life with more
s about 400,000 people
There are about 85,000
0), and 165,000 persons
gricultural sector. Some
n building and construc-
commerce and transport,
in the public service and
or 478,000 people (about
4.2).
e Danish organizational

Table 4.1 Active population by i

	1
Manufacturing	
Handicrafts	
Agriculture	
Construction	
Commerce	1
Transport	
Public service	1
Private service	1
Total	10

Source: Nyt tra Danmarks statistik 1

Table 4.2 Gross domestic product 1988 (percentages)

Manufacturing	
Agriculture	
Public works	
Construction	
Commerce	
Banking	
Transport	
Private service	
Public service	

Source: National statistics.

system is anchored in the commer
and humanitarian interests, leisure,
of the basis for the organizationa
society is so relatively homogeneou
the Lutheran State Church is d
political point of view, is of seco
Internationally, Denmark is in
organizing. Only a little less than

Chapter 4

The organizational system

Henning Bregnsbo

Introduction

The organizational system in Denmark is an integrated part of Danish society as a whole, and Denmark likewise is an integrated part of modern western society with political, social and economic pluralism incident to it.

The decades before World War I saw the breakthrough of industrialism in Denmark, somewhat later than in the leading western industrial countries, and far into this century agriculture remained the dominant industry. Agriculture was considered the 'natural' industry in a small country like ours with only (about the turn of the century) two million inhabitants and with no raw materials and other preconditions for industrial developments. Today agriculture has been pushed back by — among others — the manufacturing industry, but it still plays a major role both politically and economically as a foreign currency-earning industry and as a supplier of raw materials to the manufacturing industry.

Denmark today has a population of 5.2 million inhabitants and a total labour force of 2.8 million people, one third of whom are women. There are about 7,000 manufacturing firms, the majority of which are 'small' firms with between ten and fifty employees. In the Danish debate one often hears complaints about the lack of really large firms, so-called industrial 'locomotives', to inject Danish business life with more dynamism. The manufacturing industry employs about 400,000 people (15–16 per cent of the total labour force). There are about 85,000 agricultural holdings (in 1977 there were 128,000), and 165,000 persons (well over 6 per cent) are employed in the agricultural sector. Some 183,000 people (7 per cent) are employed within building and construction, about 430,000 people (16–17 per cent) in commerce and transport, and no less than 832,000 persons are employed in the public service and administration sector. In the private service sector 478,000 people (about 18 per cent) are employed (see Tables 4.1 and 4.2).

A large and politically important part of the Danish organizational

Table 4.1 Active population by industry 1970, 1980 and 1987 (percentages)

	1970	1980	1987
Manufacturing	19.0	15.7	15.5
Handicrafts	6.0	4.4	4.5
Agriculture	11.4	7.9	6.3
Construction	9.7	7.7	7.0
Commerce	14.3	12.0	11.3
Transport	5.3	5.0	5.2
Public service	19.0	30.8	31.9
Private service	15.3	16.3	18.3
Total	100	100	100

Source: Nyt tra Danmarks statistik 1988 no. 262.

Table 4.2 Gross domestic product (at factor cost) by industrial origin 1978 and 1988 (percentages)

	1978	1988
Manufacturing	18.0	20.0
Agriculture	7.0	4.0
Public works	2.0	2.5
Construction	7.5	6.0
Commerce	14.0	13.0
Banking	4.0	4.5
Transport	7.0	6.0
Private service	18.5	21.0
Public service	22.0	23.0
	100	100

Source: National statistics.

system is anchored in the commercial sphere, but other things – cultural and humanitarian interests, leisure, sports and religion – constitute part of the basis for the organizational system. On the other hand, Danish society is so relatively homogeneous – we speak the same language, and the Lutheran State Church is dominant – that this sphere, from a political point of view, is of secondary importance.

Internationally, Denmark is in the front rank when it comes to organizing. Only a little less than 10 per cent of the Danish population

Table 4.3 Membership of employees' vocational organizations

	Number of members
LO, The Danish Confederation of Trade Unions	1,420,225
Special Workers' Union (SID)	310,374
Metal-Workers' Union	137,532
Federation of Civil Servants and Salaried Employees' Organizations (FTF)	317,556
CO II Civil Servants' Central Organization	28,934
Union of Teachers	64,329
CO I. State Civil Servants	54,798
Professional Associations (AC)	93,263
Various 'outsider' organizations	118,527

Source: Statistical Yearbook 1989

Table 4.4 Occupation and membership of vocational and non-vocational organizations (percentages)

Type of organization	%
Vocational	
Trade unions	52
Employers' organizations	2
Organizations within agriculture, fishery etc.	6
Business and trade organizations	5
Non-vocational	
Area:	
Health, sickness	11
Property	19
Housing	10
Radio and TV	8
Environment	5
Humanitarian affairs, charity	7
Religion	4
Culture	9
Consumer affairs	31
Leisure: hobbies, athletics, sports	41
Vocational organizations	55
Non-vocational organizations	81
All organizations	90

Source: Damgaard, p. 62

does *not* belong to any organization whatsoever. Fifty-two per cent of the population belong to a trade union (the corresponding figure for Norway, for example, is 36 per cent), and of the vocationally active part of the population rather more than 75 per cent belong to a trade union.

More than 73 per cent of the population are members of more than one organization. In all there are about 2,000 national organizations in Denmark.

Usually it is the partners in the labour market that catch the big headlines.

The Danish labour market

In the private labour market two associations are dominant, The *Danish Confederation of Trade Unions* (LO) (Landsorganisationen i Danmark (LO)), and the *Danish Employers' Confederation* (DA) (Dansk Arbejdsgiverforening (DA)). They are normally referred to as the 'main' organizations of the labour market. LO has rather more than 1.4 million members (less than half of whom are women) corresponding to well over half of all wage-earners. LO is the umbrella organization for a large number of trade unions. The largest one is the *Special Workers' Union in Denmark* (SID) (Specialarbejderforbundet i Danmark (SID)) with 318,000 members. Other large unions are the *Union of Commercial and Clerical Employees in Denmark* (HK) (Handels- og Kontorfunktionærernes forbund i Danmark (HK)) with 311,000 members, most of whom are women, and the *Danish Metal-Workers' Union* (Dansk Metalarbejderforbund) with 139,000 members, mostly men. About 100,000 members of LO are employed by the state; about 318,000 are employed in the municipal sector and well over 900,000 in the private sector. In the labour market there are also a couple of 'outsider' unions which by the established unions are named 'yellow' by themselves 'free' or 'Christian'. Once in a while there is a bitter strife, and the 'free' and 'Christian' unions are advancing, though so far they constitute no more than a bad omen for the established unions.

Opposite LO one finds first and foremost DA, whose members can be local as well as national employers' organizations or individual firms. DA has rather more than 22,000 members distributed over 151 organizations and 45 individual firms. The largest member organization is the *Federation of Danish Mechanical Engineering and Metalworking Industries* (Jern- og Metalindustriens Sammenslutning). DA's members employ about 515,000 persons (310,000 blue-collar workers, 205,000 white-collar workers) most of whom belong to LO; but less than half of the LO membership work for employers that are members of DA, meaning that the degree of organization is much higher on the labour side than on the employer side. The agricultural employers' local and regional organizations are organized in the *Federation of Agricultural Employers' Associations* (SALA),

Sammenslutningen af Landbrugets Arbejdsgiverforeninger (SALA).

The two partners negotiate agreements every second or third year covering wages and work conditions for the coming two- or three-year period. The negotiations are conducted along strictly formal lines and often have the character of a ritual dance, the function of which is also to satisfy the psychological needs of the members. Great national interests are involved, and the importance of wage restraint is vigorously underscored by the government and its economic advisers. An important – though not always understood or accepted – argument is that wage restraint is a precondition for more jobs.

If the partners do not reach an agreement the official conciliation board (Forligsinstitutionen) enters the action. The task of the conciliation board is to try to bring the negotiating partners together again, and if possible put forward a draft settlement that stands a reasonable chance of being accepted by the partners. The conciliator, the chairman of the conciliation board (Forligsmanden), can await a breakdown, but he can also on his own initiative enter the negotiations at an earlier stage. The partners are by law bound to appear when called in, and the conciliator has the right to postpone a notified conflict for a period of two weeks, and even longer if important national interests are deemed to be in danger. Finally, in a conflict situation, the conciliator can demand that a ballot be taken for a proposal for a total settlement drafted by himself be taken as a whole. The ballot rules make it difficult, in practice, to reject such a proposal, and the conciliator always seeks to work in a certain harmony with the two opposing partners and may even give up putting forward a compromise proposal if he finds that the two partners are too far away from each other. They may even have advised him to stay out.

Several times the Folketing has had to interfere in order to avoid a major conflict threatening important national interests. The practice is that the conciliator's draft settlement (having been rejected by one or both partners) is made into a law by the Folketing. Politically, the most difficult situation arises when a draft settlement has been rejected by the workers and accepted by the employers.

Outside LO there are a large number of other wage-earner unions, the largest being the *Federation of Danish Civil Servants' and Salaried Employees' Organizations* (FTF) (Fællesrådet for Danske Tjenestemands- og Funktionær-organisationer (FTF)) with about 370,000 members, the *State Civil Servants' Central Organization I* (CO I) (Statstjenestemændenes Centralorganisation I (CO I)) with about 70,000 members (the 'silver cords'), the *State Civil Servants' Central Organization II* (CO II) (Statstjenestemændenes Centralorganisation II (CO II)) with about 35,000 members (the 'gold cords'), the *Teachers' Confederation* (LC) (Lærernes centralorganisation (LC)) and the *Confederation of Professional Associations* (AC) with 80,000 and 120,000 members respectively.

The opposite parties for these latter organizations when negotiating wages and work conditions are, for the most part, the state and the municipal authorities. But it is always the negotiations between LO and DA that attract the main attention, and the results in that area, or the expected results there, play an important role for all others, though during the last few years a certain shift of emphasis can be noticed away from the LO-DA area corresponding to the relative growth outside the sphere of these two organizations. While the negotiations are taking place everybody watches everybody else, as it would be embarrassing to accept conditions afterwards being trumped over by others. The informal contacts and understandings among the negotiators on all sides are therefore of great importance.

In actual fact the Danish labour market is remarkably quiet. In 1988 there were only 157 strikes in all, with about 30,000 employees involved and 96,500 workdays lost. 1988 was a normal year, while 1985 on the other hand was unusual with 820 strikes, involving 581,000 employees and 2.3 million lost workdays.

The relative peace in the labour market can be considered a reflection of a fundamental harmony in society at large. The partners in the labour market maintain close relations with the political parties. On the part of LO there are narrow formal links to the Socialdemocratic party, and if political factors wished to fan the flames it could be easily done. On the other hand LO has, in fact, in many political situations a right of veto on the party. The fundamental harmony has to do with a more or less agreed upon understanding of Denmark's fundamental economic and financial position, which can be solved only by restraint and moderation by all involved. Of course, fundamental agreement at the elite level is one thing; understanding and acceptance at the mass level is another. The situation is further complicated by the general weakening of the political system that has taken place since the 1960s and 1970s; (see below).

Industrial organizations

The manufacturing industry's mouthpiece is the *Federation of Danish Industries* (IR) (Industrirådet (IR)). It was founded in 1910 after a palace revolution in the then *Copenhagen Industrial Society* (Industriforeningen i Kjøbenhavn) which, in the opinion of the fast-growing Danish (relatively) big industry sector, devoted itself too much to industrial art and small industry at the expense of the larger manufacturing industries.

Under the umbrella of the IR are to be found a very large and heterogenous number of trade organizations, e.g. (to take a few at random) the *Association of Electronics Manufacturers in Denmark* (Elektronikfabrikantforeningen i Danmark), the *Association of Biotechnological Industries in Denmark* (Foreningen af Bioteknologiske Industrier i Danmark) and the *Trade Association for Soap, Perfumes, Toiletries and Similar Products* (Brancheforeningen for Sæbe-, Parfumeri-, Toilet- og kemisk-tekniske Artikler (SPT)).

A number of things contribute to giving industry political strength. For one thing there is industry's narrow, though informal, ties to the liberal-conservative parties which for nine years now have formed the government – mainly the Conservative Party and Venstre, Denmark's Liberal Party. Another reason is the obvious functional importance of industry, which has a 20 per cent share of the national gross factor income. Finally, there is Denmark's huge foreign debt of about 300 billion Danish kroner, accumulated through the last 25 years with continuous deficits on the balances of payments. This is a debt which, to a very high degree, limits the freedom of economic action on the part of Danish politicians and gives very little elbow room to financial initiatives. Through recent years this debt has played an increasing role in the public debate, and the manufacturing industry ('increased export') is seen more and more by the public as the saviour. It all leads in one direction, namely that industry can look forward to increased political responsiveness to its wishes.

Illustrative are the events in the biotechnological area in 1987–88, when very restrictive rules made it difficult to carry out outdoor experiments with gene-manipulated plants. The restrictive law had been passed in response to vigorous 'green' arguments among the public and in the press at the time of the passing of the law. Criticism came from the large biotechnological firm Novo-Nordisk (at the time still two independent firms) and others, and from the biotechnological industry warnings given about the – possible – necessity of moving experiments, production and jobs abroad. The trade association, the above-mentioned Association of Biotechnological Industries, also took an active part in the debate.

The then Minister for Environmental Affairs, Christian Christensen, promised to 'look into' the matter, and in fact soon after came forward will a bill with modifications to the original law satisfying the large biotechnological firms.

Agricultural organizations

As mentioned above, Danish agriculture has been dethroned from its all-powerful position round the turn of the century. The manufacturing sector has grown, as have the private service and public sectors. The party representing agricultural interests above all, Venstre, has correspondingly lost its dominant position in Danish politics. However, both are still powerful political actors.

Agriculture's share of the GNP today amounts to about 6 per cent, and the number of holdings is 80,000 as against 140,000 in 1970, which means that individual holdings are much larger now than they used to be. Today the average figure is 34 hectares. About 7 per cent of the active population are employed in agriculture. In comparison the average figure for the EC countries is 8.6 per cent, but with large national variations: England, Holland and Belgium with under 5 per cent, and Greece, Portugal, Spain, Ireland and Italy with between 29 and 11 per cent of the active population in agriculture.

Agricultural interests in Denmark are represented by the *Danish Agricultural Council* (Landbrugsrådet) in the same way that IR represents the manufacturing industry. The Agricultural Council is an umbrella organization for a large number of agricultural organizations formed on the basis of size of holding, region, primary produce, etc. These are the *Federation of Danish Farmers' Unions* (De Danske Landboforeninger) comprising 125 local unions with 90,000 members; the *Danish Smallholders' Associations* (De Danske Husmandsforeninger) comprising six regional federations of smallholders' associations with a number of local unions with 30,000 members in all; and the *Central Cooperative Committee of Denmark* (Danske Andelsselskaber, formerly De samvirkende danske andelsselskaber) comprising thirty-three cooperative companies and cooperative organizations. The largest among these (measured by turnover) are the *Danish Dairy Federation* (Danske Mejeriers Fællesorganisation); the *Federation of Danish Slaughterhouses* (Organisationen Danske Slagterier); and the *Danish Cooperative Farms' Supply* (Dansk Landbrugs Grovvareselskab (DLG)).

What gives agricultural interests their political clout is fundamentally agriculture's (relatively decreasing) functional importance to society. Furthermore agriculture has narrow bonds, especially to the Venstre party. Also important is the general respect for agriculture, Denmark's traditional main occupation through centuries. Finally, the organization of agriculture around family holdings and cooperatives gives it a special position of high legitimacy, generally not accorded to the manufacturing industry.

There are a number of legislative restraints of trade in the agricultural sector against full commercial exploitation, amalgamations and joint-stock activities, The efficiency of the present structure in the agricultural sector is being debated, and a softening of the restrictions is advocated by some observers, but breaking with proud traditions may prove difficult politically.

The public sector

The public service and administration sector employs no less than 32 per cent of the total labour force and comprises 832,000 people (the whole labour force being 2.6 million persons). It goes without saying that the men and women of this sector possess great political potential and exert influence by virtue of their sheer number.

The size of the public sector is much debated, and there seems to be wide agreement that the sector is too large and ought to be slimmed down in favour of, especially, the industrial (exporting) sector. The growth of the public sector has taken place alongside the development of the Danish welfare state; the phenomenon of 'big government' is well known elsewhere, of course, but is more prominent in Denmark than in most other countries. OECD figures show that in Denmark there are 161 public employees to every 100 employed in the manufacturing industry (IR did not hesitate in publicizing the figures); the corresponding figures being for Sweden 147, for USA and UK 86, for France 76, for Italy 69, for West Germany 51 and for Japan 26.

Despite broad agreement in principle about the desirability of slimming down the public sector, it is difficult in practice to gain political support for concrete measures. Usually the Social Democrats (bearing the main responsibility for the development of the welfare state) and the Socialist Party to the left of the Social Democrats stand guard round the public employees. It is a motley crowd that makes a living in the service of the public authorities. There are professionals, clerical employees and blue-collar workers organized in various LO unions, among them members of SID and Danish Metal Workers Union. Quite a number are organized in the *Danish Municipal Workers' Union* (Dansk Kommunalarbejderforbund), an LO organization with 120,000 members, most of whom are women. Many are organized in the *Danish Council of Nurses* (Dansk Sygeplejeråd), an FTF organization with an overwhelming majority of women among its 40,000 members, and many – 55,000 – are civil servants and organized in COI. The primary school teachers are, for the most part, public employees and are organized in the *Union of Teachers in Denmark* (Danmarks Lærerforening), an FTF organization with 65,000 members.

The opposite party to these organizations, the public authorities at large, is in principle tripartite. This has been so since the Municipal Reform Act of 1971, which delegated a large amount of political decisions to the primary municipalities and the regional councils. The political consequence of the reform was a diminishing of power relative to the organizations. The primary municipalities themselves are organized in the *National Association of Local Authorities* (KL) (Kommunernes Landsforening (KL)) comprising 273 municipalities, i.e. all except Copenhagen and Frederiksberg. It represents the interests of the municipalities *vis-à-vis* the central authorities, the regional councils and the private organizations and the trade unions. Fourteen regional councils are organized in the *Danish Country Councils' Association* (ARF) (Amtsrådsforeningen (ARF)). The majority of the public employees (75 per cent) are employed by the primary municipalities and the regional councils, the rest (25 per cent) are employed by the central state authorities. The Municipal Reform Act of 1970 gave to the municipalities extended freedom of action in various areas, though in actual fact the central authorities often intervene with administrative prescriptions, which on the other hand are always negotiated with KL and ARF beforehand. Municipal and regional life has become more partisan since 1970, and all in all a fruitful (seen in an interest organization perspective) political pluralism has been born.

Patterns of interaction

The Danish organization world is a many-headed phenomenon. The most important organizations are the ones mentioned above, whose members belong to the organizations by virtue of their jobs and private economy. There are many other organizations based on jobs and private economy besides those mentioned, and there are cultural, social and humanitarian organizations, and organizations anchored in leisure, sport, religion and environmental affairs. Many organizations have contact with the political system only sporadically, while the large economically based organizations are in constant, daily contact with public authorities.

This regular, intimate, day-to-day contact is an old phenomenon in Danish politics. In 1966, a quarter of a century ago, an observer wrote the following about the Agricultural Council and its president:

> It is unthinkable that a bill concerning agricultural problems is laid on the table of the Folketing without it having been previously submitted to the Agricultural Council for its opinion. When in parliamentary committee the president may again present himself and communicate the arguments of agriculture, and when the law is in the hand of the administration he may send his representative to the administrative office handling the law, or more simply, the law may be given to one of his sundry suborganizations for this organization to implement (Andersen, 1966).

A narrow, regular, intimate cooperation between public authorities and a private interest organization is neither a novelty nor a rarity, and was not so either in 1966. The remarks about the Agricultural Council and its president could just as well have been said about the other large organizations and their leaders. The cooperation is advantageous to both parties, and Danish society would not be able to function without the cooperation between the organizations and the political system, but – there is no denying it – one can get wary from a democratic point of view when powerful organizations are given too much scope. The organizations can offer the public authorities special knowledge, often in technical areas, and by cooperating the organizations give legitimacy to political and administrative decisions in relation to their members.

Much research demonstrates (with figures for frequency of interaction, etc.) that the dominant organizations are the large, economically well equipped organizations within the labour market, the manufacturing industry, agriculture and the public sector.

They leave their marks on law-making in all its phases, and they even take it upon themselves to administer and implement the political decisions once they are made (cf. Andersen, quoted above). They have narrow contacts with the Folketing, the government and the civil service whether local or national, and they are represented in law-preparing commissions and committees in which Danish politics abounds. The large organizations do not have to beat the drums to get a hearing; the doors are, as a rule, wide open.

Outside the established system of organizations, however, a new development has taken place. A new, more amorphous, fluid system has come into existence; its members are 'movements', activist groups, 'green' and environmental groups, 'grass roots' and diverse *ad hoc* groups operating at local, regional or national levels. They gain their political strength from fluid, often uninformed attitudes and moods in the public at large. The media, not least the TV, give impetus to this system. It can be argued that we are witnessing a shift in the balance of power from the established system of organizations to this new, 'alternative' system of organizations. The shift may not be as profound as the media would like us to believe. And there is another development which has changed the balance between the political system proper and the traditional organizational system – in favour of the last one, but even more in favour of the 'alternative' system. What I have in mind is the weakening of the party system, which begun about 1960 with the formation of the Socialist Party by former communists who liberated themselves from the small orthodox Danish Communist Party. The liberation was rewarded by the voters, and a large opposition to the left of the Social Democratic party was created making its continued cooperation with the center parties difficult. In 1972 the Progress Party was formed, with Mogens Glistrup as leader, at the extreme right. That party too had electoral success and made difficulties for the centre parties. And since then other small parties have gained access to the Folketing, where they balance on the 2 per cent electoral barrier, always in need of raising their profile. The end result is a diminished political efficiency. Behind it all lies, in the last analysis, changed attitudes in the population at large. The electors are less inclined towards political faithfulness than in former times, the electorate drifts more than it used to from one general election to the next. The fundamental harmony characterizing Danish politics prior to 1960 and 1972 is weakened, but still exists.

Illustrative of the political system and the role of the organizations is the story of the restrictive Shops Closing Hours Act. Through many years it has been hotly debated, with unorganized consumer interests confronting very well-organized producer and personnel interests. For many years HK and the organizations of the shop-owners succeeded in blockading all attempts at liberalizing the law. Now a certain, modest liberalization has been carried through the Folketing, probably under the influence of unorganized, but numerous, consumers, many of whom are women working outside the home. The saga of the Shops Closing Hours Act illustrates the actual veto power the large economically based organizations possess over weakly organized or unorganized consumer interests. Another illustrative example is the epoch-making Educational Act of 1958, which opened the way for the egalitarianization and democratization of the Danish school system that we have today. The teachers' unions fought – successfully – through many years against repeated political attempts at reforms more in keeping with popular demands and ambitions. The two cases show that it is in fact possible for large economically based, more often than not conservative, organizations to veto law-making through prolonged periods of time, often years, when more general popular interests are unorganized or weakly organized. But, on the other hand, their veto power can be broken, namely when democratic strength and ambitions in combination with structural changes (more women working out of the home, increased demand for higher education) have grown strong enough to sweep away organizational conservatism.

The European dimension

In October 1972 it was decided by referendum that Denmark should join the EC (together with the UK). Prior to the referendum there had been a hectic and emotional campaign, and a pro-EC decision seemed at the time to hang by a slender thread. Norway, at the same time, actually voted no. The result, however, was in fact a very solid victory for the pro-EC forces. But through the years the Danish electorate has had a very ambivalent attitude towards the EC. The opposition, both before the referendum and before and after a second referendum in 1986, has been very strong. Denmark has always (like the UK and Greece) been 'sceptical', and the electorate has been divided in its attitudes towards the EC across party lines. The Social Democratic Party, in particular, has been a house divided against itself. The party's dilemma has manifested itself during elections to the European Parliament when many Social Democratic voters (the sceptics) have deserted their party. Danish electoral behaviour at the European level has been a mixture of party and referendum behaviour. Now a change seems to be on its way. The Social Democratic voters seem to be about to abandon their scepticism, and in the population at large the pro-EC forces seem to be gaining the upper hand. The more positive attitudes among the electors have their counterpart in a sharply increased interest among organizations and individual firms in the EC. One important factor is undoubtedly the Delors plan for an economic and monetary union and the coming single market. After a weak start these subjects have increasingly become the topic of the day in the political and economic debate.

Until recently, and maybe still, Danish organizations mainly relied upon gaining influence in EC matters through the national political system, the government, the Folketing and the civil service. In the

Table 4.5 The Danish electorate's changing attitude to the EC (percentages)

	January 1989	March 1989	May 1989	June 1989	Referendum 1972
For EC	48	48	50	57	57
Against EC	36	31	34	33	33
Don't know	16	21	16	10	10
Total	100	100	100	100	100

Source: Worre, Berlingske Tidende 29-7-1990, Gallup poll

Table 4.6 The social democratic voters' changing attitudes to the EC (percentages)

	January 1989	March 1989	May 1989	June 1989
For EC	57	61	60	63
Against EC	43	39	40	37
Total	100	100	100	100

Source: Gallup and Berlingske Tidende 29-7-1990

Folketing there is a market committee which, at least formally, has a central position in EC matters and is an important target for the organizations. Furthermore, a number of administrative committees around specific EC matters like customs affairs, fishery and environmental matters have been established. In all, twenty-eight committees have been established. In some of them relevant organizations are directly represented. To other committees the organizations supply information through their contacts, with civil servants actually manning a given committee. In general it is safe to say that there has not been great interest among Danish organizations in procuring influence on the EC authorities by working directly in Brussels. Many Danish organizations are members of the relevant Euro-groups, but here also their interest has been lukewarm, although again a change may be on its way. Danish agriculture, however, has by its membership of COPA, the Committee of Professional Agricultural Organizations of the European Community, obtained considerable influence, and COPA is in general considered the most effective and professional interest organization at the EC level. The Danish manufacturing industry is represented in Brussels by IR and DA sharing an office in Brussels, and is increasingly seeking influence via its membership in UNICE, the Union of Industries in the European Community. Danish trade unions are represented in ETUC, the European

Trade Union Confederation. The Danish Teachers' Association has had its own representative in Brussels since 1987, the *Danish Contractors' Association* (Entreprenørforeningen) since 1988, the *Maritime Association* (Rederiforeningen) since the middle of the year 1989 and the *Office and Retail Trade Employers' Federation* (BKA) (Butiks- og Kontorvirksaomhedernes Arbejdsgiverforening (BKA)) since the end of 1989. LO is considering establishing a representation of its own, and HK at its latest congress at the end of 1989 decided to establish its own office in Brussels. A number of Danish municipalities have established their own offices in Brussels, among others Århus, Odense and Ålborg. The aim is to support local business and is seen as an expansion of the tasks performed by the municipal business support departments. One task would be to procure for local firms money from the EC structural funds, and by so doing procure jobs at home. The above-mentioned municipal interest organizations, the KL and the ARF, have established an EC secretariat in common in 1989, situated (for reasons of economy) in Copenhagen, not in Brussels. One individual Danish firm, the Danish Sugar Refineries, has its own representation in Brussels, and has in fact obtained money from an EC fund for the establishment of a factory in Haderslev. Another Danish firm, Danfoss, has gained success in that its own standards for thermostats have become European standards. The EC commission ordered the standards from the European standardization organizations CEN and CENELEC, and by paying for the R&D Danfoss succeeded in influencing the final recommendations. The toy manufacturing firm LEGO has also procured for itself favourable standardizations. Two other Danish firms, the shipping firm A.P. Møller and Carlsberg, are represented in the private organization European Round Table comprising in all forty-one large European enterprises, among others Phillips, Siemens, Fiat, Olivetti, Hoffman La Roche, Volvo and Unilever, which have been influential in launching the ideas for the European single market.

Conclusion

The Danish organizational system consists of approximately 2,000 national organizations. Add to this many local organizations and a very large number of basis or operational units. Danish society is organized to a very high degree, and only a very limited number of Danes do not belong to some organization or other. Most organizations are apolitical, though some may act politically once or twice during their lifetimes.

However, quite a large number of organizations within the different economic sectors of society are politically active year-round. The same is somewhat true of some individual firms. During the last couple of years the interest in the EC has exploded.

Denmark is in no unique position among the industrial nations of the western world. We are talking of differences of degree, and differences due to specific structural and other circumstances. Danish agriculture has, for historical and traditional reasons, an extremely powerful political position in the Danish organizational world. The manufacturing industry had its breakthrough relatively late; but industry has consolidated its political position especially since the war, and perhaps especially during the last decade. The dominant position of the Social Democratic Party during the decades up till roughly 1980 has led to the Scandinavian-style welfare state of today and in conjunction with it a very large public sector. The organizations within the fishing industry are strong due to the geographical position of the country and the relative importance of the fishing industry, also seen in a European perspective. Danish organizations have not, until recently, taken a strong interest in EC matters, but have relied upon influence via national channels. The Danish electorate (like the British and Greek electorates) has shown much scepticism towards the EC, but a change may be on its way; among other things the Social Democratic voters seem increasingly to accept the EC as a positive fact. The break-up of Eastern Europe, the coming single market and the plans for an economic and monetary union all seem destined to influence Danish society, including its organizational system, profoundly.

References

Andersen, P. Nyboe and Poul Dam (eds) (1966), *Det danske samfund*, Det danske forlag, Albertslund.

Berlingske Tidende 29/7 1990.

Buksti, Jacob A. (1983), 'Bread-and-Butter Agreement and High Politics Disagreement', *Scandinavian Political Studies*, vol. 6, no. 4, 261–280.

Buksti, Jacob A. and Nørby Johansen, L. (1977), *Danske organisationers hvem-hvad-hvor*, Politiken, Copenhagen.

Cadan, Steen m.fl. (ed.) (1990), *Arbejdsmarkedets håndbog*, AOF, Copenhagen.

Chrisophersen, Henning (1989), *Tanker om Danmark i det nye Europa*, Børsens, Copenhagen.

Damgaard, Erik (ed.) (1980), *Folkets veje i dansk politik*, Schultz, Copenhagen.

Due, J. og J. Steen Madsen (1989), *Når der slås søm i*, Jurist- og Økonomforbundet, Copenhagen.

Fivelsdal, E. et al. (1979), Interesseorganisationer og centraladministration, *Nyt fra samfundsvidenskaberne*, Copenhagen.

Hækkerup, H. og J. Hartvig Pedersen (1987), *Arbejdsmarkedsforhold*, Busck, Copenhagen.

Meyer, Poul (1975), *Offentlig forvaltning*, Gad, Copenhagen.

Nyt fra Danmarks Statistik (1988), no. 262.

Van Schendelen, M.P.C.M. and J.R. Jackson (1987), *The Politicisation of Business in Western Europe*, Croom Helm, London.

Statistical Yearbook (1989), Danmarks Statistik, Copenhagen.

Viemose, Søren (1990), *Lobbyisme*, Gyldendal, Copenhagen.

Worre, Torben (1987), 'The Danish Euro-Party System', *Scandinavian Political Studies*, vol. 10, no. 1, 79–95.

Chapter 5

Parties, voters and the EC

Steen Sauerberg

Danish ambiguity towards the EC

The Danish voters, together with the British, have always had a much more reluctant view of European integration than their co-citizens in the European Community. This reluctance is clear from the opinions that have been obtained bi-yearly since 1973 by the common EC effort of opinion polling and published as EUROBAROMETERS.

For the first seventeen years of Danish membership there was a relatively stable pattern of ambiguity, with oscillations between positive and negative evaluations of the Common Market. But there was never enthusiasm or a solid majority that found membership of the Common Market 'a good thing' for Denmark. It was not until we entered into the 1990s that this attitude changed, and the group evaluating membership as good is approximately three times as large as the group that evaluates membership as bad for the country. But there is still a solid group that considers membership of the EC 'a bad thing' – in autumn 1991 it was 20 per cent of the adult population.

This might not seem too alarming for pro-Europeans, especially with the latest positive turn. But it is still exceptional in an EC context. It is clearly the most negative attitude among the twelve member countries. Only the United Kingdom has, for periods of time, had more negative attitudes. From 1976 to 1985, in particular, there was even a prevailing negative majority pointing to the Common Market as 'a bad thing for the UK' (EUROBAROMETER, Trends, 1991, pp. 69–87).

In other words, Denmark and the UK are in a separate category: that of the two reluctant Europeans. In the 1970s it was the accepted wisdom that it was the newcomers to the six old EC countries that were most reluctant about European integration and could least match the enthusiasm of the old EC'ers. They were thought to be merely accommodating. So far, however, it has not really turned out this way and, besides, the new member countries of the 1980s, Greece (1981), Spain and Portugal (1986) were all very fast to develop favourable EC

Table 5.1 Attitudes to the Common Market in the member countries, autumn 1991, ratios

Strongest pro-Europeans												The reluctant Europeans
P	NL	L	I	B	GR	D	E	IRL	F	UK	DK	EC
38.5	29.3	26.3	19.5	17.8	12.2	11.5	10.4	9.5	7.0	3.8	3.0	9.0

Source: EUROBAROMETER no. 36, early release, no page numbers.

Note: The question asked was: 'Generally speaking, do you think that (your country's) membership of the Common Market has been a good thing, a bad thing, or neither good nor bad?' The no reply/equally good varies between 20 and 30 per cent. The answers are based on around 1,000 interviews per country and obtained in late October/early November 1991. The ratio means 'good'/'bad'. Hence a ratio of 9 means that there are 9 times as many answering 'good' as 'bad'.

attitudes; they are even above average, with Portugal in an absolute leading position. In almost all their attitudes the Portuguese are the keenest integrationists in the EC.

When you examine other indices for Danish and British enthusiasm in European integration, the picture is fairly monotonous. These countries have the lowest scores in their support for a European Union, common policies and the prospects of going through the next phases of the unification, as hammered out in Maastricht, December 1991. In the UK there have been larger oscillations in the acceptance of the EC and an increase in scepticism about extended EC cooperation, not to mention the idea that 'a group of non-popular elected bankers should sit at *their* table and decide the monetary politics of Britain', as Mrs Thatcher has repeatedly said as part of her anti-EC campaign. It might seem puzzling, but at the same time that Mrs Thatcher and the majority of the Conservatives have become more negative towards the EC cooperation, while the voters in Britain have become more positive.

The Danish and British reservations were shown in Maastricht, where the treaty for further cooperation was codified as changes and amendments to the EC treaties, notably the EEC treaty. It was essentially an elaboration of the three phases of the Delors plan which was started on July 1st 1990, with the commencement of the inner market becoming effective on January 1st 1993. Without going into details, the treaty contained innovations such as

- upgrading environmental protection standards by putting them under majority decisions;

- extension of common policies on consumer protection, health, education and culture;
- expansion of the rôle of the EC ombudsman;
- introduction of the principle of subsidiarity (what can be done at home should be done at home); and
- strengthening the social dimension (employees' rights).

The last of the above mentioned innovations – more protection for employees – was too much for the Conservatives in power in the UK. As Prime Minister Mr John Major stated when he reported the outcome of the Maastricht meeting to the House of Commons: 'I was not prepared to risk Britain's competitive position as the European magnet for inward investment. I was not prepared to put British jobs on the line' (PB122/91, p. 4).

The British tone was harsh, and was meant to be. But it became too much for the eleven other member countries. They decided to go forward without the UK. In Denmark, there was a political majority to back the social efforts within the EC framework. 'The social dimension in EC' comprises mainly issues of workers' welfare and protection (article 118A in the EEC treaty).

The main points of interest, however, are the proposals to strengthen the monetary and (foreign) political cooperation. Of some significance are also proposals to strengthen the role of the parliament in order to reduce the so-called democratic deficit in what is often perceived as a bureaucratic EC.

But again objections were made by the British. And this time they got the support of the Danes. Neither of the two countries would commit themselves to a common currency, the ECU, from 1996 or, at the latest, by the end of the decade. By accepting the ECU cooperation a country would also have to comply with a European Central Bank, the European Monetary Institute and other financial institutions.

> THE HIGH CONTRACTING PARTIES declare the irreversible character of the Community's movement to the third stage by signing the new Treaty provisions on Economic and Monetary Union (Protocol to Amendments to the EEC treaty, Maastricht 1991, p. 81).

The ten countries did commit themselves.

The British and Danish reservations comply with the attitudes of the voters in the two countries. As a special service to the delegates to the meeting, a fast, preliminary version of the EUROBAROMETER, Autumn 1991, was presented. It included the latest opinion polls on exactly these questions, the developments of which had been followed for some time. The results show an overwhelming majority for an increased European cooperation, as well as massive support for the EC. Only British and Danish voters have some reservations: the British voters have

Table 5.2 Attitudes towards the monetary and political EC-union, Autumn 1991. Pct.

1st column: % in favour 2nd column: % not in favour	B		DK		D		GR		E		F	
	+	–	+	–	+	–	+	–	+	–	+	–
European Central Bank	59	16	47	40	55	23	63	10	56	16	61	16
Single Currency	62	18	35	54	45	32	61	14	58	18	64	18
EC responsible for foreign policy	60	16	40	48	55	24	61	15	54	17	55	22
EC responsible for security/ defence	70	11	47	42	67	16	65	14	63	13	66	16
Co-legislation	73	7	49	38	61	17	69	7	65	10	67	14

1st column: % in favour 2nd column: % not in favour	IRL		I		L		NL		P		UK		EC12	
	+	–	+	–	+	–	+	–	+	–	+	–	+	–
European Central Bank	52	15	62	14	48	29	67	19	57	11	39	41	55	22
Single Currency	54	17	69	12	48	35	58	31	53	15	40	42	54	25
EC responsible for foreign policy	46	21	70	10	55	23	60	27	48	19	41	38	55	23
EC responsible for security/ defence	47	23	75	8	65	17	76	15	63	9	50	33	64	17
Co-legislation	55	11	79	6	53	20	70	18	67	5	51	27	64	15

Source: EUROBAROMETER 36 – Autumn 1991: Early release, no page numbers.

Note: The exact wording of the question was: 'The Council of Heads of State and Governments of the European Community has called for intergovernmental conferences to discuss details of a European Economic and Monetary Union and of a Political Union. I am going to read you a number of statements. For each one, please tell me whether you are IN FAVOUR/NOT IN FAVOUR of . . .'

- As an Economic and Monetary Union, the European Community having a common European Central Bank, with the heads of national central banks on its Board of Directors
- Within this European Economic and Monetary Union, a single common currency replacing the different currencies of the Member States in five or six years' time
- As a Political Union, the European Community being responsible for a common policy in matters of security and defence
- The European Parliament having the right to decide, together with the Council of Ministers representing the national governments, on the legislation of the European Community.

The answers are based on around 1,000 interviews per country conducted in last October/early November 1991.

a majority against both a central bank and a single European currency. Amongst the Danish voters there is also a majority against a single currency but, surprisingly, not against a European Central Bank. Instead, there is a unique majority against the EC being responsible for foreign policy. No Danish objections were made at this point, however, despite the inclusions of such steps in the treaty.

The practical consequence of the British stance is that they may only enter the Economic Union if pressed by political necessity, including the pressure of their membership *per se*. But their opposition to complying with EC labour market rules is clearly a matter of who is in government. With Labour in government, there is little doubt that the British would join warmheartedly in the social endeavours. In other words, there has been a complete change of positions in British politics. In the 1970s Labour was reluctant about EC integration and the Conservatives were enthusiastic. In the 1980s the situation was reversed.

The Danes had a pragmatic approach about how to handle their reservations. They plan a referendum in 1966/97 before attempting to join the common currency. It is a practical solution, but it is also demanded by the Danish constitution (§ 20), since it will hand over part of Danish sovereignty to a supra-national body. In the treaty under the 'Protocol on certain provisions relating to Denmark' it is stated that: 'The Danish Constitution contains provisions which may imply a referendum in Denmark prior to Danish participation in the third stage of Economic and Monetary Union' (*op. cit.* p. 85).

The same applies to the procedure necessary before the parliament may ratify the treaty of Maastricht. Hence there will be a Danish referendum on acceptance of the treaty in 1992, and one in about 1996 on the third state of the EMU. There have already been two referenda – in 1972 and 1986 – on the EC in Denmark because of these constitutional grounds. It has become a habit to hold referenda on the EC.

A short history of Danish attitudes towards the EC

The relatively lukewarm attitude to the European cooperation is important to bear in mind, in order to understand not only the complex attitudes towards the EC, but also the political consequences of these attitudes, such as political behaviour at elections and referenda.

But before exploring these political implications, it is worth exploring the developments of the attitudes towards Danish membership in the European Community.

In 1961 Denmark applied for the first time, together with the UK, for membership of the EC. From 1961 until mid-1970, the issue was dormant. Around half of the voters supported joining the EC and only a fraction of voters (less than 10 per cent) did not want to join, whereas more than a third had not made up their minds.

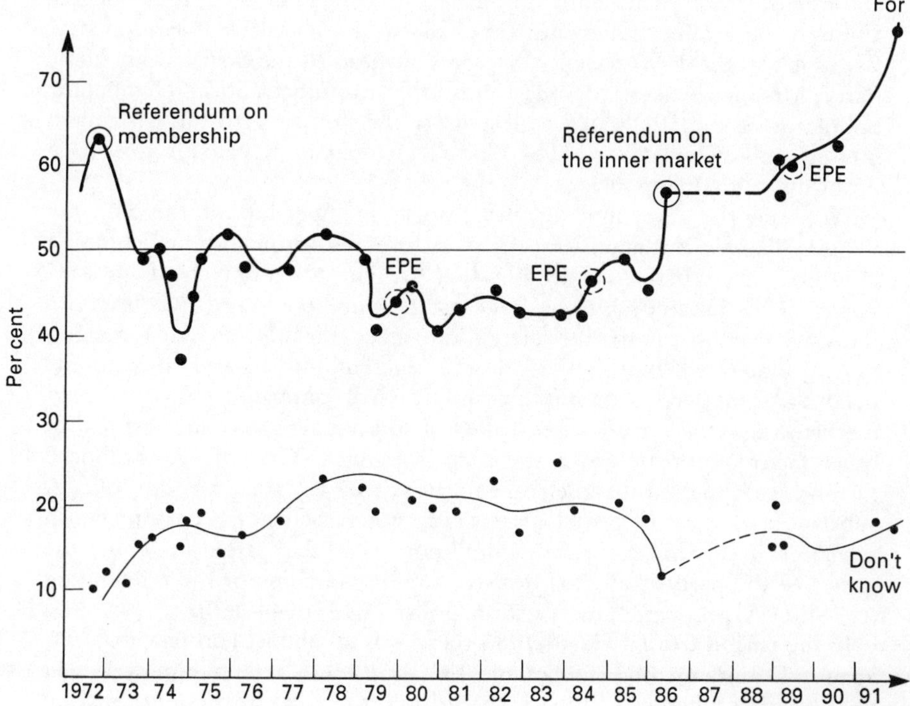

Figure 5.1 'If today you had to vote on Danish membership of the European Common Market, would you vote for or against Danish membership?'

Note: Opinion polls by GALLUP. Approximately 1,000 respondents per poll. Figures are found in the appendix. The figures for referenda are the actual votes. No polls from January 1986 to January 1989.

In the late 1960s negotiations for a closer Nordic cooperation continued, but were shipwrecked in early 1970. Thus the contacts with the EC were revitalized and the possibility of another application for membership emerged. All of a sudden, the anti-EC feelings accelerated. This was partly due to the high expectations of realizing the old, nostalgic Nordic dream and the consequent disappointment with its failure. To cope with the anti-EC feelings, a referendum was decided upon as early as spring 1971, to be held one and a half years later. The reason for the referendum was a severe split over the issue of membership in the biggest party, the Social Democrats, and a minor one in the party holding the prime minister post at the time – the Social Liberals.

The politicians hoped, in vain, to keep the EC issue out of the forthcoming national, general election that was to take place in the autumn of 1971. This split amongst the voters, and to some degree amongst the leading politicians, especially in the Social Democratic party, is still felt in the 1990s. Hence, the present head of the Social Democratic Party, Mr Sven Auken, together with other prominent Social Democratic politicians of the 1990s, were elected for the first time to the parliament on an anti-EC platform. The Social Democrats have still got their problems with EC policies.

To forge the campaign against Danish membership of the EC, the Peoples' Movement against the EC was formally formed at the beginning of 1972. They had considerable success, but the number of anti-EC voters never became quite as large as the number of pro-EC voters in the time leading up to the referendum, even through an AIM opinion poll around two months before the referendum showed an anti-EC majority. This led to an instant and massive campaign from the pro-marketeers, as they were often called. The campaign was successful. But other factors contributed to the success as well. First of all, the Social Democrats appealed to their sceptical voters to vote for the EC. A substantial amount of Social Democratic voters had not been for Danish membership before the referendum, nor were they after it. Thus, the stance of the party itself was decisive for the outcome of the referendum (OBSERVA pre- and post election polls, DDA 004–006).

In the period from 1972 to 1986 there was an almost constant majority against Danish membership of the EC. In 1986 a referendum was held to determine whether Denmark should join the road to the inner market and other undertakings that would lead to a closer integration within the EC. Formally it was named the European Common Act and consisted of changes and amendments to the European treaties in very much the same manner as the treaty of Maastricht.

With a fairly thin margin, 56 per cent for and 44 per cent against, it was accepted. When it really matters, the voters seem to be pragmatic and want to stay where they feel the bread is. The outcome was somewhat of a surprise, since the Social Democrats had recommended a 'no' and there were solid anti-EC attitudes on which to build. But the campaign came too late. During the last ten days or so of the campaign, the no-sayers were gaining in strength and the yes-sayers were losing. With a slightly longer campaign and the same trend, the Common Act would had been defeated in another ten days. But it was not.

Instead, there was an acceptance of the road to closer integration after 1986. There is almost a consensus that Denmark is part of the EC, and that anti-EC sentiments should be expressed and instrumentally channelled into a critical watch-dog function within the community.

Nevertheless, there is still a relatively clear-cut difference between the parties in their policies towards European integration. This picture has not changed very much since 1971: the pro-European parties have been the Liberals, the Conservatives and the Centre Democrats, whereas the strongest opposition to Danish involvement in the EC has been the

Table 5.3 Party vote and attitudes to EC, January 1991 (percentages)

	Attitudes towards the Common Market			Total	N
	Yes	No	Don't know		
PRO-EUROPEANS					
Liberals	87	9	4	100	138
Conservatives	82	9	9	100	109
Center Democrats	(84)	(14)	(2)	(100)	(32)
CONDITIONAL EUROPEANS					
Progress Party	(74)	(18)	(9)	(100)	(31)
Radical Liberals	(65)	(11)	(24)	(100)	(22)
Social Democrats	48	39	13	100	302
ANTI-EUROPEANS					
Soc. Peoples Pty	19	72	9	100	79
Small (left wing) parties	(24)	(76)	(0)	(100)	(29)
All	56	28	16	100	968

Source: Survey of AGB Gallup conducted nationally by personal interviews for the Election-research group.

Note: The actual wording of the question was: 'If there were to be a referendum on Danish membership of the EC today, would you then vote *yes* or *no*?' Conclusions for the figures in parentheses have too weak a base for statistical use, but the results do fit into a repeatedly found pattern. The Christian People's party, with only 16 respondents, has not been reported on.

Socialist People's Party together with the other left-wing parties, whoever they might have been in the period of time between 1971 and 1991.

The group of anti-European parties has also got support from a small non-socialist party: the now almost extinct Georgist Single-Tax Party. But support has also come from politicians from parties that are somewhat split over the EC issue. These parties could be labelled 'conditional Europeans' and consist primarily of the Social Democrats and the Radical Liberals. Both parties have suffered severely under internal struggles over EC policies, and seem to be close to the end of the road as far as directly negative, or at least very sceptical, attitudes towards the EC are concerned. On the other hand, the situation has not been all that unpleasant for the Social Democrats – especially in their position in opposition since 1982 – since they have had the *de facto* power over EC policies. There has always been a majority for any of their proposals concerning greater integration. They have had the hand on the break of the speed of Danish integration into the EC.

There are two parties that have been rather unstable in their stance towards the EC. The Christian People's party have vacillated between pro-European and conditional-European attitudes, whereas the Progress Party started out being mostly pro-European, but relatively quickly exposed more reluctant attitudes. On the other hand the Progress Party recommended a pure and clean *yes* to the package with the inner market at the 1986 referendum. For the 1992 referendum on the Maastricht treaty, however, the party recommends their voters to put their crosses against *no*. This recommendation is not in line with their voters' attitudes and possible intentions.

Otherwise, there is very good correspondence between the European policies of the parties and the attitudes of their respective voters, and this has been the case ever since 1971. The rank ordering has been very stable. The development for all parties, with the exception of the Progress Party, is first of all an increase in the acceptance of the EC. Especially the Social Democratic politicians and voters have moved. For the referendum on the Maastricht treaty, they even recommend a *yes*.

The European Parliamentary elections of 1979, 1984 and 1989. Two party systems: a national and a Euro-party system

With the widespread anti-EC attitudes amongst voters, it is hardly surprising that these attitudes are reflected in the voting behaviour in the European Parliamentary Elections (EPEs), especially since the People's Movement Against the EC has become more than a movement and is actually running as a party.

It was expected that the People's Movement would have lost most of their momentum after the 1986 referendum, which they had declared to be the last chance to get out of the EC. And certainly this state of affairs was confirmed by findings in the opinion polls taken in the months prior to the election where the pro-attitudes had taken the clearly dominant position. This expectation, however, was not realized; changes in the election results from 1984 to 1989 were marginal and mostly due to national party fluctuations.

The outcome in mandates closely reflects the outcome in votes since the election system at EPEs, as is the case in the national general elections, is one of a rather extreme proportional representation (law no. 746 of December 1988). As a result, there are two different party systems in Denmark: a national party system and a Euro-party system.

This situation is unique for Europe and it is not only due to the uniqueness of the People's Movement Against the EC, but also due to the difference between the election laws in Denmark and the UK. Had the UK not had elections in single constituencies, the UK would have been in the same situation with a national and a Euro-party system. In 1984 the Alliance won 18.5 per cent of the votes in the UK, but gained

Table 5.4 Results of the European Parliamentary Elections in Denmark, 1979, 1984 and 1989. Percentage and mandates

	EUROPEAN PARLIAMENTARY ELECTIONS			NATIONAL ELECTIONS		EP MANDATES		
	1979	1984	1989	1988	1990	1979	1984	1989
PRO EUROPEAN								
Liberals	14.5	12.5	16.6	11.8	15.8	3	2	3
Conservatives	14.0	20.8	13.3	19.3	16.0	2	4	2
Centre Democrats	6.2	6.6	7.9	4.7	5.1	1	1	2
Christian Peoples Pty	1.8	2.7	2.7	2.0	2.3	–	–	–
Total Pro-European	36.5	42.6	40.7	37.8	39.2	6	7	7
CONDITIONAL EUROPEAN								
Progress Party	5.8	3.5	5.3	9.0	6.4	1	–	–
Social Liberals	3.3	3.1	2.8	5.6	3.5	–	–	–
Social Democrats	21.9	19.5	23.3	29.8	37.4	3	3	4
Total Conditional European	31.0	26.1	31.3	44.4	47.3	4	3	4
ANTI EUROPEAN								
Socialist People's Party	4.7	9.2	9.1	13.0	8.3	1	1	1
Small (left wing) parties	6.9	1.3	–	4.8	5.2	–	–	–
People's Movement against the EC	20.9	20.8	18.9	–	–	4	4	4
Total Anti European	32.5	31.3	28.0	17.8	13.5	5	5	5
TOTAL	100	100	100	100	100			
TURNOUT	47.8	52.4	46.1	85.7	82.9	15	15	16

Source: Official election statistics (SE 1984: 13v, SE 1989: 11, SE 1990: 19)

no mandates. In 1989 the Greens won 14.0 per cent of the votes, but they did not gain any mandates either.

Explaining the outcome: who are the anti-marketeers?

The profile of the anti-marketeers has generally been rather clear and consistent. Ever since the heated debates over Danish membership of the EC at the time of the referendum in 1972, the anti-marketeers have mostly been

- younger,
- better educated,
- students or employees in the public sector,
- living in Copenhagen or bigger provincial towns.

In European elections and referenda, the electorate of the parties with a conditional stance towards the EC is rather bland in their socio-economic background. They do, though, stand out as slightly less educated and as living in provincial towns. These are mostly Social Democrats who stay with their party when the debate on EC becomes intense.

The pro-European parties attract elderly people in rural districts employed in the private sector of the economy. The composition of this electorate is, however, more complex, as a more detailed analysis would show. The pro-European electorate consists of two major groups: urban, rather well-educated high-level employees and self-employed, and a rural group of farmers and others connected to the primary sector.

A focus on the anti-Europeans shows that they are more interested in politics than the average voter, they are opposed to nuclear energy, they feel that the police should be checked a little more, but also that the state should have more control with private investments. In short, they express anti-authoritarian and leftist attitudes.

In 1972 they were part of the 1968 syndrome. It seems the message has been passed on and there are countervailing undercurrents to the young, otherwise prevailing, right-wing wave.

A closer look at the voters for the anti-European parties shows that the pattern is genuine in the sense that the attitudes are not a simple syndrome. In other words, it is not the case that if a voter has a negative attitude towards nuclear energy, then everything else, including anti-European attitudes, can be explained. The different attitudes are additive in a fairly complex way and not reducible to this one factor.

Part of the complex pattern shows that an extremely high probability for voting for an anti-European party is found among voters with anti-nuclear attitudes, with middle-level education, leftist orientation, and in their thirties and forties. Voters who would never dream of voting for

Table 5.5a Socio-economic background of the pro/anti party groups at the 1984 EPE: percentage difference in the groups

	Pro European	Cond. European	Anti European	N
Male	−2	−2	+3	279
Female	+2	+2	−3	258
18–24 years	−10	−4	+14	76
25–29	−7	+2	+4	48
30–39	−7	−4	+11	117
40–49	−2	0	+2	79
50–61	+12	2	−14	105
62–	+5	−4	−12	112
Lower education	−1	−2	−7	192
Medium education	+1	+2	−6	225
High education	−6	−15	11	117
Copenhagen	−6	−8	14	133
Provincial town	−2	+5	−1	275
Rural areas	12	0	−11	128
Public sector	−10	0	10	140
Private sector	10	−1	−8	280
Not in work	−2	+1	1	216
All	37%	29%	34%	536 = 100%

Source: AIM Telephone survey on the day before and on the day of the election (DDA 807).

Note: The percentage difference in the group means e.g. that 48 (14 + 34) pct. of the voters in Copenhagen voted for an anti-European party. In the sample the anti-European party voters are over-represented.

an anti-European party have pro-nuclear power attitudes (or do not know about it), subscribe to law-and-order, are for little state intervention in private investments, and either very interested in politics or not interested at all.

It is clear that anti-nuclear attitudes are the best predictor for voting for anti-European parties. Anti-nuclear attitudes are the core of a green/environmental stance, so by stretching the argument slightly, one might say that voting for the People's Movement, the biggest and most central of the anti-European parties, may be considered voting for a green party.

Returning to the party level, it could be claimed that with the People's Movement against the EC, Denmark has a green party on the European level, but none on the national level. The UK would have had a similar

Table 5.5b Political interest and attitudes at the 1984 EPE (percentages)

	Pro-European	Cond. European	Anti-European	Did not vote	All
Interest in politics:					
Very interested	15	16	27	8	15
Some interest	49	45	43	30	41
Little interest	32	36	28	47	37
No interest	4	3	2	15	7
	100	100	100	100	100
Anti- Law & order	13	21	40	27	25
Pro- Law & order	74	61	42	56	58
Don't know	13	18	18	17	17
	100	100	100	100	100
Pro-nuclear	40	18	7	16	20
Anti-nuclear	38	70	85	65	64
Don't know	22	22	8	19	16
	100	100	100	100	100
Socialist	18	50	62	35	40
Non-socialist	58	24	16	24	31
Don't know	24	26	22	41	29
	100	100	100	100	100
N =	198	156	182	244	780

Source: AIM Telephone Survey on the day before and on the day of the election (DDA 806)

Note: The exact wordings of the questions were:

- How interested are you in politics?
- Do you think there is a need for more control with the methods of the Police?
- If there were to be a referendum on Nuclear Energy, what would you vote?
- Do you think the state has too little control over private investments?

phenomenon if the British election system were one of proportional representation.

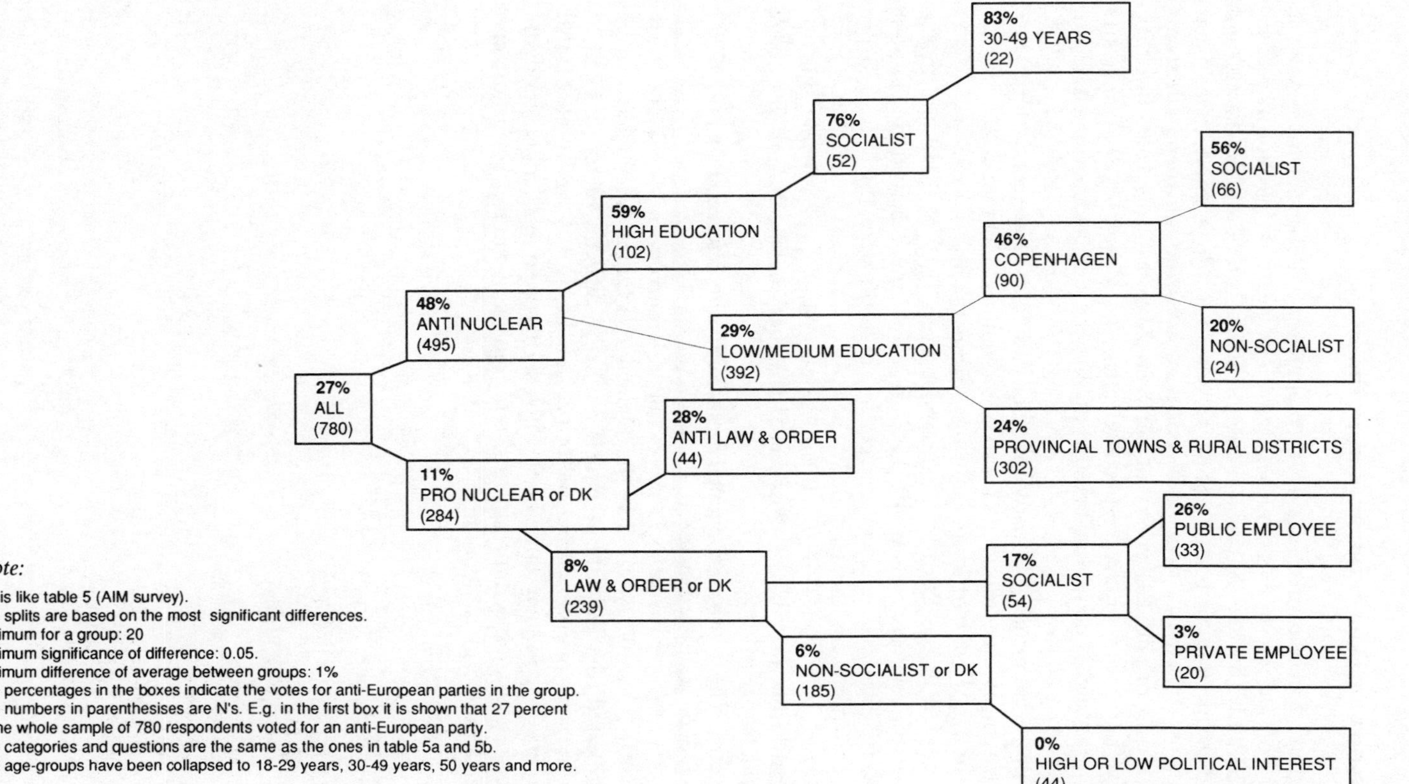

Note:

Basis like table 5 (AIM survey).
The splits are based on the most significant differences.
Minimum for a group: 20
Minimum significance of difference: 0.05.
Minimum difference of average between groups: 1%
The percentages in the boxes indicate the votes for anti-European parties in the group.
The numbers in parenthesises are N's. E.g. in the first box it is shown that 27 percent of the whole sample of 780 respondents voted for an anti-European party.
The categories and questions are the same as the ones in table 5a and 5b.
The age-groups have been collapsed to 18-29 years, 30-49 years, 50 years and more.

Figure 5.2 Attitudes and votes for anti-European parties at the 1984 European Parliamentary Election: AID multivariate analysis

The future of Danish integration in the EC

The future for Danish resistance to main-stream European integration is bleak. For the referendum on the Maastricht treaty, a rejection is recommended only by the Socialist People's Party, the Progress Party, and perhaps some minute parties. They account only for a good 15 per cent of the votes. That is a very weak position, even though there still seems to be a core of anti-EC voters of between 20 and 30 per cent. But they will be hard to mobilize, especially since the People's Movement has largely stopped functioning because of internal heterogeneity in political outlook.

Finally, the grand old lady of the People's Movement, Mrs. Else Hammerich, is a co-founder of a new movement, Denmark '92, that has a declared goal of working critically within the EC framework.

She served in the European parliament from 1979 to 1989 and in the last election she contested, the EPE in 1984, she received the highest number of personal votes ever recorded in Denmark: 156,145 or 8 per cent of all votes in the election.

Her withdrawal in 1989 from the Peoples Movement was perhaps not the final blow to it, but it is expected that her co-founding of Denmark '92 will be so.

Hence a YES to the EC from Denmark in the referenda of both 1992 and 1996/7 can be expected.

In practical terms, a NO at either referenda would also be very awkward. It would mean that the Danish conditions would have to be re-negotiated, the benefits of which might be difficult to see. Instead, it seems that the overwhelming majority of politicians – and perhaps also the voters – put their faith in the belief that their moderate, good old friends, the other Nordic countries, will join us in the EC before the end of the decade and millennium.

Appendix Table 1 Attitudes towards the Common Market 1961–91

Year	Month/day	For %	Against %	Don't know %	Total %
1961		50	9	41	100
1962		46	8	48	100
1963		47	8	45	100
1964		50	7	43	100
1965		52	6	42	100
1966		54	5	41	100
1967		56	6	38	100
1968	September	57	8	35	100
1970	January	54	10	36	100
1971	October	49	17	34	100
1971	April	41	25	34	100
1971	June	37	28	35	100
1971	August	40	28	32	100
1971	September	42	29	29	100
1971	October	42	29	29	100
1971	November	40	29	31	100
1971	December	38	31	31	100
1972	January	38	33	29	100
1972	February	40	33	27	100
1972	March	42	31	27	100
1972	April	44	30	26	100
1972	May	44	30	26	100
1972	June	44	32	25	100
1972	August	44	33	23	100
1972	September	47	33	20	100
1972	October 2, Referendum	57	33	10	100
1973	February	51	37	12	100
1973	May	46	43	11	100
1973	October	42	43	15	100
1974	March	42	42	16	100
1974	May	38	43	19	100
1974	August	31	53	16	100
1974	October	37	45	18	100
1975	April	40	41	19	100
1975	August	45	41	14	100
1976	March	40	43	17	100
1977	May	39	43	18	100
1978	April	40	37	23	100
1979	February	38	40	22	100
1979	May 26–May 30	33	48	19	100
1979	December	31	39	30	100

Appendix Table 1 cont.

Year	Month/day	For %	Against %	Don't know %	Total %
1980	May	36	43	21	100
1980	December	33	48	19	100
1981	May	35	46	19	100
1982	March	35	42	23	100
1982	December	35	48	17	100
1983	September	31	43	26	100
1984	April/May	34	47	19	100
1984	May/June	37	42	21	100
1985	May	39	40	21	100
1985	December	38	44	18	100
1986	February 27 'Package'	50	38	12	100
1986					
1987					
1987					
1988					
1988					
1989	January	48	36	16	100
1989	March/April	48	31	21	100
1989	May	50	34	16	100
1990	June	57	33	10	100
1991	May	57	24	19	100
1991	October	63	19	18	100

Source: 1961–1985: Material by Gallup. 1989–1991: Art. No. 57 for Berlingske Tidende by Gallup. 1972 and 1986: Official election statistics.

Note: From 1986, it is 'easier' to adhere to the 'For' definition, as the question to 'Against' is phrased 'resign'. If the answer to the question of resigning is 'No', it counts as 'For'.

The exact wordings of the questions were:
If you were to vote on adherence to the European Common Market today, would you vote for or against Danish adherence?
If you were to vote on Denmark's resignation from the EC, would you vote for or against resignation?

Chapter 6

Parliamentary control of the executive

Niels Jørgen Nehring

Introduction

When in 1973 Denmark acceded to the European Communities we had implicitly to decide whether we considered our relationship with the Community a domestic or a foreign policy matter. If our relationship were to be considered a matter of domestic policy, parliamentary control and participation in the decision-making process in line with the Danish legislative procedure should be applicable. This procedure stipulates three readings by the Danish parliament (the Folketing) in plenary sitting, and usually parallel debates to be held in the relevant parliamentary committees – a procedure which ensures a politically and factually thorough debate of the matter. If our relationship with the Community were perceived as a foreign policy matter, the participation of the Folketing would be much more limited, in as much as the field of foreign politics in pursuance of the Danish Constitution is a government matter, and the Folketing merely a forum to be informed and consulted. In principle, the consultation does not bind the government. But, this said, there should be no delay in adding that in practice this principle has been considerably narrowed down.

However, the reason for the outlined fundamental difference between the two spheres is clear. The character of the majority of Community acts is legislative, either because they are, in the form of regulations, directly applicable in the Member States, or because as directives they presuppose transformation into national laws. It is a well-known fact that law-making is parliament's main sphere. However, in foreign policy matters the negotiating position *vis-à-vis* other states calls for a scenario where the government enjoys a considerable liberty of action, which has not been hampered by parliamentary shackles. It is furthermore necessary that information concerning the government's negotiating strategy should not be freely available to its negotiating partners.

As far as Denmark is concerned, the solution was a compromise making allowance for both viewpoints, but logically limiting both to a certain extent. In pursuance of this compromise, which was laid down in the acts transforming the Treaties of Rome into national laws, a special committee – the parliamentary Market Relations Committee – was set up under the purview of the Folketing, where the government and the Folketing would debate matters appertaining to Denmark's policy towards the European Community. In principle, the rules of procedure established in 1972 have been in force ever since, albeit with certain minor adjustments as a consequence of experience gained and developments in European cooperation. The key element of the procedure is that prior to the adoption by the Council of Ministers of matters of far-reaching scope and importance, the government prepares a so-called introduction, i.e. an outline of the framework within which the government will negotiate. The introduction is oral, and normally made by the minister who is to negotiate the matter in the Council. The subsequent discussion in the committee will, if necessary, elucidate some obscure points, and members of the committee may make political intimidations of an advisory character to the government. Following the debate on the matter, it is established whether a majority of the members of the committee has pronounced against the government's introduction. If this is not the case, the minister concerned may negotiate in the Council within the framework thus stipulated. This system is at times called 'negative parliamentarism'.

In matters outside the category of 'matters of far-reaching scope', the government briefs the parliamentary Market Relations Committee, which now and then may debate the matter in question. When later a decision can be taken on the matter, and the government presents it on the basis of an introduction, the preceding debate will often prove to have been a useful preparation for the committee's final decision.

However, it is no surprise that a regime governing such an important sphere is subject to criticism and pressure. The Danish regime is critized from outside as well as from within. From outside, because this very visible regime governing relations between government and parliament has at times been considered by our partners in the Community to hinder cooperation. From within, because this ever growing body of laws has evaded the usual thorough legislative procedure. Let us examine whether the criticism is fair, and if so, what can be done to counter it.

A couple of times the parliamentary Market Relations Committee has attracted international attention. This has happened, for instance, when a Danish minister during a meeting of the Council of Ministers has exhausted the latitude given him at his meeting with the parliamentary Market Relations Committee, and he consequently has to reserve his position till he has had renewed contact with the Committee. In such situations other Member States construe the Committee as an institution obstructing cooperation. This is not a fair judgement. Other governments are also accountable to their parliaments. But the forms of this accountability might differ, and often they are less visible than the Danish regime.

The fact that often Danish governments are minority governments, which in all matters are forced to procure the necessary support of the parties of the Folketing, exposes the Danish decision-making process. Furthermore, differences in politico-administrative tradition play a role in this respect. In Denmark there is a tradition that laws, regulations and administrative provisions are subject to a thorough and detailed processing. Usually, this diminishes the problems which might crop up in the implementing phase. In the Community, Denmark ranks among the Member States having the best statistics in terms of implementation of adopted acts.

The fact that Denmark is one of the smaller Member States might also challenge Denmark's policy *vis-à-vis* the Community in terms of quality. There is no doubt that the major countries, simply by virtue of their political weight, enjoy a larger degree of latitude in the negotiating process. The smaller countries should seek to counterbalance this phenomenon. One of the ways to do it would be to introduce a larger element of consistency and internal logic into the national policies towards the Community. The dialogue between the government and the Folketing, taking place in the parliamentary Market Relations Committee, seeks to fulfil this objective.

The legislative procedure is also subject to current criticism from within. Since Denmark's accession to the Community in 1973, the body of laws has grown and become more complex and the integration process has made a major step forward, not least as a consequence of the Single Act. This has fuelled the internal discussion on whether the national EC legislative procedure entirely fulfils the preconditions which in reason must be laid down. The basis for comparison is, as mentioned, the national legislative procedure. In general terms, the procedure outlined above has been adjusted on several concrete points, but the 1972 pattern has been preserved. One reason is the realization that allowance must be made for the two basic, but partly conflicting, considerations, namely parliamentary participation in the decision-making process and the government's liberty of action.

The Single Act, and in particular the many proposals of the White Paper, have put heavy pressure on the Danish as well as on other Member States' decision-making systems. The tight deadlines, and not least the fact that a larger number of matters will be adopted by majority decisions, occasioned considerations as to whether the rules are still adequate. In the years between 1973 and the Single Act the procedure was subject to various adjustments, which generally resulted in a more exhaustive briefing on the part of the government. An ever increasing number of oral introductions by ministers were accompanied by factual notes to the Committee, particularly in technically complicated matters.

The deadline for the notice convening a Committee meeting was also extended. Special mention should be made of a scheme under which the government and the parliamentary Market Relations Committee agreed during each presidency, i.e. every six months, to select a number of proposals for a directive concerning internal market matters, which should be subject to a particularly thorough procedure. This implies that the proposals concerned, usually between five and ten, prior to their adoption in the Council are debated by the Folketing in plenary sitting under a procedure commensurate with the first hearing of national bills. This scheme permits a more thorough debate of principles as a supplement to the more targeted deliberations undertaken by the Committee, typically a few days before the meeting of the Council.

This amendment, together with the other changes of the procedure which were made after the adoption of the Single Act, has not silenced the internal debate. This can hardly be expected as long as the Community's dynamic development of recent years continues.

However, a few fundamental problems shall be reviewed here: first, the continued integration of economy and politics in the European cooperation. Denmark's formulation of its policy towards the European Community is partly based on the fiction that politics and economy are separate spheres. The procedures outlined above apply to the economy, i.e. the commercial policy. However, the point of departure for foreign policy matters is that this is a government matter where the Folketing acts in an advisory capacity only. Even though this description is no longer exact, the government still enjoys a greater liberty of action in foreign policy matters. The procedure governing the dialogue between the government and the Folketing is more of an advisory one, and deliberations are undertaken after the international event concerned. However, in practice the reality of politics does not respect this dividing line, and there are clear indications of a growing disrespect. In concrete terms, this has given rise to difficult considerations when the distinction between the Community's policy in the field of external trade and its foreign policy became obscure. A relevant case is the introduction of measures to protect trade on foreign policy grounds. Naturally, the topical key example is Eastern Europe. Here, there are no real misgivings occasioned by convergence of politics and economy — on the contrary. But the fact remains that the Danish procedures are not geared to the present situation. They are applicable with certain adaptations only — and this probably applies to several other countries too.

Another example is the meetings of the European Council, which deal partly with politics and economy, and partly hold debates of far-reaching, fundamental scope, but which in a way are difficult to wrap up in formal procedures. Before the Prime Minister participates in a meeting of the European Council, he briefs the parliamentary Market Relations Committee on his expectations of the deliberations and result of the meeting. However, compared to the processing of acts in the Council of

Ministers, the basis for deliberations is far more vague. Only in exceptional cases is there a concrete proposal to consider. There may be communications from the Commission, but typically these are new ones which the national administrations have not had the opportunity to debate. In certain cases, the most concrete basis for the briefing can be a letter from the president of the European Council, briefly outlining his expectations of the outcome of the meeting. This, together with the usual reports from embassies in other capitals, forms the basis of the Prime Minister's briefing of the parliamentary Market Relations Committee. On the other hand, the Committee may claim that, even though no formal decisions in the form of EC documents are to be made, decisions of principle, and often of far-reaching scope, will be made, in which the Committee has not been properly involved. In order to counter these objections as far as possible, the Prime Minister's briefing seeks to concretize his expectations in such a way that it is to be compared with the ministers' usual introduction. Basically, this is, however, a field where parliamentary control can hardly ever be effected satisfactorily.

On balance, the Danish regime outlined above seems – despite allegations made off and on that it is obstructing cooperation – seems to be a wholehearted and fairly successful attempt at solving a complicated problem: to incorporate parliamentary participation/control into a process which is still to a wide extent characterized by being deliberations between sovereign states.

There is reason to believe that the Danish experience outlined above might prove useful to the Community's efforts in finding models to solve the problem of 'the democratic deficit' – even though primarily this term alludes to the European Parliament.

Chapter 7

Sovereignty

Niels Jørgen Nehring

It is no wonder that the concept of sovereignty has appeared so often in the fervent discussion of recent years concerning European integration. The term sovereignty is rather wide. It is used in particular in two senses: a vague political one and, to a certain extent, a more exact legal one. In the discussions concerning the strength of the integration the plea for sovereignty is a powerful means. It refers to the entire identity of the State concerned, its history and institutions. The purpose of this reference may be manyfold. But, more often than not, they are restrictive. In the legal sense, the concept has a certain exactitude, at any rate within the borders of the individual country. Comparative studies on the definitions of sovereignty would no doubt reveal certain differences.

One of the more specific references to the concept of sovereignty is made in section 20 of the Danish Constitution, which deals with the relinquishment of sovereignty to international authorities. The inclusion of this provision in the Constitution in 1953 aimed precisely at enabling Denmark to accede to international organizations of a supranational character.

As regards contents, section 20 constitutes a rule of procedure stipulating the preconditions for the relinquishment of powers, which in pursuance of the Constitution are conferred upon Danish authorities, to international authorities. Such relinquishment may be effected provided that a majority of five-sixths of the members of the Danish parliament (the Folketing) vote in favour thereof. Where it is not possible to muster a qualified majority of this size – but a majority nevertheless – the Folketing must take the issue to the country, and the outcome shall be binding. This variation of the rule in the form of a referendum was applied in 1972 when Denmark joined the European Community. At that time, it was doubtful whether the accession presupposed any relinquishment of sovereignty within the meaning of section 20 of the Constitution.

The assessment made in connection with the Single Act concluded that the Act did not call for any further relinquishment of sovereignty, and that consequently the procedure laid down in section 20 of the Constitution should not be applied. Some politicians and academics took a different stance, but small wonder, since to a certain extent the interpretation of section 20 is *ipso facto* a matter of opinion. Instead, an advisory referendum was held in 1986, where, in advance, the most important political parties had announced that they would respect the outcome of the referendum.

PART III: ECONOMIC POLICY

Chapter 8

Internal market policy

Peter Nedergaard

Introduction

In the White Paper from the Commission of 14 June 1985 on completion of the internal market, the measures that need to be taken are classified under three headings: the removal of physical, technical, and fiscal barriers. The objective of the Internal Market Programme is to remove these barriers for individuals, goods, services and capital.

Only for some of the issues covered by the White Paper have there been analyses or publicly articulated estimations regarding the costs and benefits for Denmark. Costs in this respect are mainly supposed to be connected with the elimination of physical barriers, public procurement, capital movements and the proposals on approximation of indirect taxation, whereas benefits are supposed to be connected with the removal of technical barriers in industry and free mobility for services.

Costs

The removal of the *physical border controls* in the Community immediately put into question the already existing Nordic Passport Union between Finland, Norway, Sweden and Denmark, which enjoys strong public support.

At the same time, the idea of less border control has created some public fear about accelerated drug trafficking, terrorism, etc. This fear has been stimulated by a campaign financed by the customs officers union.

If, however, the problems of drug control, terrorism, etc. can be dealt with in an effective manner, and if the approximation of the EFTA countries like Norway and Sweden to Community legislation includes a passport union, *then* the removal of the physical border controls will probably be regarded as being more beneficial than costly by the Danish public opinion. In that case, the much less restrictive border controls will pose some visible benefits to the people living in the border region of

Germany and Denmark, and to lorry traffic, (see below). On the other hand, the limitation of the controls of the Danish-German border still means that some 'hard' decisions have to be considered at government level, because of the important 'spill-over' effect from less border control to tax approximation (see below).

In an analysis of the sectoral impact of the Internal Market in Denmark, by J. Kongstad and L. Larsen (1990), *public procurement* is perceived to play a moderate role in the following sectors: Boiler Making (NACE 315), Office Machinery and Data Processing Equipment (NACE 330), Insulated Wires and Cables (NACE 344), and Locomotives and Tramways etc. (NACE 362). For all these sectors, relatively high import penetration ratios prevail simultaneously with public procurement, emphasizing that this practice in general is relatively open to foreign suppliers. Nevertheless, it is worthwhile posing the question about how and to what degree these sectors might be influenced by the internal market. To a large extent the answer to this question depends on the competitive position of the public procurement dominated sector *vis-à-vis* their competitors within the Community.

By combining the actual competitive position with its change during the last ten years, a dynamic dimension is added to the picture of the sectors dominated by public procurement. The analysis made by Kongstad and Larsen (1990) shows that only the Locomotive and Tramway sector turns out to be both a weak performer and a sector which has had a declining competitive position in the 1980s, while other weak performers like the Office Machinery and EDP-Equipment sector and the Insulated Wires and Cables sector show no sign of change in the competitive position.

The status quo competitive position applies both to an average performing sector like Boiler Making and to a strong performing sector like Telecommunications Equipment. Therefore, the conclusion is that the impact on the sectors dominated by public procurement in Denmark seems to be both encapsulated and moderate. So, it can be argued that the public procurement-dominated sectors in Denmark will be relatively better off in the internal market than will the average industries in the Community.

This can be illustrated by the fact that sensitive sectors in Denmark in general have taken up 4 per cent of all new jobs during the 1980s, while the sensitive sectors (as identified by the Commission, 1988) in the Community in the same period as a whole lost 19 per cent of the new jobs.

The costs of *capital movements* for Denmark as perceived by the Danish Parliament (especially the opposition parties) are caused by some indirect effects of free capital movements. First, there has been no agreement reached in the Council on obligatory information to the Danish tax authorities about interest revenue on foreign bank accounts held by Danish taxpayers. Secondly, it can be difficult to uphold the so-called

Table 8.1 The importance of technical trade barriers to export from Denmark to other member states

Number of employed	Without importance (%)	Minor importance (%)	Some importance (%)	Very important % calculated	Total
0–49	45	33	22	100	51
50–299	33	45	22	100	40
more than 300	19	31	50	100	16
Meat products	14	36	50	100	14
Wooden beds	82	9		100	11
Agricultural machinery	24	57	19	100	21
Pharmaceuticals	0	33	67	100	6
Machinery in food and chem. ind.	58	27	15	100	26
Radio transmitters and receivers	0	33	67	100	6
Electric machines	36	50	14	100	14
Cheese prod.	34	44	22	100	9
TOTAL: Pct.	37		26	100	
Number	39	40	28	107	

Source: Breum and Forsberg (1989), p. 119.

'real interest tax' on Danish pension funds. In 1990, the real interest tax is expected to contribute DKK 18 billion in revenue to the Danish state budget.

Due to the Internal Market Programme the last major cost for Denmark deals with the effects on state revenue, too. In a much debated publication from several ministries (Finansministeriet *et al.*, 1989) the loss in state revenue is calculated to be about DKK 40 billion if an *approximation of Value Added Taxes and Excise Duties* comes into effect, as proposed by the Commission in 1987.

As mentioned in the White Paper, Denmark (and Ireland) rely heavily on indirect taxation. At the same time, neither of the bigger political parties perceive the income tax system to be able to bear the substantial extra tax burden. Therefore, approximation of the indirect taxation in the Community presents Denmark with a budgetary problem that is more difficult to solve than in most other Member States.

The question to tax approximation has been one of the most important issues in the Danish debate on the internal market. To a certain extent this debate has overshadowed other proposals in the White Paper.

Benefits

The perceptions of Danish industrialists of the importance of the *technical barriers* to export from Danish industry have been ascertained in a survey based on a questionnaire, involving a small but carefully selected number of enterprises, representing different sizes and locations (Breum and Forsberg, 1989). Table 8.1 presents the answers to the basic question in the survey.

Three-quarters of the industrialists who took part in the questionnaire felt that technical trade barriers to export were of no or minor importance to their enterprises, although the larger firms estimated trade barriers to be a more important obstacle to export than did the smaller ones. In addition, technical trade barriers seemed to be more important in certain product groups than in others.

Sixty-five enterprises estimated the costs caused by the technical trade barriers in their export to other member states. For the average enterprise these costs amounted to DKK 455,000 in 1988, which corresponded to 0.5 per cent of their average sales to other Member States (see Table 8.2).

The free mobility in *services* are of significant importance in transport and finance. During the 1980s, the Danish lorry sector has been characterized by over-capacity. If, therefore, the demand for transport services will increase as expected in the internal market, the present over-capacity will possibly disappear.

A precondition for an increasing demand for Danish road transport services is that the sector will be able to compete on more equal terms. Thus, if the Danish road transport sector is to reap the benefits of the internal market the social regulations in the road transport sector have got to be harmonized at a higher level than the present average level in the Community (Trafikministeriet, 1989).

The liberalization of financial services is expected to bring about substantial welfare gains in the Community as a whole. From the point of view of Danish enterprises and households, the benefits consist of cheaper financial services.

To the Danish financial market concepts like 'overbanking' and 'overmanning' have been ascribed, because of the less than optimal competitive situation on the market. As a consequence the costs of running the Danish bank sector are relatively higher compared to most other member states (Industriministeriet, 1989).

With the aim of exploiting more economies of scale in the financial sector, in 1991 five major Danish banks merged into two. Yet it still remains to be seen whether cheaper financial services will be the result. If not, it is supposed that banks from other member states will enter the Danish market for bank services offering low cost loans, credits, etc., to the Danish consumers.

Whether the first or the second scenario are realistic or not, financial services are expected to become cheaper in the more integrated internal

Table 8.2 Size of costs caused by technical trade barriers in export to other member states

	Number of employed			
	20–49	50–129	300	More than average
Total costs in 1988 for the whole enterprise (in 1,000 DKK)	198	464	1,369	455
Decomposition:				
Administrative costs	110	102	245	125
Production costs	27	301	473	191
Finance costs	25	7	526	83
Marketing costs	13	51	125	43
Other costs	23	3	0	13
Costs/sale to other member states (%)	2.36	1.56	0.25	0.53
TOTAL number	30	27	8	65

Source: Breum and Forsberg, 1989, p. 128.

financial market in the 1990s, benefiting especially households and small and medium sized enterprises.

Conclusion

On the *cost side* of the balance of costs and benefits for Denmark, first, one finds the removal of the physical border controls, which put into question the very existence of the Nordic Passport Union. If, however, the approximation of the EFTA countries like Norway and Sweden to the Community legislation will include a passport union, the removal of physical border controls will probably be regarded as more beneficial than costly by the Danish public opinion.

Secondly, concerning the public procurement sectors in Denmark, the impact of the internal market seems to be both encapsulated and moderate. It can be argued that the public procurement-dominated sectors in Denmark will be relatively better off in the internal market than other industries in the Community.

A third estimated cost for Denmark in the internal market is the indirect effect of free capital movements. On one hand (so far), no agreement has been reached in the Council on obligatory information to the Danish tax authorities about interest revenue on foreign bank accounts held by Danish taxpayers. On the other hand, it can be difficult to uphold the so-called 'real interest tax' on Danish pension funds.

Due to the Internal Market Programme the last major cost for

Denmark deals with the effects on state revenue, too. If the Council accepts an approximation of Value Added Taxes and Excise Duties as proposed by the Commission in 1987 the loss in state revenue is calculated to be about DKK 40 billion. But the loss will (naturally) be less substantial when the 1987 proposals are changed in a seemingly more 'flexible' direction.

On the *benefit side* of the balance of costs and benefits for Denmark in the Internal Market, one finds the gains reaped by Danish industry of an elimination of technical barriers. Although the size of benefits seems to be relatively small, judged from a survey involving a little more than a hundred enterprises, the benefits still exist. In total, the costs caused by technical trade barriers in export to other Member States correspond to 0.5 per cent of the average sales in the enterprises asked in the survey.

The free mobility of services in the internal market is expected to have a significant effect on transport and finance. The Danish lorry traffic sector hopes for an increasing demand for transport services in the export sector, however, if the social regulations in transport are harmonized at a higher level than the present average level in the Community. For small and medium sized enterprises and Danish households, the liberalization of financial services is expected to bring about a substantial reduction in the prices for financial services. The more competitive climate in the internal financial market will either force the Danish banks to reduce prices, or bring about price reductions by the presence of banks in Denmark from other member states.

References

Breum, Poul and Jørn Forsberg (1989), *Tekniske handelshindringer*, Jysk Teknologisk Forlag, Århus.

Commission (1988), *The Social Dimension and the Internal Market, Social Europe*, special edition, Brussels.

Finansministeriet *et al.* (1989), *Redegørelse vedrørende dansk afgiftspolitik og det indre marked*, Stougaard Jensen, København.

Industriministeriet (1989), *Dansk erhvervsliv på vej til det indre marked, Stougaard Jensen*, København.

Kongstad, J. and L. Larsen (1990), 'The Sectorial Impact of the Internal Market in Denmark', forthcoming in *European Economy*, Brussels.

Trafikministeriet (1989), *Vognmandserhvervet og det indre marked – en brancheanalyse*, København.

Chapter 9

Industrial and technology policy

Lise Lyck

Introduction

The fundamental economic reason for the existence of an industrial policy is to be found in market failures which lead to mis-allocation of resources. One type of market failure is connected to externalities resulting in huge differences in cost and benefit seen from the viewpoint of a state and from a private economic perspective. The existence of externalities often implies simple regulation of production in the form of regulation of price and quantity. Another type of market failure has to do with market power as a result of the degree of concentration due to large-scale economics, which implies that prices and quantities decided in a market differ from what is wanted from a social point of view. Also, asymmetric information can result in market failures from a social point of view. Therefore the core element in industrial policy is normally connected to the competition situation and to political attitudes to competition.

According to one industrial policy orientation, the principal task of industrial policy is to set and generate a framework for production which establishes a wanted degree of competition among corporations. According to the opposite industrial political orientation, the state has to be actively involved in order to secure and even to decide the wanted degree and kind of competition.

It is a question to which the attitudes are very different in the single countries, and consequently it is also a question characterized by international disagreement. A market-oriented industrial policy implies a minimal intervention in the markets, and the function of the policy is only to ensure that the market mechanism functions.

The opposite point of view is found in an industrial intervention policy due to which it is an important task for the state to influence the allocation in order to achieve regional and distributive objectives of the society. An active industrial policy can also pursue strategic, more future-oriented purposes for specific sectors such as, for instance, transportation and high-technology industries, or it can follow a more conservative strategy giving subsidies to industries which are backward due to structural changes of demand. Furthermore, it will always be a question for political discussion if a national or a more international policy is called for.

In short, many different attitudes to the need and kind of industrial policy-making exist, which is why it a difficult task to establish a coherent and effective policy.

EC industrial policy

The Treaty of Rome (1957) did not call for an EC industrial policy. In fact most of the industrial policy topics such as state aid, cartels, etc. were seen as hindrances to attaining a common market, but as time passed different industrial policy instruments have come into use.

According to Swann (1988) four elements of EC industrial policy can be identified:

1. Creation of a European industrial base, i.e. a real common market

This has always been a fundamental task and an economic rationale for the EC. The removal of tariffs, quotas and other hindrances for trade and free movement of production factors are central to the creation of an industrial base. Most of the Single Market directives are also closely connected to the establishment of a European industrial base, and the directive on public procurement and the establishment of free capital movement are particularly decisive factors for realizing a comprehensive, functioning European industrial base.

2. Promotion of business integration

The purpose has been to encourage the creation of European corporations. For some time the EC has not been successful in this area because of both practical problems in overcoming the fiscal and legal difficulties which inhibit cross-frontier mergers and other forms of cooperation, and of different attitudes to competition/concentration in the single EC Member States. There has been strong pressure within the EEC to evolve policies at community and national levels which would hasten the process of integration and lead to the emergence of large corporations which could compete with the giant enterprises of the US and Japan. On the other hand, it has also been recognized that the Community needs a policy which can deal effectively with the concentration of economic power.

The question of competition is especially dealt with in article 86 of the Rome Treaty. It provides no general power to prohibit mergers. The Commission was originally given power to deal with abuse of a dominant market position, but not to prevent a dominant position should it arise. Now, however, the Commission can veto a merger. For many years mergers were an exception. It was a result of the refusal of the EC Commission to accept the cartels for synthetic fibres proposed by Commissioner Etienne Davignon in the end of the 1970s. However, the introduction of the internal market has led to the number of mergers rising considerably and increased concentration and integration.

3. *Instruments to close the technological gap between the EC and Japan and the US*

In 1980 European anxiety about the lack of competitiveness due to the technological gap between Europe and Japan and the US began to be a real concern in Europe. The Commission argued that Europe's position as a world economic power required both the removal of barriers within the EC to create greater efficiency through increased competition and large-scale economics and the protection of Europe's high technology industries. In 1982 the European Council rejected this approach in favour of a proposal which focused on specific areas of technology in which the EC lagged behind, and devoted increased financial resources to programmes of cooperation.

The core element of the EC research and development and technology policy is the provision of financial resources to promote cooperation in all Member States, between research centres and universities on one hand and industrial corporations on the other hand. The main instrument has been framework programmes which involve multi-annual plans embracing all the specific well-known EC research and technology programmes and include objectives, the types of activities envisaged and the extent of the financial commitment. The first took place from 1984 to 1987.

In 1987, at the revisal of the Treaty of Rome, research and technology development were added to the Community's future aims and competences.

The second framework programme ran from 1987 to 1991 and provided for action in eight areas: quality of life; information and communication; modernization of industry; biological resources; energy, science and technology for development; marine research and European scientific cooperation. About 0.2 per cent of the Community's GDP was devoted to the framework programme.

4. *Sectoral policies to address the problems of industries encountering structural difficulties*

This kind of industrial policy dealing defensively with declining industrial sectors has taken place in the EC for some long time and includes regulation of the steel sector, textiles and shipbuilding. Furthermore, the agriculture and the fisheries policy could be mentioned as examples.

The measures for intervention have been: 1) Financial aid to diminish capacity; 2) to facilitate the movement of capital and labour into other industries; 3) to increase the efficiency of the rest of the industry. But protective measures have also been applied. The instruments have often been introduced as temporary, but have turned out to be of a more permanent nature.

The steel industry has been regulated via a comprehensive and systematic policy by the Commission and the EC in general. In relation to the published objective the results have been unsatisfactory: 'The EC steel regulation has delayed adjustment and protected EC steel production and has not succeeded in bringing about what it was supposed to' (BMWi-Dokumentation, No. 287, February 1988).

Concerning textiles, the Commission has tried to control external trade with regulations. The Multi-Fibre Arrangement has existed since 1977 in a still more restrictive form: The industry has grown in the shade of regulation and the objectives for the restructuring of the industry have not been achieved.

Concerning shipyards, the objectives were to prevent oversubsidization and to harmonize the national subsidy levels. The sixth directive on assistance to shipbuilding permitted state aid if the industry diversified into more economically promising activities. The industry has only to a small degree developed enough competitiveness to keep up with the non-European world ship production, and from a European fraction of world ship production of two-thirds, the production fraction is reduced to one-tenth.

Danish industries – main structure

Table 9.1 presents the structure of Danish industrial production in 1973, when Denmark joined the EC, and in 1990. Services have increased and manufacturing diminished proportionally, as is the case in most other countries. The importance of the primary sector has increased heavily because of oil production in the North Sea. Furthermore, construction went dramatically down at the end of the 1980s due to overbuilding in the mid-eighties followed by economic and financial crises.

Statistical information on manufacturing industry with more than 20 employees shows:

- the total size of the industry is about 2,500 corporations and 6,500 plants;
- 5 per cent of the corporations have more than 500 employees and 55 per cent of the turnover;
- 2 per cent of the corporations have more than 1,000 employees and that corporations of real world size are not found;
- Denmark has three core manufacturing industries: the iron industry,

Table 9.1 GDP in 1973 and 1990 in 1980 prices, billion DKr

	1973	%	1990	%
GDP total	275	100	397	100
Agriculture etc. and minerals	14	5.1	38	9.5
Manufacturing	57	20.7	72	18.2
Electricity, gas and heating	3	1.1	68	1.7
Construction	29	10.5	23	5.9
Private services	119	43.3	171	43.1
Public services	53	19.3	86	21.7

Source: Statistisk 10-Årsoversigt 1991.

the food, beverage and tobacco industry and the chemical industry. The food and beverage industries are the original industrial complex;

- 1 per cent of the plants of the main manufacturing industries employ 20 per cent of those employed in the manufacturing industries.

Danish industrial policy

Since World War II Denmark has followed what in Bela Belassa's terminology is called an outward development strategy, which does not imply favouring export over import substitution but rather a strategy providing similar incentives to production for domestic and for export markets.

Danish industrial policy has been market-orientated and the state has not interfered much. The function of the state in relation to production has been to provide for a comprehensive and well-functioning infrastructure and a well-educated labour force, and not to compete with the private sector. In other words the state set the framework and followed a non-interventionist strategy, with the private sector deciding allocation.

In the 1980s new technology ushered in a new phase in production and administration. Most of the labour force was not able to use this technology, and the problem was seen as an infrastructural one. It resulted in the decision of a Technology Programme in 1982, which in the following years included a large part of the amounts used for industrial policy purposes. This was at the end of the eighties followed by other programmes with a special focus (biological production and foods) and with greater emphasis on support for increasing export and the organization of networks, etc. The policy developed into a structural policy, with allocative impacts and adjustment to the EEC Internal Market. At the end of 1989 industrial policy changed dramatically back to the old pattern because of a political compromise in order to have the

Finance Act passed, and because of pressure from large corporations and industrial organizations. Most of the support at the company level was cut away, and Denmark has now the lowest industrial subsidies in relation to GDP in the EC.

The problem concerning industrial policy is narrowly connected to the objectives of the policy (is it primarily seen as a means for stabilization, or for adjustment?). Furthermore, it is highly dependent on the attitudes and views concerning uncertainty, imperfect information, effects on market prices and bureaucracy. Both the lack of awareness of these concepts and the different opinions of these concepts have resulted in different and unstable decisions on what should be the role and the instrument of Danish industrial policy. An efficient industrial policy demands greater responsibility in the political decisions, as the effects of an industrial policy demand a larger time perspective than an election period to be realized. In the 1990s the industrial policy has been nearly without intervention, except for the areas governed by EC policies and the housing policy.

References

Balassa, Bela (1961), *European Integration*, London: Macmillan.

Balassa, Bela (1975), *Theory of Economic Integration*, Allen & Unwin.

Balassa, Bela (1981), *The newly Industrializing Countries in the World Economy*, New York 1981.

Balassa, Bela (1989), *A Conceptual Framework for Adjustment Policies*, Working Papers, The World Bank.

Cecchini, Paolo (1988), *Europe 92*, Børsens Forlag, Copenhagen.

Davis, Evon, Geroski, P.A., Kay, J.A., Manning, Alan, Smales, Carol, Smith, S.R. and Szynanski, Stefan (1989), *1992: Myths and Realities*, London: Centre for Business Strategy, London Business School 1989.

Den industripolitiske udfordring, *Samfundsøkonomen* temanr. 4, Copenhagen 1990.

EF-Kommisionen, Hvidbog om gennemførelse af det indre marked, Bruxelles 1985.

EF-Kommisionen, En europæisk udenrigspolitik for 1990'erne, *Bulletin for EF*, Supplements 3/91.

Helpman, E. and Krugman, P. (1989), *Market Structure and Foreign Trade: Increasing Returns, imperfekt Competition and the Internal Economy*, MIT Press.

Industriministeriet (1989), *Dansk industripolitik på vej til det indre marked*, Copenhagen.

Industriministeriet (1989), *Strategi 1992*, Erhvervspolitisk redegørelse, Copenhagen 1989.

Industripolitik i et åbent og konkurrencebaseret miljø: Retningslinier for en EF politik, *KOM* (90) 556, 1990.

Jacquemin, A. (1987), *The New Industrial Organization*, Oxford: MIT and Oxford University Press, 1987.

Kristensen, Søren Brøndum, *Industripolitik med særligt henblik på danske erfaringer*, Samfundslitteratur, Copenhagen 1990.

Lyck, Lise (ed.) (1990), *The Nordic Countries and the Internal Market of the EEC*, Nyt Nordisk Forlag, Arnold Busck, Copenhagen 1990.

Pelkmans, J. (1984), *Market Integration in the European Community*, The Hague: Martinus Nijhoff Publishers.

Samfundsøkonomen 1991:5.

Samfundsøkonomen 1991:7.

Statistisk 10-års oversigt 1989.

Chapter 10

Competition law

Evan Sølvkjær

The principles of Danish law

Until 1 January 1990 competition law was based on the Monopolies and Restrictive Practices Supervision Act 1955 (the Monopolies Act) and the Prices and Profits Act 1974.

The purpose of the Monopolies Act was '... by means of public supervision of monopolies and restrictive practices to prevent unreasonable prices and business terms and to ensure the best possible conditions of the freedom of trade'.

The Prices and Profits Act was a kind of supplement to the Monopolies Act with the aim '... by means of supervision of prices to contribute to economic stabilization and through similar measures as regards rates, fees and profits to contribute to implementation of an incomes regulation within the sectors involved in line with the incomes political objectives for the society as a whole'.

But in a wider sense, competition law has included – and still does – other statutory regulations:

- Statute No. 252 of 8 June 1977 on price marking and display (cf. Consolidation Act No. 492 of 4 July 1989, as amended);
- The provisions on prices etc. of Statute No. 54 of 25 February 1976 on electricity supply;
- The provisions on prices, etc. of Statute No. 382 of 13 June 1990 on heat supply;
- Statute No. 216 of 8 June 1966 on competitive tendering;
- The EC competition rules laid down in Article 85 and 86 of the EEC Treaty, the Regulations pursuant to Article 85, and the EC rules on competitive tendering.

Competition Act 1989

The Competition Act was passed by the Danish Parliament on 7 June 1989 and came into force on 1 January 1990. Like the previous legislation, the Act is based on public access and control.

This implies that anti-competitive practices – whether in the form of agreements or by virtue of a certain conduct – are basically allowed as part of commercial activities, but also that such practices must be visible and are subject to control and to measures against harmful effects taken by the competent authority.

In section 1 of the Competition Act, the purpose of the Act is described as follows:

> The purpose of this Act is to promote competition and thus strengthen the efficiency of production and distribution of goods and services etc. through the greatest possible transparency of competitive conditions and through measures against restraints of the freedom of trade and other harmful effects of anti-competitive practices. Accordingly, in step with the increasing internationalization, the aim is to ensure a development of the market structure based on competition and efficiency.

In contrast, the EC competition rules are based on prohibition against anti-competitive agreements which have a substantial influence on trade between Member States and against abuse of dominant position, with exemptions, however, in the series of regulations concerning certain categories of agreements, and with the possibility of individual exemption in pursuance of Article 85(3).

Public access

The principle of public access implies that information about monopolies and restrictive practices must be available to anybody. This principle is reflected in Section 1, Section 5 on notifications (which accordingly – except for trade secrets – is available to the public); Section 7 on submission – at the request of the authority – of prices, discounts, bonuses etc.; Section 8 on investigations of markets structures, prices and business terms, and on publication of the results of such investigations; and in Section 9 on publication of prices, discounts, bonuses etc. In addition to this there is the general public information about decisions made according to the Act.

When the Bill was introduced to Parliament and during the parliamentary debate, importance was attached to making transparency (public access to information about market structures) the main instrument for achievement of the purpose of the Act: to promote competition and thus strengthen the efficiency of trade and industry. Creating transparency ensures easy access for producers, dealers and consumers to relevant information about prices, business conditions and other information about competition.

In the general remarks on the Bill it is indicated that the need for measures to regulate competition is considered less and less pronounced as the market transparency is increased.

By an amendment of the Act (which came into force on 1 June 1992) the extended public access has, however, been considerably limited. The amendment was based on experience from the administration of the Act.

The amendment repeals the general public access to cases treated by the Competition Council, except where the request for access concerns notified agreements and decisions, or such information which the Competition Council has ordered enterprises to submit concerning markets where competition is not sufficiently workable.

The Competition Council will still be entitled to publish information through reports on market investigations etc. Information on technical matters, including research, production methods and products, and matters pertaining to individual customers in enterprises which are under the jurisdiction of the Danish Supervision of Banking, Insurance and Securities is not to be disclosed, however.

In addition, the Council can decide to conceal other types of information if an enterprise may suffer a considerable financial loss, and 1) if other enterprises etc. will be able to derive an unjustified competitive advantage from the disclosure, or 2) in case of other special circumstances. No. 2) is similar to the provision prior to the amendment, but No. 1) is an innovation.

The amendment also implies that as a principal rule, decisions which concern right of access to documents and concealment cannot be brought before the Competition Appeals Tribunal.

The principle of control implies an established supervision of monopolies and restrictive practices and intervention against unreasonable effects on the market and against abuse of dominant position. The legal authority for control and intervention is laid down in Sections 11, 12 and 13 of the Act.

Binding resale prices

One prohibitory provision is contained in Section 14, however, according to which enforcement of binding resale prices is prohibited and under penalty.

Negotiation/orders

The rules on control are based on Section 11: 'If the Competition Council finds that an anti-competitive practice is exerted on a certain market, which entails or may entail harmful effects on competition and accordingly on the efficiency of production and distribution of goods or services etc. or restraints of the freedom of trade, cf. Section 1, the Council can attempt to terminate the harmful effects through negotiation'. The words '. . . the Council can attempt to . . .' indicate that it is up to the Competition Council's judgement as to whether measures should be taken.

If it is decided to take measures, the first step is always initiating negotiation with the enterprise/organization concerned in order to try to terminate the anti-competitive practice. Only once negotiation has been tried without a satisfactory result can an order be issued which may imply total or partial termination of agreements, decisions, etc., or force a company to supply specified buyers with goods or services on the terms usually applied by the enterprise concerned to similar sales. Where such an order is made, the enterprise is, however, always entitled to demand payment in cash or adequate security, cf. Section 12 of the Act.

Price regulation

If an anti-competitive practice entails that a price or profit, whether in level or duration, clearly exceeds what would be obtainable on a market with workable competition, the Competition Council can decide that a given price or profit must not be exceeded, or that specified calculation rules shall be observed in connection with the calculation of prices and profits (Section 13).

Such a decision can only be made for a period of up to one year at a time, but may – after reconsidering – be prolonged by a new order. Assessment of a price or profit shall be based on the conditions of such enterprises which are operated with appropriate technical and commercial efficiency, and the enterprise concerned shall be able to meet the necessary costs and to obtain a profit reflecting the risk involved in manufacturing and sale of the product or service, etc.

The assessment is based on the calculation for the individual and specified product or service (the cost-price principle), but the Competition Council may deviate from that principle in the assessment of prices and profits within production sectors with intensive research and development. The expression 'if justified by weighty reasons' gives a definite indication that taking the total production into consideration – with due respect for the legitimacy of allowing the transfer of costs from one product to another – before drawing a conclusion on the price calculation, is a specific deviation from a principle rule. The provision is a continuation of the law and practice prior to the Competition Act. An addition to the Monopolies Act in 1983, according to which wider latitude was allowed in cost allocation, was based on the conditions of the pharmaceutical industry, where it was considered justifiable to debit the price/profit of one product with expenses for research and development of the manufacturing of other (new) products.

In the remarks on the Bill it is emphasized that '. . . direct regulatory measures against competition should as far as possible be avoided. A too circumstantial and rigorous regulation will inevitably result in freezing of the market structure and consequently in undesirable effects on costs and prices, etc.'. As regards the access to control prices and profits, it is indicated that such access is 'subsidiary compared to other measures'.

With regard to this it should be mentioned that the debate in Parliament resulted in the insertion of provisions on measures to ensure the freedom of trade, and the fact that it was established by the passage of the Act that the Secretariat of the Competition Council should have an independent position – and twice as many employees (about a hundred, compared to the fifty which had been recommended in the Bill) – indicates that the legislators considered it likely that the need for control/measures might be more pronounced than assumed in the remarks on the Bill.

The significance of previous practice

The powers to intervene laid down in the Competition Act have almost the same substance as the powers pursuant to the Monopolies Act in force from 1955–1990. Accordingly, the practice which has evolved by virtue of the Monopolies Act is of great importance – as a guiding instrument – in the administration of the Competition Act.

The scope of the Act

According to Section 2, the Act applies to commercial enterprises and associations of such enterprises, including liberal professions and financial enterprises (banks and insurance companies and business activities, which under special provisions are subject to control or approval by public authorities – but as far as such activities are concerned, the rules on intervention (Sections 11–14) do not apply. Furthermore, the Act applies (with the exception of Sections 11–14) to business activity performed by a central or local government administration, which consists in supply of or demand for goods or services, etc., of importance for competition within trade and industry.

According to the preceding Monopolies Act and Prices and Profits Act, the supervision of restrictive practices and price conditions of banks and insurance companies was placed under the Danish Supervision of Banking, Insurance and Securities. But as mentioned, this sector is now included, like all other business sectors, under the scope of the Competition Act.

As previously stated, the powers of intervention (by means of orders issued by the Competition Council) do not apply to business activities regulated or performed by public authorities – in contrast to the other provisions of the Act, such as the rules on notification of agreements, preparation of reports on investigations, etc. – but these activities are covered by Section 15, according to which the Competition Council may approach the competent public authority and point to the potentially harmful effects on competition. Such communication shall be published.

Wages and labour relations

Explicit exemption is made in the Act as far as this field is concerned. However, the obligation to submit information on request applies in full. (Clarification in that respect can be of great importance for the assessment of costs, etc., in relation to the competitive situation).

The obligation imposed on the enterprises to submit information

In connection with creating transparency in market structures, and when measures need to be taken against anti-competitive practices and abuse of dominant position, the instruments used by the Competition Council are the access to demand relevant information from enterprises, associations, etc., and the immediate obligation imposed on the enterprises to make notification of restrictive agreements and decisions which have a dominant influence on a certain market.

The Competition Council

The Council consists of a Chairman appointed under the Royal Seal and fourteen members appointed by the Minister of Industry. The Chairman and seven of the members must be independent of commercial interests.

A secretariat under the management of a Director is attached to the Council to attend to the current administration and preparation of the cases.

Appeal

The decisions of the Council can be appealed to the Competition Appeals Tribunal, and the decisions of the Tribunal can be brought before the courts of law.

Penalty provisions

Infringement of the obligation to make notification, submission of incorrect or misleading information, and omission to comply with an order is subject to a fine.

EC law and Danish law

The EC competition rules are immediately applicable in the member countries, i.e. they guarantee rights to and impose obligations on the enterprises (and citizens) concerned as well as the member states.

The authority of the national courts of law to enforce the EC competition rules follows from the immediate effect of the rules, and is exercised parallel with the powers of the EC Commission and the national competition authorities.

In the BRT-II case (judgment of 30.1. 1974) the EC Court of Justice stated that, '. . . as the prohibitions laid down in article 85(1) and article 86 are inherently certain to create immediate effects on the conditions of private citizens, these articles give rise to immediate rights for those governed by the law, and whom the national judicial authorities are committed to protect.'

Accordingly, it rests with the national courts of law to prove an infringement of the prohibitions and, in connection with the nullity effect, to settle an action for damages. But the national courts of law are not in a position to grant exemption in pursuance of article 85(3) because of the Commission's exclusive authority in that respect, cf. article 19(1) of Regulation No. 17/62.

In order to promote a workable and efficient competition policy, the Commission seeks to increase and facilitate the decentralized decision procedures to the greatest possible extent, and therefore the Commission intends to publish a statement on application of articles 85 and 86 by the national courts of law.

The national competition authorities are also entitled to apply the prohibitions of article 85(1) and article 86 as long as the Commission has not initiated procedure in the case, cf. article 9(3) of Regulation No. 17/62.

Only the German Competition Act contains a provision which empowers the German competition authorities to apply the EC rules, and in practice they only use these powers in connection with a parallel application of the national competition rules.

Even though implementation of the 'internal market' does not imply alignment of the national competition rules with EC law, it is obvious that most member countries – except for Denmark, the UK and the Netherlands – as well as the other Nordic countries have more of less adopted the principles which conform to the principle of prohibition laid down in articles 85 and 86.

As all member states have a national competition law, one cannot preclude the risk that a conflict may arise between national and EC competition law, whether the national rules are based on prohibition or control.

The EC Court of Justice has clearly established the principle of the absolute priority of EC law (the Costa-ENEL case).

Even though the criterion of trade between member states in article 85(1) and article 86 aims at separating EC law from national law, there may be borderline cases where the application of national law will collide with the practice developed by the Commission.

The question of possible conflict between EC law and national law may in particular come up when the Commission has decided to prohibit an agreement etc. in pursuance of article 85 (1) or to grant an exemption in pursuance of article 85(3).

If, on the other hand, the Commission has given a negative clearance, the national authorities continue to have complete power to use their national legislation.

As regards agreements etc., which the Commission has decided to prohibit in pursuance of article 85(1), the EC Court of Justice has clearly established the principle of priority of the EC law (the Walt Wilhelm case – judgment of 13.12. 69).

According to the Court of Justice there is a conflict if the application of national law impedes an unlimited and equal application of EC law. On the other hand, the Court of Justice establishes that, in principle, there is nothing to prevent a parallel application of national law and EC law, provided that a Regulation pursuant to article 87(2)(e) of the Treaty has not been adopted and that the application of national law does not impede the unlimited and equal application and effects of EC law. Conflicts between EC law and national law should be settled according to the principle of priority of the EC law.

In connection with the appeal case involving the television companies BBC, ITP and RTE, which concerned an infringement of article 86 as regards the companies' refusal to submit information about coming television programmes for the use of an inclusive edition (Magill TV Guide), the Court of First Instance found that EC law has priority over such national rules on copyright which prevent the competing enterprise from getting access to the market concerned.

The relation between EC competition rules and Danish competition law has come up in a number of cases, i.e. in connection with the Commission Regulation No. 123/85 on block exemption to certain categories of motor vehicle distribution and servicing agreements, but it has never resulted in any actual conflicts.

The competent Danish authority in relation to the EC competition law is the Secretariat of the Competition Council.

References

Sølvkjær, Evan (1990), *Konkurrenceloven med kommentarer*, Jurist- og økonomforbundets Forlag, Copenhagen (in course of publication).
Sølvkjær, Evan (1984), *Monopolloven med kommentarer*, Jurist-og økonomforbundets Forlag, Copenhagen.
von Eyben, W.E. (1980), *Monopoler og priser*, C.E.C. Gad, Copenhagen.

Chapter 11

Agricultural policy

Peter Nedergaard

Introduction

The Common Agricultural Policy (CAP) was a primary reason for Danish membership of the European Community in 1973. Even though the importance of Danish agriculture had been declining in terms of export and employment *vis-à-vis* Danish industry and services, the agricultural sector was and still is of major importance in Denmark.

The situation in Danish agriculture before 1973 was gloomy. Since the CAP was established at the beginning of the 1960s Danish agriculture had lost substantial market shares on the export markets in the Community, especially in Germany and Italy. A phrase was coined to illustrate the situation in the Danish agricultural sector before 1973: that of being put in a 'waiting-room'.

Benefits

After the membership of the Community, the representatives of the Danish government became defenders of the basic principles in the CAP and the traditional price support policy regime. In a report from 1983, the official Danish attitude towards the CAP was said to rely on the following points of view (Betænkning fra Udvalget vedrørende . . ., 1983):

- to uphold the fundamental principles of free trade together with the Community preference, common finance, and free competition on equal terms,
- to uphold the price support policy as the main instrument in securing the farm incomes,
- to let the expenditure of the agricultural budget be governed by the agricultural policy, and not the other way around,
- to use the agricultural expenditures as efficiently as possible, and

Table 11.1 Annual income transfers and net welfare induced by the CAP, Denmark (in million ECU)

	1980	1981	1982	1983	1984	1985
Balance of tax expenditures	249	259	319	166	442	477
Budget and trade balance	631	606	820	859	990	887
Net welfare[1]	309	365	449	493	511	362

1. Unweighed summation of change in producer and consumer welfare and taxpayer expenditure.

Source: Brown, 1989, p. 58.

- to examine the necessary adaptions of the agricultural policy within the framework of the basic principles.

The official Danish attitude towards the CAP represents a broad consensus of agricultural interest organizations and shifting governments, and the attitude clearly mirrors the Danish benefits of the CAP in terms of annual income transfers and net welfare induced. Whether one considers 1) the balance of tax expenditures, 2) the budget and trade balance, or 3) net welfare, the result turns out to be beneficial for Denmark, if one looks at the years 1980–85 (see Table 11.1).

Thus it is not so much a question of costs and benefits for Denmark as a question of the CAP being more or less beneficial. The more the price support mechanism is weakened, the more the agricultural expenditures are allocated to alternative structural purposes, and, in general, the more the agricultural expenditures are put under external or internal pressure, the less beneficial the CAP is for Denmark.

Some of the major issues in the present debate on the future of the common agricultural policy in the Community will be examined in the next sections from this official Danish cost-benefit point of view.

GATT negotiations

Officially, the present GATT negotiations began in Uruguay in 1986. The negotiations were scheduled to end in December 1990.

Contrary to former GATT negotiations, the ongoing round of trade talks deals with agriculture. The purpose here is to implement a more market-oriented agricultural policy on a global level.

From a Danish agricultural point of view considerable interests are at stake during the GATT negotiations. These interests are compounded with the potential effects for the present CAP regime, while the CAP is at the top of the agenda. The United States , in particular, and a number of agricultural exporting countries are pressing for changing the CAP in a less 'supportive' direction.

As mentioned above, for Danish agriculture the ideal outcome of the GATT negotiations will be a CAP left as unchanged as possible. On the other hand, considering the strong external pressure, the Agricultural Council of Denmark (Landbrugsraadet, 1990) representing the major interest organisations in agriculture accepts binding agreements on a gradual reduction in the agricultural support level and a strengthening of the GATT regime, if the basic principles of the CAP are left unaltered.

Yet a number of preconditions still have to be fulfilled before a new GATT regime is settled. These preconditions are as demanded by the Agricultural Council:

1. The objectives of agricultural policies continue to be those of income stabilization and food supply at reasonable prices.
2. Binding rules have to cover *all* agricultural policy instruments with important direct or indirect effects on trade.
3. Agreements must take their background from calculations on the total agricultural support with a system of fixed but reversible world market prices.
4. The 'two price' system of the CAP shall be restored.
5. Steps should be taken toward a stabilization of the world market for agricultural products covering minimum export prices, maximum national stocks, and procedures for notification and consultation in GATT.
6. Veterinary and phytosanitary rules should be harmonized at a high level.

The Internal Market

Danish agriculture is estimated to have the necessary potential to exploit the possibilities of the Internal Market, even though adaptations in the sector are needed and problems have to be faced (Landbrugsraadet, 1988).

In general, Denmark's major debt burden has imposed higher interest rates on the agricultural sector and other economic sectors. Economic integration and the liberalization of financial services are supposed to compensate for the former economic disadvantages based on earlier Danish agricultural policy.

On the demand side, the removal of mobility barriers in the Internal Market will give the export-oriented Danish agricultural sector the means to fully exploit comparative advantages that may exist. At the same time, higher growth rates and structural funding of the southern European Member States are to some extent expected to raise the demand for agricultural products and agro-industrial equipment.

Problems will arise, too, during the Internal Market process due to the forthcoming harmonization of veterinary and phytosanitary rules. The present level of veterinary and phytosanitary regulations in Denmark having to be harmonized at a lower level may cause problems with agricultural exports to the United States and Japan.

Reforming the CAP

The above-mentioned status quo attitude of Danish agriculture and governments toward the present CAP regime does not take into consideration that fundamental changes to market support arrangements from unconditional price schemes have already emerged in the late 1980s.

Various means have been used to reduce expenditure, including a reduction in support prices, a decline in the amount of production receiving support, and the introduction of offsetting production levies. Although forecasting future changes in the CAP presents substantial difficulties, the continuation and extent of recent supply management schemes and production levies are nevertheless likely integral elements of a CAP in the 1990s, as well as the introduction of a more targeted income support policy and a nationalization of some of the agricultural support costs.

The more the traditional price support policy of the CAP is tempered down, the less the CAP will provide benefits for Danish agriculture. That is not to say, however, that the CAP will not be beneficial for Danish agriculture as long as the foreseeable alternative to the CAP is even worse.

Conclusions

The CAP was a primary reason for Danish membership of the European Community in 1973. Since then, Danish governments and agricultural interest organisations have been defenders of the basic principles in the CAP and the traditional price support policy regime.

The official Danish attitude clearly mirrors the Danish benefits of the CAP in terms of annual income transfers and net welfare induced. Thus the CAP is not so much a question about costs and benefits for Denmark as it is a question about whether the CAP is more or less beneficial.

Considering the ongoing GATT negotiations, the optimal solution for Danish agriculture will be a CAP left as unchanged as possible. If, however, adjustments are considered because of strong external pressure, they must be gradual, all-encompassing, and pay respect to the original objectives of the agricultural policies.

Danish agriculture is estimated to have the necessary potential for full exploitation of the comparative advantages of the Internal Market free of barriers for goods and services. However, problems are expected to arise in the Internal Market process due to the forthcoming harmonization of veterinary and phytosanitary rules, as the present level of regulations in Denmark having to be harmonized at a lower level may cause problems with agricultural exports to the United States and Japan.

The above-mentioned status quo attitude of Danish agriculture and governments does not take into consideration that fundamental changes of the traditional price support policy have already emerged in the late 1980s. The more the traditional price support policy of the CAP is tempered down, the less the CAP will provide benefits for Danish agriculture. That is not to say, however, that the CAP will not be beneficial for Denmark as long as the foreseeable alternative to the CAP is even worse.

References

Betænkning fra Udvalget vedrørende landbrugets økonomiske vilkår og udvikling, En fremtidig landbrugspolitik – nogle mere langsigtede perspektiver, (1983), Betænkning nr. 993 København.

Brown, Colin (1983), *Price Policies of the CAP: Retrospect and Prospect*, Statens Jordbrugskonomiske Institut, Rapport nr. 1, København.

Landbrugsraadet (1988), *Det indre marked og dansk landbrug*, København.

Landbrugsraadet (1990), *GATT – forhandlingerne og EF's landbrugspolitik*, København.

Chapter 12

Fisheries policy

Peter A. Friis

Introduction

The European fishing industries are facing growing problems and the organization of the EC Common Fisheries Policy is being strongly questioned. All the EC countries engaged in fisheries are confronted with large groups of dissatisfied fishermen and others representing the fishing industry. The dissatisfaction not only concerns the EC quota policy, but also the administration of declining resources resulting from reductions in the overall quota of the most important species of fish allocated. Furthermore, these groups are dissatisfied with the lack of dynamics and development within the fishing industries. The current disproportion between too few resources and too large a fishing capacity within the Community inevitably leads to conflicts among fishermen from different countries.

Reductions in the fishing quotas are necessary and less interesting than policies expanding the fishing industry. Instead of striving towards constructing the best possible resource policy in the EC, the politicians have agreed to the least unacceptable solution.

Such a solution is only implementable because the fishing sector constitutes a relatively small part of the European economy. Nevertheless, in some parts of Europe this sector is predominant.

The EC politicians are facing the problem of having to revise the current policy and construct a new one. Before 1 January 1993 the Commission is to present a report evaluating the past ten years of common fisheries policy. This report is subsequently to be used as a basis for assessing whether the current arrangements are to continue till the end of 2002, at which time all temporary arrangements are scheduled to expire.

The following account of the EC fisheries policy analyses, from a Danish perspective, both the Community's fisheries policy and the Danish fisheries policy and the problems Denmark is facing.

EC fisheries policy

The third and last part of the EC Common Fisheries Policy, apart from the resource policy, was agreed upon in January 1983. Guidelines concerning the other two major components – structural policy and market policy – had already been agreed upon.

The administration of the Common Fisheries Policy has three objectives:

1. To utilize all fish stocks optimally in terms of catch and market exploitation in such a way that steady returns are continuously ensured;
2. To maintain the largest possible degree of employment and level of income in those coastal regions that are depending on fishing or are in a poor economic position;
3. To ensure that the EC fishing capacity is adjusted most optimally to the basic resources.

Resource policy

The objective of the resource policy is to determine Totally Allowable Catches (TAC) in the EC fishing zone. Allowable catches of each relevant stock are determined on the basis of biologists' recommendations. The Commission then works out a proposal for TAC which the Council upgrades for socio-economic reasons.

The TAC are distributed among the member countries on the basis of the percentage distribution, the quota-key which was instituted in 1983, and organized according to three different considerations:

- Consideration of the different countries' traditional home fisheries during the period from 1978 to 1983.
- Special conditions in those regions that were especially dependent on fisheries and fishing industry.
- The loss of fishing rights that each member country suffered by the introduction of 200 nautical miles fishing limits.

The resource policy furthermore covers a range of technical means to ensure that small fish are given a chance to grow. The regulations include size of mesh networks, minimum sizes, closed zones, and side-catches. Finally, the resource policy covers agreements with third countries on mutual exchange of quota.

The resource policy is enforced by a small number of EC fisheries inspectors. Furthermore, each member country is responsible for seeing that its fishing industry observes the rules. However, the EC has very limited possibilities for sanctioning infringements.

During recent years the resource policy has been facing growing criticism, not only in Denmark but in all the Community's fishing nations. The reason is that the overall objective – to preserve the fish stock – has not yet been achieved, and nothing seems to indicate that the policy is capable of achieving this goal in the foreseeable future.

One of the major complaints concerns the methods applied by biologists to assess the stock. Critics claim that these methods, by applying the so-called single species approach, are neither taking into account the ecological processes in the sea nor the different species' mutual competition for food. A new method, the multi-species approach, includes these aspects, but it is still being developed and is not yet applied when assessing fish stocks. The main problem is that it is impossible to maximize all fish stocks at the same time – which is exactly what the current system attempts to do.

A general problem with the EC fisheries policy is that right from the beginning it has been closely linked to the agricultural policy. The conditions for agriculture and aqua-culture are somewhat similar, while the conditions for catching fish and for fish to reproduce have very little in common with agriculture. Nevertheless, the same structure is applied to both sectorial policies. Agriculture and fisheries are in many ways linked up, e.g. in the Treaty of Rome, Article 38: 'Agricultural products . . . are products of the soil, livestock, and fisheries as well as first time refined products of these'. It is impossible to apply the same type of policy to increase production within fisheries as that applied to agriculture. When the Treaty of Rome was formed the primary objective was to increase the European countries' self-sufficiency in agricultural products, and contrary to most of the other economic activities the common agricultural policy was not based on the principle of free market grouping. The same applied to fisheries, but the major problem was quite different: administration and distribution of scarce natural resources. Subsidized fisheries result in growing catches and perhaps over-fishing, which will ultimately jeopardize the resources.

Structural policy

The major objective of the structural policy is to support an expedient development of the fishing fleet, the infrastructure of fisheries and aqua-culture. More than 50 per cent of the funds allocated to the EEC 5-year structural programme is reserved for renewal and modernization of the fishing fleet, while approximately 10 per cent is reserved for temporary laying up or cessation of fishing vessels. Another 10 per cent is marked for the development of projects studying aqua-culture.

Critique of the structural policy

The EC has concluded that 40 per cent of the fishing fleet is redundant compared with the TAC and the Community is thus supporting reductions in and cessation of fishing vessels. In this situation it is surprising that the Community at the same time supports new constructions of fishing vessels. Half of the structural programme's budget is allocated to new constructions. This may seem absurd when the aim is to cut down the fishing fleet almost by half.

Also, the structural regulations recently agreed upon are questionable. They imply that the construction of new fish processing plants in certain member countries can be subsidized by up to 75 per cent at the same time as other countries are having problems with an overcapacity of fish processing plants. In this case subsidies are merely transferring production and work places from one part of the Community to another or simply increasing competition for the same amount of scarce resources.

Market policy

The purpose of the market policy is to achieve uniform, high quality fisheries products and to ensure the producers a reasonable income through a system of minimum prices and import duty. During the last five years, the EC has been working on a new statute on hygiene which is expected to be passed before the internal market is established. The rules covering fisheries products rest on a system which is based on self-regulation.

The existing system of minimum prices could be criticized for largely being superfluous at a time when the relationship between the market for and supply of quality fish is growing. In practice this system often functions as a safety net under fish of such poor quality that they could not be sold at all. The system of minimum prices may be justifiable in relation to a number of largely unutilized species. It might also be rational in the future to apply it to shore fishing and to fish caught by tools especially designed to protect the environment, such as long-line fisheries. The EC import duty on fish has had a significant impact on where the fish is processed and on consumer prices. In some cases the import duty on raw materials used by the EC processing plants is higher than on imported semi-products and manufactured goods. Thus the effect of the system is quite contrary to its purpose.

The importance of fisheries in Denmark

Denmark is evidently the EC country to which the fisheries sector is relatively most important. The sector constitutes 1 per cent of the gross national product, employs 20,000 people and accounts for almost 7 per cent of the Danish export, amounting to approximately 1.7 billion ECU. On the Danish island of Bornholm and in a number of towns on the west coast of Jutland, fisheries are of decisive importance to the local economy.

The problems of Danish fisheries

Most of the problems confronting Danish fisheries are caused by reductions in TAC for cod. In the beginning of the 1980s the quota was 160,000 tons, but today it has been cut down to 85,000 tons. This reduction in the single most important resource to Danish fisheries has implied that the Danish fishing fleet is much too large. This problem, which by no means is a unique Danish problem but also applies to all the other countries around the North Sea, has been attempted to be solved partly through the EC structural policy and partly through a cessation scheme initiated by the Danish Ministry of Fisheries. As a result of these measures 10 per cent of the Danish fishing fleet, measured by number of fishing vessels and by tons, disappeared from 1987 to 1989.

However, the capacity of the fishing fleet is still too large compared with the allowed amount of catches. Consequently, each day has its bankruptcies and there is no money to be spent on renewing the fishing fleet and its tools.

But what is perhaps even worse is the rigidity of the fishing industry and its lack of dynamics. The sector shows neither optimism nor any belief in future development. Consequently, the average age of fishermen is rising.

Another unfortunate consequence of the difficult situation within fisheries is that a large number of EC fishermen are violating the laws as they occasionally feel more of less forced to disregard the rules for discards, minimum size of fish and quotas.

Other problems confronting Danish fisheries are reduced catches in internal Danish waters, which may either be caused by over-fishing or by pollution.

The various groups within the Danish fisheries sector are convinced that the problems could be solved over time by removing the quota system, which has not proved capable of producing the expected effects. In replacement more technical measures such as larger mesh networks, separation gratings in trawlers, etc., which effectively preserve the resources, should be introduced. In addition to this, the size of the EC fisheries fleet should be dramatically reduced in all the member countries.

The Danish Ministry of Fisheries does not yet possess any competence in questions concerning fisheries. This applies to competence in connection with regulations comprising internal Danish waters, national waters, i.e. within the twelve nautical miles limit. Outside this territory, regulations must be in compliance with the basic EC law and hence also the internal Danish allocation of quotas.

Simultaneously with the evolving integration process of the EC, the national Danish authority concerning fisheries is being reduced. It can merely be characterized as the remains of pre-federal systems.

After the year 2002 neither Denmark nor any of the other member countries can operate with other rules than those of the general EC law. From this time all national exceptions and temporary arrangements are expected to expire. This does not imply, however, that Denmark cannot introduce different quota schemes to overcome the current serious problems of rentability and overcapacity characterizing the fishing industry. The Danish Ministry of Fisheries has thus worked out a proposal for the testing of a new licence system which is based on marketable quotas for larger fishing vessels (more than 12 metres). Iceland and New Zealand, for example, has already gained quite some experience with such systems (Individual Transferable Quotas). However, so far no decision has been made to implement such an experiment.

Assessment

The EC preservation policy does not preserve and it contains a wide range of contradictory sub-policies. Some of them are strongly characterized by being copies of the agricultural policy and are not created by people with special insight into the specific preconditions and problems of fisheries.

However, no examples of obvious policies for solving the problems currently exist. In a long-term perspective, ITQ solve the problems of renewal and capacity, but do not abrogate the quota scheme's large problem of discards. A viable long-term solution to the problems of fisheries policy would imply a scheme making it profitable for a limited number of fishermen to assume responsibility for the reproduction of the living resources of the sea.

References

Churchill, R.R. (1987), *EEC fisheries law*, Martinus Nijhoff Publishers.

EF's Fiskeriplitik. Europanoter, Kommissionen for de Europæiske Fællesskaber, No. 3, 1991.

Frost, H. and Lynge Jensen, C. (1991), Fisheries Regions in Nordic Countries, in 'Når fisken svigter', *NordRefo* no. 2, Copenhagen.

L'Hostis, D. (1990), Fisheries management, market relations and regional production, in 'Nar fisken svigter', *Nordrefo* no. 2, Copenhagen.

Nyheim, K.A. (1990), *De nordiske land som fiskerinasloner*, Markedsforskning, Norges Fiskerihøjskole, Tromsø.

Schmiegelow, H. (1990), EF's fiskeripolitik og dens betydning for Norden. Report from the 22nd Nordic conference on fisheries, Copenhagen.
Tepstad, I. and Engsæter (1991), *EF's kvotepolitik og Norsk fiskenæring*, Vestlandsforskning, Sogndal.
Tørring, P. (1991), EF's groteske fiskeripolitik, *Nordrevy* no. 3.

Chapter 13

Transport policy

Eigil Waagstein

EC transport policy

In connection with the implementation of the EC's internal market, a common European transport policy is being outlined.

The Council has adopted the main lines for the creation of a common internal transport market. According to these an internal market without quantitative regulations must be established no later than 1992, just as competition restraints should be removed during a transitional period.

In the traffic sector the process of liberalization and harmonization of technical standards is progressing quickly. Fiscal harmonization is, however, advancing more slowly.

This has to do with the fact that decisions in the Council regarding quantitative regulations and technical standards are normally reached by qualified majority, whereas decisions regarding tax changes require unanimity.

In 1988 the Council decided that cross-border road traffic is to be completely liberalized as from 1 January 1993, as Community permissions for the transport of freight by lorries should only be issued on the basis of qualitative criteria. Up till then, a gradual harmonization of the rules and a removal of the remaining competition restraints will take place. Thus common decisions on drivers' driving and resting times have been passed, as well as on weight and dimensions of commercial vehicles.

The Commission has furthermore put forward a proposal about common gas and diesel oil excise duties. In the petrol field target rates for the size of the excise duties have been made, which the countries, in principle, are supposed to approach. This implies that countries above this rate are only permitted to change the rate in a descending direction, whereas countries with a tax under the rate are only permitted to change it in an ascending direction. Thus the aim for unleaded petrol is a rate of 445 ECU per 1,000 litres. As to diesel oil, it is suggested that the taxes of the member countries should have a range from 245 to 270 ECU per 1,000 litres. In addition to competition equality, the proposals are aiming at a limitation of the emission of green house gasses.

The aim of the Commission is to change the principles of collection for vehicle taxes in relation to business transport from a principle of nationality to a principle of territory, so that the taxation is carried through according to where the driving takes place and not to where the vehicle is registered.

Work is being carried out in the Commission on the suggested separation of the running of the national railway companies into two sectors, one operated on a commercial basis and the other on a subsidized one. The purpose of this is to create homogeneity between the countries and equal conditions of competition for the commercial sectors of the railway companies.

It is assumed that the infrastructure costs are separated from the rest of the economy, and that fees are to be paid for the use of the railway track. The intention is also to liberalize the carriage of goods by rail, thus allowing private forwarding agents to use the railway network.

Rail transport in principle is supposed to be self-financing. The ways of rail transport in question first of all are freight transport, international passenger transport, and other long distance transportation by railway of passengers between large population centres.

The national subsidization for the above-mentioned commercial sectors of the railways is supposed to cease by the end of 1992. It will, however, be permitted to give subsidies out of social considerations to other parts of the rail sector.

For environmental reasons, the EC is intensively planning the transfer of long-distance forwarding from cars to rail or cargo vessels. Measures leading to the development of the concept of combined car and railway traffic are also being promoted.

Air traffic within the EC is, incidentally, being extensively liberalized. This has meant a steep increase in the number of flight concessions, which sharpens competition within air traffic.

Danish transport policy

In 1987, in continuation of the political decision about a fixed link across the Great Belt, the Danish government put forward a traffic policy plan of action.

With the decision about the Great Belt link a clarification of the most important Danish traffic policy question of decades was reached, as the link is positioned in the most important traffic corridor between East and West Denmark, where the traffic up till now has been obliged to use ferries. Because of this there was a need to establish a planning basis, taking into account the sharply changed situation to be brought about by the establishment of the Great Belt link.

The plan of action implies a considerable extension of the overall motorway network. With the adjustments later added to the plan, a continuous motorway connection between Copenhagen in the East and the port of Esbjerg on the West coast of Jutland will be constructed before the end of the decade. In addition to this a motorway connection from the Danish-German border to Northern Jutland is to be constructed.

The motorway connection from Elsinore and Copenhagen to the ferry harbour of Rødby at Fehmarn Belt has just been finished. An important element in this respect is a newly constructed motorway bridge of a length of 3 kilometres between the islands of Zealand and Falster.

The Great Belt link implies the elimination of a considerable bottleneck for railway traffic. The plan of action outlines the possibilities this will bring about for the introduction of new rolling stock with possibilities of increasing travelling speed.

The plan of action has been followed up by concrete planning from the Danish State Railways (DSB). These plans involve a considerable improvement of the rail service between Copenhagen and the major Danish towns, with new timetables and considerable reductions in travelling time caused by the Great Belt Link and high-speed trains. In the freight field DSB suggests increasing marketing efforts with offers of combined traffic solutions and shorter freight transport times. These plans will be implemented in stages.

Considerable investments in new rolling stock of the so-called IC3 type are taking place, as a result of several years of development.

An unclarified element in the planning has been the continuation of the railway connection between Denmark and Germany, as an extension of the railway connection between the Danish-German border and Hamburg depends on decisions to be reached by the German federal authorities and Deutsche Bundesbahn.

A cessation of the subsidization of freight transports is suggested in the traffic policy plan of action, as neither car nor rail covers the total socioeconomic costs of transport. A need for subsidization of passenger transport by rail will, however, continue to exist, as the Danish State Railways have an obligation to provide a rail service of a magnitude far beyond what the revenues can provide for.

The plan of action states that locally the economic basis of the collective means of transportation, i.e. bus or train, may be weakened by a migration of passengers. Therefore there is a need for the traffic companies to carry out continuing productivity and service improvements and increase their marketing efforts. Furthermore, an increased cooperation between the traffic companies on the subject of fares is suggested.

Bicycle traffic is rather important in Denmark. Over the last few years large investments in the expansion of the cycle path network have taken place. New cycle paths have been established both in the cities and along the main highways. In the plan of action a further expansion of the network along the main highways is recommended.

The fixed Great Belt Link brings about a drastic reduction in the intensive ferry traffic between East and West Denmark. This traffic is to a large extent taken care of by Danish State Railways. It is therefore suggested in the plan of action that planning for the disrupting of the ferry service is carried out.

DSB has now arranged a programme for re-training of the ferry staff, and agreements with the staff organizations have been reached, ensuring that the staff are kept on right up to the last day of the ferry service. Furthermore, the possibilities of using the remaining ferries on other routes are being explored, for instance across the Fehmarn Belt and to the Baltic States.

Environmental policy strategy

The Danish government published its plan of action for environment and development in 1988 as a follow-up to the report *Our Common Future* (The Brundtland Report) from the World Commission on Environment and Development. In 1990 the recommendations of this report were utilized in an environmental plan of action for the traffic area.

In the plan of action targets are put forward for energy consumption and for the emission of polluting materials from the traffic sector for the period up till the year 2030. Thus the target for energy consumption and emission of CO_2 is a stabilization as compared to the 1988 level reached before the year 2005 and a reduction of 25 per cent up till the year 2030. As to the emission of NO_x and HC the target is a reduction of at least 40 per cent before the year 2000, a reduction of 60 per cent before year 2010, and a further reduction up till the year 2030. The sooty air pollution in the cities is to be reduced by half up till the year 2010 and a further reduction up till the year 2030 has been planned.

The transport sector consumes about 15 per cent of the total energy consumption in the industrialized countries, and contributes 10–15 per cent of the CO_2 emission. The contribution of other polluting materials to the total pollution is typically: CO_2 70–80 per cent, HC 40–50 per cent, NO_x 30–60 per cent, lead 60–70 per cent, SO_2 10–20 per cent, and soot particles 10–20 per cent.

In the plan of action prognoses are advanced for traffic growth in Denmark up till the year 2030, showing a considerable increase in traffic volume, especially in the freight field. Thus passenger traffic is expected to increase by 46 per cent and freight traffic 106 per cent. Nevertheless, only a moderate increase is expected in the energy consumption (14 per cent) and the CO_2 emission (15 per cent) of the transport sector. A reduction of 10 per cent and 52 per cent, respectively, applies to the emission of NO_x and HC. As opposed to this, the emission of soot particles will increase by 28 per cent. The problems of emission of CO_2 and lead will practically cease to exist.

The reason for these results is technological development, making constant improvements to the energy efficiency of vehicles. In addition to this comes the effect of the US norms for the emission of polluting materials, introduced in Denmark as from 1989.

However, the targets for energy consumption, emission of CO_2, NO_x and soot particles will not be reached unless further initiatives are carried through. Several suggestions for the realization of the targets are therefore put forward in the plan of action.

These suggestions include the California requirements for cars with petrol engines, increased demands on the limitation of emissions from cars with diesel engines (US standard 1994), introduction of diesel oil with low sulphur contents, electrification of the railways, application of natural gas as fuel, and additional improvements of the energy efficiency for all means of transportation.

Furthermore the plan points to the possibilities of converting a major part of the freight transport to rail, and increasing efforts in supporting public traffic and cycle transport, etc.

The establishment of the fixed links across the Great Belt and the Sound, which will shift the traffic away from ferries, will also contribute to the environmental targets put forward. The background for this is the considerable energy consumption by the ferry service. Even though the new links will generate new traffic as compared to a situation with continued ferry service, this will not counterbalance the reduction in energy consumption and emissions brought about by the ferries.

The investments in traffic infrastructure

Every year the Danish government announces a ten year plan for investments in the public and semi-public sectors. The plan is based on the investment budgets of the State, the municipalities and the public companies.

The public investment plan is used to determine the total public investments and to fix the order of priority for the investment projects within the frame fixed.

The government has laid down some general rules to ensure an efficient allocation of the public investment resources. The rules are outlined in three main groups:

First, in connection with the establishment of the public investment plans a balancing of the total investment requirements and the expected activity in the construction sector must be carried out. The purpose of this is to avoid overheating in the construction sector leading to bottleneck problems and wage drift. The investment plans will at the same time be coordinated with the expenditure policy aims, put forward for the total current and capital budgets of the State and the municipalities.

As employment current account and debt problems are significant for the Danish macroeconomic situation, the aim is, by means of allocation of investment resources, to fix an order of priority between the public subsectors, taking into account the best way of solving the balance problems of society. Therefore the investments are evaluated on their immediate consequences for imports, exports and employment. The degree to which the investments support the competitive power of the economic life, for instance in reducing production costs or encouraging technological development in companies, is, however, also taken into account. Investments in infrastructure is one example.

At the fixing of order of priority within each sub-sector it is recommended to use different project evaluation methods (cost-benefit analyses etc.). The aim of this is to implement the projects giving the highest benefits and solving the different problems by using the least possible resources. This kind of project evaluation has up till now primarily been used only in the traffic sector.

The total investments in the public investment plan for the period 1991 till 2000 is on average 45 billion DKK yearly, compared to the total Danish gross national product of around 850 billion DKK in 1991. The traffic sector accounts for, on average, 7 billion DKK yearly, of which the investments in the fixed links across the Great Belt and the Sound amount to an average of almost 3 billions DKK yearly. The investments in telecommunication amount to 3.5 billions DKK yearly.

Fixed links

In 1987 the Danish Parliament passed a bill to establish an 18 km-long combined road and rail link across Great Belt. This strait separates a number of East Danish islands, including Zealand where the capital of Copenhagen is situated, from the rest of Denmark. The car and rail traffic across this strait has so far been served by an intensive ferry service.

The total construction costs in 1991 prices are 22 billion DKK. The construction work is expected to be completed in 1997. The project is organized by a state corporation which finances the construction work by raising loans on the capital market. Repayment of the loans takes place through user payments.

For the rail link this is done by a fixed yearly payment from the Danish State Railways; for the road link by means of tolls paid by the motorists. The Great Belt link is the first Danish traffic project to be financed by means of user payments.

In the spring of 1991 the Danish and Swedish governments have agreed to establish an 18 km-long road and rail connection across the Sound between Copenhagen and the city of Malmoe in Southern Sweden. The traffic across the Sound is today served by ferry services.

The investments in this link are estimated to 19 billion DKK at 1991 prices. The construction works are expected to be started in 1993 and completed around the turn of the century.

Financing for this link will also take place by raising loans. Subsequently the Danish and Swedish state railways on the one hand, and the motorists, on the other hand, will repay the loans.

A corporation owned by the Danish and Swedish states will conduct the construction of the fixed link.

With the present ferry services, Great Belt and the Sound today act as economic barriers, which restrain economic development in the regions in question.

The decisions about the fixed links across Great Belt and The Sound are to be seen in the context of the expectations of the EC internal market. In order to benefit from the elimination of the internal borders of the EC, efficient traffic links are necessary.

Taxation in the Transport Sector

The total revenue of the State in the form of excise duty deriving from the transport sector amounted in 1990 to just above 21 billion DKK corresponding to just under 3 per cent of the yearly Danish GDP.

More than half of the revenue derives from the collection of the registration fee. The excise rates are constructed on a progressive scale so that luxury cars yield a proportionally higher duty. The registration fee is assessed as 180 per cent of the value of the car; however, it may be reduced if environmental and traffic safety devices are installed. Lorries weighing over 4 tons, as well as buses and taxis, are exempted from the fee.

Apart from the registration fee, owners of both cars and lorries pay an excise duty based on the weight of the motor vehicle. This duty is calculated according to the net weight and the permitted total weight of private cars and lorries, respectively. This excise duty contributes approximately one quarter to the total tax revenue.

The remaining quarter of the tax revenue comes from the collection of petrol and diesel oil duties, excise duty on number plates, and excise duty on third party liability insurances.

The petrol and diesel oil excise duty is collected at a rate of 2.90 DKK per litre leaded petrol and 2.25 DKK per litre unleaded petrol. For diesel oil the excise rate amounts to 1.76 DKK per litre. Companies liable to pay VAT, however, are fully reimbursed by the tax authorities for the excise duty on diesel oil.

In addition to the excise duty mentioned, custom duty and VAT on the vehicles sold are also collected.

In total the Danish tax level in the transport area is deemed to be very high for private car traffic. Compared with the other EC countries this high tax level on private cars results in car ownership in Denmark being below the EC average. In Denmark in 1989 there were approximately 350 cars per 1,000 inhabitants against approximately 500 cars per 1,000 inhabitants in France and Germany.

Since lorries are exempt from registration fees and pay no duty on oil, the excise burden on the road haulage sector is rather low in Denmark compared to other European countries.

Measures are being taken to get the Danish excise on motor vehicles more in line with the average EC level. In 1990 petrol excise duty decreased by 1.0 DKK per litre. The tax reduction was introduced primarily to limit the extensive border shopping at the Danish-German border. Furthermore, legislative preparations have been made for lowering the reimbursement of the excises on diesel oil consumed by lorries.

In Denmark tolls are not collected for the use of the road network. This situation, though will be changed as from 1997, when the fixed motorway link across the Great Belt is completed, as the link will be financed by user payments.

Subsidies in the transport sector

The total subsidies for the Danish transport sector in 1989 amounted to around 7 billion DKK. Private car transport is not included in this, having a negative element of subsidization as a result of the heavy taxation.

The Danish government has put forward strategies for a cessation of the subsidies, thereby creating equal competition between the different means of transportation. The idea is that the full economic responsibility for the socioeconomic costs triggered off by transportation, including accident and environmental costs, will be imposed on the different means of transportation.

It will, however, be possible to depart from the principle of full economic responsibility to the extend it is decided to include social and regional policy considerations.

In 1989 the subsidies per ton kilometre to freight transport amounted to:

Lorries	0.10 DKK
Railway, mixed cargo	1.40 DKK
Railway, wagonload cargo	0.25 DKK

The subsidies are made up as the difference between on the one hand the fare revenues from the railway traffic and the excise duties on lorries, and on the other hand the current and capital expenses connected with railways and roads. Environmental costs are left out of account in the figures above.

To reduce the element of subsidization in lorry transports, the government has proposed a lowering of the present reimbursement of the diesel oil excise duty for companies liable to pay VAT. The excise rate amounts to 1.76 DKK per litre. As a counterpart to the reduction of the subsidies for lorry transport an improvement of efficiency is planned for the Danish State Railways, aiming at changing unprofitable activities into profitable ones.

For passenger transports the subsidies per passenger kilometre are assessed as follows:

Private cars	– 0.20 DKK
The Danish State Railways	0.49 DKK
Private railways	1.35 DKK
Regional bus companies	0.60 DKK
Regional airports	0.20 DKK

It is expected that the need for subsidies to the Danish State Railways will decline over the years to come, as a result of the fixed links across the Great Belt and the Sound and because of the introduction of new timetables based on high-speed trains. The improved infrastructure will increase the level of competition for the railways as compared to air and car traffic, just as completely new traffic will be generated between the Danish provinces and to and from neighbouring countries. The railways will therefore profit from higher revenues. It is therefore estimated that it will be possible to achieve a balance between revenues and operating costs as from the middle of the 1990s. It will, however, probably not be possible to obtain a commercial balance covering investment costs as well.

As to the private railways, the government has put forward a suggestion of reducing the subsidies, just as initiatives have been taken towards the municipally owned bus companies aiming at rationalization of the service and thereby reductions of the deficits of the companies.

References

Bill on construction of a fixed link across the Sound (1991), The Danish Parliament, Copenhagen.

Group Transport 2000+ (1990), *Transport in a fast changing Europe*. The EC, Brussels.

Report on traffic economics (1989), Ministry of Finance, Copenhagen.

Expenditure analyses 1990, Ministry of Finance, Copenhagen.

The Government's plan of action covering environment and development (1990), Ministry of Transport, Copenhagen.

Traffic policy plan (1987), Ministry of Transport, Copenhagen.

Chapter 14

Energy policy

Peter Hoffmann

The Danish energy scene

Before the first oil crisis of 1973–74 Denmark was almost entirely dependent on imported energy, especially oil. Denmark has no indigenous hard coal resources. Indigenous crude oil and natural gas were discovered in the North Sea and together with renewables these sources today cover almost half of the country's total primary energy consumption.

Total primary energy consumption declined dramatically after the first and – especially – after the second oil crisis. Energy consumption today is at the level of 1972, while GNP has increased by 35 per cent. During the 1970s and the beginning of the 1980s there was a marked change from oil to coal, especially in power stations. During recent years natural gas and renewables have made progress. Primary energy consumption today consists of 47 per cent oil, 40 per cent coal, 8 per cent natural gas and 5 per cent renewables.

On the end-use side of the energy balance the characteristics are a relatively low share of industrial energy consumption (21 per cent) and a relatively high consumption of district heating (13 per cent) half of which is CHP (heat from combined heat and power stations).

EEC energy policy

EEC activities in the energy field up to 1988 were relatively few, and their impact on energy policies of the member countries seem to have been limited. Two exceptions are nuclear policy, regulated according to the EURATOM treaty, and coal policy, regulated according to the ECSC treaty.

The reason for this situation is obvious. Unlike foreign trade, agricultural policy, transportation policy and – since the Single Act of 1987 – environmental policy and energy policy are not mentioned at all in The Treaty of Rome. That means that there is no direct title in the Treaty for establishing a common EEC energy policy.

Consequently the formulation and implementation of energy policy is first of all the responsibility of the member states. Most of the EEC initiatives in the energy field have taken the form of legislation – i.e. resolutions and recommendations – which are not binding for the member states.

It is worth mentioning that the EEC initiatives in the energy field up to 1988 were greatly overshadowed by the actions of the International Energy Agency (IEA). The EEC-IEA relationship has been complicated by the fact that France is not a member of the IEA.

The Single Act and the EEC initiatives to establish the internal market before the end of 1992 have given quite a new impetus to the implementation of EEC energy policy. In the White Book of 1985 energy was still hardly mentioned. But since then trade in energy, the monopolistic character of part of the energy sector, the environmental aspect of energy and the taxation of energy have become key issues in the realization of the internal market. In May 1988 the DG17 (Energy) of the Commission published a working paper, *The Internal Energy Market* (COM(88)238), which has since then been the 'bible' of EEC initiatives in the energy field.

Danish energy policy until today

As in most other European countries a formal energy policy was not formulated until after the first oil crisis in 1973–74. The first overall energy plan was published in 1976. The next came in 1981, but in the meantime important energy laws had been decided on. This was on the one hand a legal regulation of the exploitation of the Danish underground – primarily extraction of oil and natural gas – and on the other hand the Heat Supply Act calling for a detailed heat planning of the whole country, especially to utilize piped natural gas and CHP.

The overall goal of the 1981 energy plan was to obtain cheap energy with a high security of supply and manage energy consumption in such a way that the growth rate of energy consumption was less than the growth rate of the economy.

As a result of the energy plans and – just as important – as a result of market forces, the Danish energy scene has experienced a remarkable change during the last fifteen years.

The achievements very much correspond to the EEC objectives: less independence on imported oil, increased share of coal and renewables and increased energy efficiency. The achievements might have been the same without EEC energy policy initiatives. On the other hand Danish ministers of energy have frequently referred to EEC resolutions and recommendations when arguing for their own plans and for additional legislation – i.e. heat planning, subsidies for conservation measures and renewables, new energy taxes and development of the natural gas system.

The internal energy market

The internal market – or the single market – basically means one big market consisting of twelve member states with free movement of commodities, persons, services and capital. This definition was part of the Single Act of 1987.

The Commission basically looks upon energy as commodities, which should be subject to the principles of free movement. This goes not only for oil and coal, but also for natural gas and electricity. In its basic paper *The Internal Energy Market* the Commission investigates the obstacles to free movement of energy products. Their main findings are:

- the oil and the coal markets already to a great extent fulfil the requirements of an internal market, though various state subsidies are still to be removed in the coal market;
- the natural gas market and the electricity market are not subject to free movement. Transmission and distribution is based on pipes and wires owned and operated by monopolies, which do not necessarily act according to community interest;
- different national energy policies tend to distort the EEC energy market.

In order to remove the barriers to free energy trade the Commission has initiated

- drafting of directives/regulations
- various analysis of the markets
- formulation of plans to be implemented in the longer run.

The basic concept is 'integration'. This could be interpreted as an EEC-wide optimization of planning and operation. The basic question is whether this integration should be achieved by introducing competition or by increasing present cooperation. This will be discussed soon – focusing on the situation of Denmark.

Moreover, new EEC legislation on procurement, standards, taxes and environment will all have substantial impacts on the decisions taken in the energy sector.

Integration of the energy markets

Electricity

The Danish electricity supply is taken care of by 120 distributing utilities, with twelve generating companies and two companies being responsible for fuel purchase and cooperation in planning and operation. The ELSAM covers the western grid (Jutland and Funen). The ELKRAFT covers the eastern grid (Zealand). The utilities are a mixture of cooperative companies, partnerships, limited companies and municipal companies.

One common feature is that all utilities have an **obligation to supply** electricity to the consumers of a specific geographical area. They also have the **right to supply**. This means that there are no other utilities to compete with in the market.

The organizational framework of electricity supply varies between EEC member countries. But they all have in common the obligation and the right to supply. The electricity industry looks upon it as a 'natural monopoly'. The reason is the physical characteristics of electricity, being transported on designated grids and having to be generated at the time of consumption, as it cannot be stored. Its strategic importance in modern society is also stressed.

This strategic importance is the reason for each country having planned and operated its own electricity system – or systems. However, interconnections between national grids of different states have been known for years. These interconnections have been used to supplement to the national systems, especially in cases of shortfall in capacity and in order to exploit cheap hydropower in years of heavy rain and snow.

In the internal market national borders are arbitrary demarcations for energy systems and energy policies. The EEC Commission therefore aims at an overall optimization of the entire EEC electricity system. They have carried out two studies – by Merz and McLellan and by Professor Smeers. The first (Study of Operating Regimes for High-voltage Electricity Transmission in the European Community, Merz and McLellan, July 1989) is a static technical optimization. The second (*The Benefits of Integration in the European Electricity System*, Commission of the European Communities, December 1989) is a dynamic economic optimization. Both studies show substantial benefits if the electricity systems are optimized on a pan-EEC basis. The methods and results of both studies could be queried.

However, no doubt can be raised that the approach is right. If present generating capacities and nature-given comparative advantages are exploited better, the average costs would decline.

The key problem of the Commission now is how to obtain integration. Apparently they do not believe in 'the cooperative way' i.e. trying to get the electric utilities to work more closely together.

Instead they have embarked on 'the competitive way'. As a first step a new directive has been drafted, giving a right of transit through the transmission grid of other member states (*Proposal for a Council Directive on the Transit of Electricity through Transmission Grids*, COM(89)336). This right of transit is given only to generating companies or groupings of generating companies. The right is subject to various technical constraints and to a payment for the transit.

According to the directive Danish ELSAM could enter into a contract with Dutch SEP on exports (or imports). Interjacent German owners of the transmission grid should offer this grid – against payment – for the transportation of the electricity.

Denmark has a very particular position in relation to the directive. The western Danish grid is connected to Norway, Sweden and Germany, but not to the eastern Danish grid. The directive also opens for a right of transit between an EEC-member country and a third country, through an EEC country. Electricity costs and prices in Germany are high compared to the very low prices of Sweden and especially of Norway, where hydro-generation makes marginal costs in wet years almost zero.

Western Denmark, with its coal-based thermal power system, has much lower prices than Germany but higher than Norway and Sweden. Today the Danish electricity trade with Norway and Sweden is carried through within the rules of the Scandinavian electricity cooperation Nordel. Denmark is normally a net importer and the price is determined as the arithmetical average of Danish and Norwegian/Swedish marginal prices.

The transit directive opens the way for trade between Norway/Sweden and Germany. Norway and Sweden might be interested in higher export prices than the Nordel rules allow. Germany might be interested in cheap Scandinavian power – especially as the integration of the two Germanies develops and as the requirement to burn indigenous German coal gradually is abolished.

Depending on available transmission capacity, western Denmark could become a major transit country of electricity. The benefits would be the payments for transit. The cost would be smaller amounts and more expensive imports from Norway and Sweden, the balance is difficult to estimate. The result could be higher Danish electricity prices while Germany gets a benefit and the net results for the EEC as a whole might be positive while Denmark is 'suffering'. This could especially be the case if ELSAM (western grid) is not able to participate actively in the competition due to tight capacity. If, however, ELSAM is allowed to build new capacity and utilize the Danish comparative advantages for coal fired thermal power generation – good harbours and abundant cooling water – both the EEC as a whole and Denmark could benefit from the liberalization of the power market.

The Danish eastern grid (ELKRAFT) is connected only to Sweden and neither to Germany nor to the Danish western grid. Benefits in electricity trade are generally obtained between different generating systems or areas with different consumption patterns (over time). Therefore the establishment of a connection to Germany might be appropriate – both as a means for transit from Sweden and possibly for better utilization of the ELKRAFT generation capacity.

Inducing an element of competition in electricity trade by establishing a right of transit between generators might only be the first step of the Commission. 'Common carrier', 'open access', 'third part access' are – for the Commission – synonymous concepts: the right for end-users to use the grid and buy electricity directly from a generating company of the consumers own choice.

Whether a common carrier will be introduced by the Commission is doubtful. The opposition in the electricity sector and in the national energy administrations is overwhelming. On the other hand, certain legal experts argue that a common carrier already is named in the Treaty of Rome.

The arguments of the opposition focus on the fact that capital investments in the electricity sector are substantial and have long 'lead-times'. As the capital is not divisible to any great extent, an attempt to create a 'perfect competition type of market' will lead to sub-optimal investments and operations. Moreover, engineers argue that it is technically impossible to trade electricity like tomatoes.

If the technical difficulties of a common carrier could be overcome, the increased competition might be beneficial to Denmark. Denmark today has the lowest electricity costs and prices (before tax) of the EEC. Cheap fuel and low capital costs per kW installed capacity could give substantial net benefits to Denmark, provided that there are set no political constraints to generation and trade.

If, however, a 'common carrier' were to give net benefits to the EEC as a whole, the precondition would be that energy policy, environmental policy and other policies are totally harmonized. Artificial differences in conditions for generation and trade would distort the market.

Natural gas

Along with the paper on the electricity market from 1989 (*Increased Intra-Community Electricity Exchanges: A Fundamental Step Towards Completing the Internal Energy Market*, (COM(89)336) the Commission published a paper on the natural gas market (*Towards Completion of the Internal Market for Natural Gas*, (COM(89)334). As for electricity it contains a proposal for a directive on transit. However, the whole analysis leading up to the proposal is very different.

It is concluded that while the natural gas market consists of transmission- and distribution-monopolies, a substantial part of EEC natural gas trade is already transit. Even the common carrier is analysed more systematically. It is seen as a tool to make the market more efficient 'the competitive way'. However, a study quoted – a parallel to the Professor Smeers' study on electricity – gives only limited net benefits for an open EEC natural gas market with end-user access.

In Denmark the transmission system built in the second half of the 1980s is owned and operated by DANGAS, which is a limited company wholly owned by the state. DANGAS up till now has bought all its gas from the North Sea wells of the Danish DUC (apart from a small amount in the beginning from Germany). On agreement DANGAS supplies gas directly to big consumers. The bulk of the consumers are supplied by five distributing utilities, which are partnerships with the municipalities as partners.

Unlike electricity the gas grids of western and eastern Denmark are interconnected. The western part is connected to Germany and the middle European grid, while to the east there is a connection with Sweden.

Today it is not very clear which initiatives of the Commission will be carried through in the gas sector. There is opposition in governments and in parts of the gas industry to the transit-directive – and in general to common carrier thoughts.

As the Danish transmission system exists today, a transit directive would have limited consequences. A direct link to the Norwegian system with abundant indigenous resources could change the situation and make Denmark a country of transit.

The introduction of a common carrier could be an interesting prospect for some big consumers today negotiating with a monopoly. In Denmark this would especially be the case for the power station companies. If lower prices were obtained for natural gas, making it able to compete with coal, natural gas could be an important fuel in Danish power generation, in accordance with the goals of energy and environmental policy.

However, as with electricity the society net benefits from a common carrier being introduced in Danish natural gas are not certain. American examples have shown that a common carrier benefited only big end-users. Prices for small consumers would remain unchanged or even rise.

Transparency

No doubt the most important EEC initiatives in creating an integrated European energy market are the draft directives on transit and the reflections on a common carrier. As a contribution to the smooth functioning of the markets a directive on openness regarding electricity and natural gas prices has been decided on (Proposal for a Council Directive Concerning a Community Procedure to Improve Transparency of Gas and Electricity Prices Charged to Industrial End-users, COM(89)-332).

The impact in the case of Denmark will be limited, as most energy prices are published already – including those for bigger consumers. Openness is important, but the real economic importance will not be realized until the consumers have a true choice, i.e. until a common carrier type of system is introduced. Until then generators and distributors can use the prices as references in their 'competition on performance'.

Another aspect of openness approached by the Commission is transparency in investments. Already in 1972 a council regulation calling for yearly national reports on important investments planned in the oil, the coal, the natural gas and the electricity sectors was passed. A recent proposal (Proposal for a Council Regulation Amending Regulation (EEC) No 1056/72 of 18 May 1972 on Notifying the Commission of Investment Projects of Interest to the Community in the Petroleum, Natural Gas and Electricity Sectors, COM(89)335) to strengthen these reports and to make them available to other countries has been strongly opposed by governments, who feared that this was the first step to introduce an EEC energy investment policy.

Other aspects of integration

No matter how fast or slow the integration of EEC energy markets initiated by energy legislation, the energy companies will experience the internal market in other ways. Liberalization of capital markets, common environmental standards, common technical standards, procurement rules and harmonization of taxes will change aspects of planning and operation, including those of the Danish energy-suppliers.

The draft directive on procurement in the 'excluded sectors' (energy, water, transportation and telecommunication) should be emphasized.

Danish energy companies have a tradition of looking to the world market when procuring big investments. One reason is the small domestic market. But this tradition has led to substantial savings compared to countries where a very limited number of national suppliers are automatically used.

The directive on procurement imposes a certain workload on the energy companies. Although in Denmark in the future more works and supplies will be procured internationally, no net benefits are expected by the energy sector. The procurement rules, however, might be advantageous to Danish manufacturing industries.

Energy is heavily taxed in Denmark. For most types of energy taxes amount to more than half of the price paid by residential consumers. Renewable energy and natural gas are exempted from energy tax – only VAT is paid. CHP (heat from power stations) is relatively lightly taxed. As a special feature of the Danish energy tax system, industry and other businesses are not taxed.

The result of the EEC efforts to harmonize taxes is not yet known. No matter what the result is, the removal of physical barriers to trade will force Denmark to approach energy taxes at least on the German level.

Even after the likely introduction of EEC environmental taxes, Denmark will have to adopt a system of energy taxes lower than the present, and probably with tax payment by industry. This will have substantial impacts. Tax revenue will decline. Energy projects profitable today due to the energy-tax system will experience reduced profitability. From an economic point of view this will mean net benefits for the national economy, in the sense that future energy investments will to a higher degree be determined by the degree of profitability.

It is important to stress that this concept of profitability also implies environmental external diseconomies, which might be assumed to be taken care of by EEC environmental taxes.

Conclusion

Past EEC energy measures have been few, and their impact on Danish energy policy and the Danish energy system have been only marginal. The internal market efforts to integrate EEC markets have given new inputs to EEC energy measures. These measures are not yet decisively formulated and decided upon. However, it can be estimated that consequences for Denmark can be considerable in the longer run.

The EEC internal market concept is based on a liberalistic economic philosophy. If the Danish energy sector is allowed to act without too many political constraints the internal energy market will mean net benefits for Danish society. In particular, Denmark's geographical situation and tradition for flexible energy systems are advantages in the new big market.

Chapter 15

Environmental policy

Lise Lyck

The Danish tradition and consciousness concerning environment

Denmark has a long and vivid tradition of concern about the environment both at the state level and at the individual level. Looking back at this century it is furthermore characteristic that the popular attitude to environment has been very active and in favour of more far-reaching legislation.

Back in 1916 Denmark introduced special legislation to safeguard the Danish coast and to secure public access to the coast. A law was voted for in the Danish Parliament but the safeguards for public access were weak, leading to the establishment of the first private environment association in the world, called 'Gilleleje Strandbakker' named after a town in the north of Seeland. The purpose of the association was to raise private money to buy the coastline in order to make it possible for all to have free access to the beaches and coast areas. This association still exists and has succeeded in attaining its purpose.

Most of the popular interest for environment is today channelled via the Danish Society for the Preservation of Natural Amenities, which has about 300,000 members out of a population of five million. Furthermore, many Danes are also members of Greenpeace and of the World Conservation Fund.

It must also be pointed out that Greenland is a part of the Danish realm, and that survival and life conditions in Greenland are extremely dependent on environmental care, which places a special responsibility on Denmark.

The basic principle of Danish environmental legislation is that pollution and nature-destroying activities are forbidden unless special permission is given by the authorities.

One of the major concerns in the debate concerning Danish EEC membership in 1972 was the environment. It was feared that the four basic freedoms of the EEC would imply the introduction of the European pollution level into Denmark and that foreigners, especially Germans, would buy the Danish coast areas and be a hindrance for the Danes' free access to the coast. As these questions were of great importance in the debate and could jeopardize EC membership a comprehensive and restrictive legislation was put in force in Denmark in 1972. Especially important in this context are the law dividing the nation into town and country areas; the intensification of the building and safeguarding articles of the Nature Preservation Law; the new and restrictive articles in the Weekend Cottage and Summer House Law, which forbid foreigners to own such Danish property; the country and regional legislation; the Natural Resource Law and the law of Environment Preservation.

Later on in connection with the internal market debate the environment again became the main issue. The veto access was of crucial importance for the Danish attitudes to the internal market.

Due to the weight environmental matters carry, both in the daily life of the Danes and at the political level, Denmark has argued strongly for the coming EEC environmental institution to be situated in Denmark and it is without doubt that such a decision would provoke a more positive attitude to the EEC among ordinary people.

The international development on environment

During the 1970s and 1980s environmental damage became more and more visible, giving rise to popular movements and concerns. Grassroot movements were formed focusing on environmental issues, and political parties established in order to stress the importance of the environment. The main aim of the environment movements was to place ecological considerations in the forefront and to make economic considerations more subordinate, i.e. to change the point of view on production. The aim of preventing environmentally destructive production to take place and maintaining the compensation system by which environmentally destructive production was allowed only if an economic price was paid to compensate for the damage done.

The concept of 'sustainable development' first defined in the strategy of the World Conservation Fund and later defined by the United Nations commission led by the Norwegian Prime Minister Gro Harlem Brundtland as a development which satisfies the needs of a generation without disturbing the possibilities of new generations to fulfil their needs has become a major concern since this work began in 1983.

The greenhouse effect has demanded increasing attention both at the political level and in daily life and has initiated comprehensive research projects and efforts to find new concepts of which the environment is a central part. To be mentioned are green national accounts and green criterias for investments. To conclude, both theoretically and in practice a new framework for protection is developing in which research, new concepts and political interest focus more on the environment than ever since the industrialization of the world.

Internationally, the new political development in Eastern Europe and the Soviet Union will strengthen the increased focus on environment and call for international agreements on environmental issues.

EEC environmental policy

Though density of population in the EEC is high and industrialization has been going on for many years and though income standard is high it is only recently that environmental problems have been part of the European agenda.

The Treaty of Rome did not include a common European policy or environmental goals. An environmental agenda was first discussed in Paris in 1972. At that time worldwide reports on global pollution and environmental disasters had been known for years.

In Paris EC member states agreed upon:

1. Pollution abatement should be integrated into European economic and social development.
2. Pollution should be restrained at source.
3. 'The polluter pays principle' should be the basis of environmental policy.
4. Border-exceeding pollution should be prevented.
5. Cooperation on environmental topics should be extended and improved, leading to common environmental standards and policy.
6. Research and debates on environmental issues should be stimulated.

The agenda was formulated related to Article 235 in the Treaty of Rome. In 1986 environmental policy became finally established as a Community policy in the Single European Act. (Article 100 A-B related to market considerations and Article 130 R-T concerning the traditional environment preservation matters.) The Act has three main environmental objectives:

1. Maintaining and improving environmental standards.
2. Maintaining and improving human health.
3. Caring for a cautious use of natural resources.

Environmental matters related to goods are characterized by: (1) Decisions need a qualified majority as main principle; (2) The environmental standard shall be high (Article 100 A,B); (3) Environmental guarantee related to Article 36. A member state can argue for a need for national legislation to secure labour environment but it has to be controlled to ensure that it is not a technical barrier to trade. It was Danish concern that produced the environmental guarantee; (4) Preservation clause, related to article 36.

For environmental matters in general decisions are unanimous and each member state has a veto possibility (Article 130-S); each member state is also allowed to set a national standard higher than the general one.

It has long been recognized that the internal market of the EEC would provoke increased environmental problems unless special instruments and regulations were established. The Commission required a survey and the report 'Environment and the Single Market' was published in 1989. It points out both unwanted impacts of static and dynamic character and the few positive impacts:

Static impacts:
1. Transportation of garbage.
2. Free circulation of products also from member states without thorough product control.
3. Lack of incitements to improve the environment (energy and environment duties).
4. Increased transportation of goods.
5. Increased building activities.

Dynamic impacts:
1. The well-known relation between economic growth and environment.
2. Increased investments leading to efficient use of resources.
3. The impact of environment policy.
4. The unequal economic growth in different regions.

In addition, it has to be taken into account that other EC policies have severe unwanted environmental impacts. The Common Agricultural Policy (CAP) has this effect because of the artificially high agricultural prices encouraging countries to bring more land into production and to produce intensively, thereby destroying wildlife habitats and creating fertilizer pollution. The common energy policy has the effect of encouraging alternatives to oil, including the generation of electricity by burning coal.

Concerning *air pollution* it is found that the sources of most of the pollution are cars and electricity. In spite of the prevailing efforts to reduce this pollution it is predicted to increase 10—15 per cent to the year 2010 due to economic growth: for example, border traffic of lorries will increase by 50 per cent after 1992 and lower prices of energy due to tax harmonization are expected to increase energy consumption. It is believed to be of special importance to reduce the content of carbon dioxide (CO_2) in the air.

Concerning *water pollution* it is recognized that many rivers are polluted from agriculture (diffuse sources).

Concerning *garbage* the EC capacity is too small. Yearly 150 million tons of industrial garbage are produced, of which 25 million tons are dangerous, but the capacity to deal with dangerous garbage is less than 2 million tons per year.

The report emphasizes the need of a new and more active environmental policy and recognizes the principle of sustainable development.

Though the recommendations are precise and clear it has to be remembered that the member states have very unequal pollution levels and still, too, very different attitudes to the need for a change in behaviour. A high level of consciousness on the environment is found in Denmark, Germany, France and the Netherlands while a low level is found in the UK and southern member states. This heterogeneity will cause problems for quick and efficient changes.

Denmark and EC environmental policy

Denmark is – and has been for a long time – a front runner in environmental matters. The most severe air pollution in Denmark is caused by Eastern and Southern winds, i.e. the import of air pollution from abroad. Concerning water pollution Denmark is in the forefront with the water environment programme. Denmark has also been the first member state to introduce a carbon dioxide (CO_2) duty.

A way to examine the impact of EC/Denmark advantages and costs concerning environment is to compare the about 140 environmental EC directives with the corresponding Danish environmental legislation, in order to compare the EC standard and the Danish standard for the environment. Such a comparison shows that Denmark more than fulfils EC standards. In other words, any interpretation of EC standards as maximum standards will lower the Danish environmental level.

At the same time it is to be stressed that Denmark is a small country, which – as pollution has no frontiers – makes it absurd to deal with pollution only in a national framework. As a consequence of this, every strengthening of the EC environmental standards as long as they are minimum standards will be an advantage to Denmark.

In conclusion, in evaluating EC membership from an environmental point of view it is found that EC environmental policy has had a positive influence, as Denmark has enjoyed the efforts towards a higher EC level and has not been restricted in setting up higher national standards.

Finally, it can be mentioned that Denmark has had one case for the EC Court, a case Denmark won in 1988. It was about re-using of packaging. Denmark has national rules for beer in bottles, and it was argued that it was a trade barrier. The judgement recognized that the law was an environmental standard and fair in that perspective and that the purpose was not to be a hindrance for trade.

References

Bedre beskyttelse (1989), *Natur-og miljølovgivning i 1950'erne*, (Nature and environmental laws in the fifties), Danmarks Naturfredningsforening.

Coopers and Lybrand (July 1990), *Europe Belmont-monitorer*, Det indre marked – en trussel mod miljøet?, (The Internal Market – a threat to the environment?), Danmarks Naturfredningsforening.

EC Bulletin (September 1989) *Fra ord til handling i Energihandlingsplan for en bæredygtig udvikling*, (From words to action in the Energy Plan for a sustainable development), made by N60 in the EEC-countries.

Gullman, Claus and Sørensen, Karsten Hagel (1988), *EF-ret*, (EC-law) Copenhagen: DJØF.

Christiansen, Hey and Jutta, Jahns-Bøhm (1989), *Ecology and the Single Market*, Cambridge.

Iversen, J. and Søndergaard, J. (1988), *Europas miljøproblemer*, (Europe's environmental problems).

Martens, Hans (1989), *Danmark og det indre marked*, (Denmark and the internal market), Copenhagen.

Regeringens handlingsplan for miljø- og udvikling (1988), (The Government's plan for environment and development).

Samfundsøkonomen, Globale miljøspørgsmål, 1991:8.

Chapter 16

Monetary policy

Lise Lyck

Introduction

This chapter briefly outlines the EC monetary policy, especially the EMS and the EMU and their implications for Denmark. It also examines the internal market directives of importance for capital movements and banking. Finally, gains and losses are discussed.

EC monetary policy

Following Article 102a in the Rome Treaty EC member states are obliged and have agreed to cooperate in matters of monetary policy. The aim of creating an Economic and Monetary Union (EMU) was already decided at the conference of Heads of Government of the six Founder Member States of the EC in The Hague in 1969. In the protocol it was prompted by the existence of a political will to reach this goal. It was considered a rational and natural development of trade cooperation to establish an economic and monetary union. Such a union was characterized by the free movement of goods, capital, services and persons (The four freedoms), a common external tariff, irreversibly fixed exchange rates with full convertibility between the currencies of the single member states, a common central bank and a pronounced fiscal integration, i.e. a situation in which the member states transferred economic and monetary sovereignty to the Community.

The creation of an economic and monetary union was originally mostly seen related to the Common Agricultural Policy (CAP) which is to a high degree dependent on stable exchange rates.

After Bretton Woods with its fixed exchange rate system fell apart and the EC was enlarged by the United Kingdom and Denmark the need for mechanisms and means for stability of the exchange rates among the member states were heavily felt, especially among the small member states. At the same time the first oil crisis and its immense consequences

Table 16.1 Composition of the European Currency Unit, 16 September 1984

	The composition as a percentage of the total	The composition of the ECU in national currencies
Deutschmark	32.0	0.719
French franc	19.0	1.31
Pound sterling	15.0	0.0878
Italian lira	10.2	140.0
Dutch guilder	10.1	0.256
Belgian franc	8.2	3.71
Danish kroner	2.7	0.219
Greek drachma	1.3	1.15
Irish punt	1.2	0.00871
Lux. franc	0.3	0.16

made a comprehensive coordination of the economic and monetary policy of the EC member states a political impossibility. In this situation it was only possible to narrow the bands of fluctuation around the national currency exchange rates of those member states participating in the 'Snake' arrangement (1972–79) to 2.25 per cent. The currencies developed into a Deutschmark currency zone consisting of Germany and the small EC member states.

The 'Snake' was replaced in 1978 and made operational in March 1979 by the European Monetary System (EMS). Roy Jenkins was the originator of the idea of the EMS, and it was considered an important means for both exchange rate stability and for economic integration.

The EMS is an exchange rate regime of fixed exchange rates with a 2.25 per cent fluctuation band (Italy 6 per cent) with original parities agreed on by the member states. These fixed exchange rates can be adjusted, but it requires the consent of all member states. If the national economic policy cannot keep the exchange rate within the fixed band, governments or central banks should react by diversified intervention related to the size of the divergence indicator monetary measures, drawing on credit facilities or by external and domestic policy matters.

In the EMS a much larger amount of credit became available to member states facing balance of payment problems.

The EMS also includes the European Currency Unit (ECU). The parity grid defines the value of the ECU in term of the percentage share of its component currencies in the 'basket'. In September 1984 the ECU was reformed and recalculated by making individual national divergence spreads. (see Table 16.1.)

The weight of each currency was defined as the fixed quantity of currency divided by the ECU exchange rate of currency per ECU. In spite of the ECU and the idea of the EMS the system has functioned asymmetrically: for instance, Germany has governed the monetary policy independently and the other member states have had to peg to the Deutschmark.

The economic analytical framework behind the member states' willingness to join the EMS is 'the monetary approach to the balance of payments'. Following this theory the level of output and employment in an open economy is determined *totally by the real forces* (labour force, capital stock, levels of taxes and transfers) and the level of output and employment gravitates towards their full employment levels. According to this theory, changes in the exchange rate have no lasting effects on output or employment because changes of prices and wages leave the real exchange rate unaltered.

Other economists, especially neo-Keynesians from the Cambridge school, are critical of the monetarist approach to the balance of payments and do not consider the control of inflation as the core element of the economy but allow for impacts on employment and output on changes in exchange rates.

In 1988 the EMS was criticized for its asymmetry and for the first time the idea of a European Central Bank was mooted by a government (the French) and this was taken up by Germany and Italy. The Round Table of the most powerful businessmen in Europe also announced in 1988 that a common European currency was required.

A committee under the leadership of Jaques Delors was decided by the Minister Council; the Delors Report was published in 1989 and discussed in the Minister Council June 1989. The report only includes thirty-eight pages. It has three sections. The first section deals with the history and the internal market. The second section defines what is meant by an economic and monetary union. The third section outlines the way in which the economic and monetary union should be achieved. The latter includes three stages: (1) a further coordination in EMS and enlarging EMS to all EC currencies; (2) a central bank, still allowing some flexibility of the exchange rates and (3) all exchange rates irreversibly fixed.

It is also stated in the Werner Report, 1970, that a monetary union is characterized by (1) totally irreversible convertibility among the currencies; (2) free capital movements and integration of banking and capital markets and (3) irreversibly fixed exchange rate parities. Point (1) is already a reality. In 1990 only Belgium, Spain, Ireland, Greece, and Portugal still had restrictions on capital movements. Spain, Belgium and Ireland are expected to have free capital movements from the end of 1992. Point (3) is the decisive difference for the EMS system. Concerning an economic union it is stated that the core elements of an economic union are (1) a common market for goods, services, capital and persons (the four freedoms) (2) a competion policy strengthening the market mechanisms (3) a common regional and structural policy and (4) a coordination of economic policies, especially fiscal policy, with binding rules for budget deficits.

The internal market is thought to fulfil conditions (1), but it is very much delayed and will in the author's opinion not be a reality before year 2000, if ever. The competition policy (2) has been changed, giving more room for market mechanisms. In 1988 the EC structural funds were heavily increased to increase the transfer income, especially to Greece, Portugal and Ireland, but the income differences between the member states have not decreased up till now and it is a fact that regional differences are extremely persistent: it is doubtful whether the increased transfer incomes can effectively deal with the problem. In fact it is extremely doubtful whether the EC area can develop into an optimal (efficient) economic area. Point (4) is the most difficult topic, going directly to the heart of sovereignty.

In the report it is stated that point (4) is necessary due to: (1) the small size of the EC federal budget (1 per cent of GNP); (2) large budget deficits posing a threat to fixed exchange rates and (3) common monetary policy requiring no lending or borrowing in the central bank or for outside the EC to finance budget deficits.

It is worth noticing that the report does not analyse or deal with the gains and losses of EMU. In this respect it can be mentioned, for example, that the Danish Central Bank director – one of the authors of the report – has in debates opined that the EMU will give no strong economic gains.

It is also worth noting that the report does not have the establishment of the internal market as a precondition.

Perhaps the most remarkable and most discussed is that the report stresses price stability as the main goal, i.e. copying the German system. Since the report has been published it has been very much discussed but, in short, the way of proceeding to the EMU outlined in section 3 has been followed, lining up a ratification procedure of the EMU and the principle of the EMU in the member states in 1992 and 1993.

Danish adjustment to the EC monetary policy and its economic consequences

Until the spring of 1982 Danish economic policy included small devaluations of the Danish currency, but in 1982 Denmark was only 'allowed' to devalue half of what was wanted. This ended the ruling Danish economic policy and a fixed exchange rates policy giving priority to price stability was introduced. Through 1982 the credibility of the change of economic policy was low, but it proved to be a lasting change. The monetary approach to the balance of payments was considered appropriate economic theory for Denmark to follow. In Denmark exports to GNP amount to 37 per cent and imports to GNP to 35 per cent (1990).

Table 16.2 shows inflation, economic growth and the development of unemployment in Denmark. Inflation has become very low, and Danish interest close to the German level.

Denmark has been very quick in the eighties in freeing capital

Table 16.2 Denmark: inflation, economic growth and unemployment 1980–91

Year	Inflation (GNP-deflator)	Economic growth	Unemployment
		Per cent	
1980	8.2	1.0	7.0
1981	10.1	− 0.4	9.2
1982	10.6	3.2	9.8
1983	7.7	2.1	10.5
1984	5.7	4.0	10.1
1985	4.3	3.8	9.1
1986	4.6	3.5	7.9
1987	4.7	1.3	7.9
1988	4.5	1.4	8.7
1989	4.3	1.9	9.4
1990	2.3	2.3	9.7
1991	–	–	10.6

Source: Statistisk 10-Års oversigt.

movements and in applying the directives related to the financial market. It was expected that Denmark would thus experience a positive front-runner effect, but the private financial institutions were not able to change their behaviour and routines and the Danish financial sector incurred heavy losses of a never-seen size at the end of the eighties and the beginning of the nineties: the adjustment to the EC financial structure and monetary policy is still not completely achieved.

Gains:
- EMS has contributed to greater monetary stability
- low inflation
- cheap imports
- freedom of capital movements in Europe
- no exchange cost if a common currency is decided in connection with the EMU

Losses:
- EMS with Deutschmark as reserve value has given Germany seniority
- the asymmetry gives Germany a leading position in monetary policy
- overvaluation of the Danish currency has caused lower activity level and lower employment
- low interest has increased the difference between interest and wage rates and implied substitution in production from labour to capital and increased unemployment
- Deutschmark being slightly undervalued up to the German unification and since overvaluated effects Danish economy and employment

- unnecessary high adjustment cost in the Danish financial sector
- loss of sovereignty if EMU is decided
- loss of economic freedom if EMU is decided

References

Gros, D. and Thygesen, N. (1988), *The EMS: Achievements, current issues and directions for the future*, Brussels: Centre for European Studies.

Hoffmeyer, E. (1989), Delors rapporten, *Nationaløkonomisk Tidskrift*, no. 2.

Issing, O. (ed.) (1988), *Wechselkursstablisierung, EWS und Weltwährungssystem*, Hamburg: Verlag Weltarchiv.

Kjær, H. J. (1991), *Regulering af den private sektor*, Nationaløkonomisk Tidsskrift.

Lyck, Lise (ed.) (1990), *The Nordic Countries and the International Market of the EEC*, Copenhagen: Arnold Busck.

Lyck, Lise (1991), Prisen for liberaliseringen af den private sektor 'i' *Danmark og Unionen – demokrati, økonomi og miljø*, Kai Lemberg (ed.), Akademisk Forlag.

Sharrer, H.E. and Wessels, W. (eds) (1988), *Stabilität durch das EWS*, Bonn Europa Union, Verlag.

Swann, D. (1988), *The Economies of the Common Market*, 6th edition, London: Penguin.

The Macroeconomics of 1992 (1990), Papers from the CEPS Macroeconomic Policy Group, Brussels: Centre for European Policy Studies.

Thygesen, N. (1989), Er den økonomiske og monetære union kommet nærmere?, *Nationaløkonomisk Tidsskrift*, no. 2.

Chapter 17

Fiscal/taxation policy

Per Vejrup Hansen

Introduction

From a Danish point of view the most important issue regarding fiscal and taxation policy is without doubt the proposal of fiscal harmonization within the EEC internal or single market.

Fiscal harmonization means the removal of fiscal 'barriers', which in fact means the removal of the differentials in taxation: incompatible with the idea of open borders between EEC member countries. This applies first of all to a harmonization of value added tax and excise taxes, because large differentials in commodity taxes would give rise to a large amount of cross border trade in a situation where there are no customs controls at the internal borders. Secondly, fiscal harmonization also applies to differentials in corporate taxes, because capital is in line with commodities in the sense that it is highly mobile across borders. On the other hand, there is no urgent need for changes in personal income taxation in general. Accordingly, the proposals of the EEC Commission for a harmonization of taxation concerns mainly the area of value added tax and excise duties.

Therefore the main issue will be taxation policies and, especially, the issue of a harmonization of commodity taxes *vis à vis* the creation of the internal market. The reason why this tax harmonization is a difficult task for Denmark is that the structure of taxation in Denmark is quite different from that of the other EEC member countries. This will be explained in the following section, together with a comparison of the level and structure of public expenditures in Denmark and selected EEC countries. The comparison of public expenditures might also be a relevant subject concerning the proposals for the creation of an economic and monetary union. The aim of the union is primarily to coordinate economic policies among member countries and to put a limit on the size of public budget deficits, in particular.

Table 17.1 Public expenditure as a percentage of GDP, 1987

	Consumption expenditures	Income transfers	Interest (gross)	Investments	Total
Denmark	25.5	18.7	8.3	5.3	57.8
West Germany (1)	19.8	18.4	2.8	4.6	45.6
United Kingdom	21.0	15.3	4.6	3.8	44.7
France	19.1	24.1	2.8	5.7	51.7
The Netherlands	16.1	29.2	7.2	4.6	57.1
Sweden	26.7	20.7	6.6	7.4	61.4

(1) 1986

Source: Finansministeriet, Finansredegørelse 90, February 1990 (based on OECD statistics).

The level and structure of public expenditures and taxation

In this section the size, composition and financing of the public sector in Denmark will be compared to that of West Germany, the UK, France, The Netherlands and Sweden. The conditions in West Germany are especially relevant to Denmark, because of the common border and because West Germany is Denmark's main trading partner. Although not an EEC member country, Sweden is included as a representative of the other Nordic countries.

Table 17.1 shows that the overall level of public expenditure is relatively high in Denmark compared to West Germany, the UK and France. In The Netherlands the overall level is the same as in Denmark, while the level of public spending is even higher in Sweden. By dividing public expenditure into types of transactions it can be seen that consumption expenditures are higher in Denmark than in the other EEC countries but in line with Sweden's. One reason for this could be that the participation rate of women in the labour force is higher in Denmark and Sweden, which implies that more resources are devoted to certain types of public services (such as public day care for children, old age care, etc.). Concerning transfer payments Denmark is placed at the low end. Finally, interest payments are higher in Denmark than in any of the other countries in this comparison. This is due to a large public debt and high interest rates in Denmark. The interest payments are one important item when comparing the overall levels of public expenditures; half of the overall differential between Denmark and West Germany is explained by the higher amount of interest payments in Denmark.

The level and structure of taxation is shown in Table 17.2. As far as the overall levels of taxation are concerned, magnitudes are parallel to the levels of expenditures. The incidence of total taxation is lower in West Germany, the UK and France than in Denmark. Differentials in total taxation between countries can differ from differentials in total expenditures

Table 17.2 Taxation as a percentage of GDP, 1987

	Personal income taxes	Social security contributions	Value added and excise taxes	Other taxes	Total
Denmark	25.6	1.9	17.6	6.9	52.0
West Germany	10.9	14.0	9.6	3.1	37.6
England	10.0	6.8	11.8	8.9	37.5
France	5.7	19.3	14.0	5.9	44.9
The Netherlands	9.5	20.6	12.6	5.6	48.3
Sweden	21.1	13.7	16.2	5.7	56.7

Source: Finansministeriet, Finansredegørelse 90, February 1990 (based on OECD statistics).

owing to different levels of surplus/deficit in the public sector accounts.

The most striking difference in taxation concern the composition of the different types of taxation. The difference in this composition is very significant between Denmark and the other EEC countries. The main differences are:

- that the level of personal income taxes is much higher in Denmark;
- that the contributions to social security by employers and employees are considerably lower in Denmark. In fact this type of taxation is almost non-existent in Denmark (while this is not the case for Sweden, the other Nordic country in the comparison);
- that the level of value added tax and excise taxes is much higher in Denmark, especially compared to West Germany, the UK and The Netherlands. With a common border the differential of 8 percentage points between Denmark and West Germany is a most crucial one. Taken separately, both the value added tax and the excise duties are at a higher level in Denmark.

As mentioned in the introduction, the pressure for a harmonization of taxation is especially urgent as far as the value added and excise taxes are concerned.

In spite of this, the debate about taxation policies in Denmark is at present predominantly oriented towards a reform of personal income taxation. In one respect the argument for this has to do with external relations and competitivenes, namely the role that the high marginal income taxes plays in Denmark. For high income levels (above DKR 250.000) the marginal taxation in Denmark is 68 per cent, and this might pose a barrier to the influx of labour and capital and the placement of firms in Denmark. On the other hand the amount of deductions (e.g. of interest payments) is quite high in Denmark, and for that reason the actual amount of taxation need not be higher in Denmark. The Danish Council of Economic Advisors recently made a comparative study of taxation in Denmark, Germany and The Netherlands. In this study social security contributions are taken into account together with personal income taxes, while differences in deductions are not included. It shows that average taxes on wages, including contributions to social security, are quite similar for the large majority of wage earners in West Germany, The Netherlands and Denmark. It is only fairly high incomes (above DKR 350.000) that are taxed significantly higher in Denmark than in, for example, West Germany (differences in the level of deduction are not taken into account).

Concerning corporate taxation the tax rate in Denmark was recently reduced from 50 to 40 per cent. This brought the Danish rate in line with the European average. However, in order to compare the level of corporate taxation one should also note that the tax base can differ between countries as there are different levels of depreciation allowances. These are considered to be high in Denmark compared to most EEC countries, and consequently the level of corporate taxation might turn out to be relatively low in Denmark. It should be mentioned that the personal income taxation of capital income is now higher than the corporate tax rate as the taxation of capital income still is about 50 per cent.

Regarding value added tax and excise duties, there have only been very minor steps so far in the direction of the EEC average. I shall deal with this in the following sections, in which the main issue is the considerable problems facing the Danish economy as regards harmonization, i.e. a reduction of value added and excise taxes.

The fiscal harmonization in the EEC internal market and the loss of tax revenue in Denmark

The value added and excise taxes in Denmark can be characterized as follows:

- Denmark has one single standard rate of value added tax (VAT), which is 22 per cent. In comparison, an estimate of the average EEC value added tax rate is about 14 per cent. West Germany has a standard rate of 14 per cent and a reduced rate for food of 7 per cent. In Denmark there is no reduced VAT rate for basic necessities and no increased rate for luxury products.
- Denmark has very high excise duties on alcohol, tobacco and energy, i.e. in the areas where a harmonization of rates has been proposed. From a Danish point of view the reason for these high excise duties is that they serve health and environmental policies. In January 1990 a minor reduction of the excise duty on petrol was introduced.

- Finally, Denmark has minor excise duties on chocolate, perfumery, coffee, mineral water etc., on which items the duties should be completely abolished according to the proposals by the EEC Commission. Denmark has taken minor steps in that direction lately, by abolishing the excise duties on such items as TV receivers, major household appliances, sugar etc.

The implication of a harmonization of value added and excise taxes will at first be a considerable loss of tax revenue for the Danish Government.

In January 1989 the Danish Government published an estimate of the size of the loss of revenue, based on the first proposals of a tax harmonization by the Commission in 1987. According to these proposals it would be necessary to reduce the Danish VAT standard rate to 20 per cent in order to fit it into the proposed standard band of 14—20 per cent and to introduce a reduced VAT rate for basic necessities of 9 per cent (the maximum rate). Concerning excise duties a uniform rate for alcohol, tobacco and energy products was proposed together with an abolition of minor excise duties. On the assumption of these rates the estimated loss of tax revenue would be 40 billion DKR, corresponding to 5.5 per cent of the GDP. The reduction of the VAT rate accounts for about half of this loss and the reduction of excise duties for the other half.

This is a considerable loss of revenue. Based on the figures in Table 17.2 it would be identical to a reduction of total taxation in Denmark from 52 per cent to approximately 46—47 percentage of the GDP. It far exceeds the loss of tax revenue in any other EEC country.

In 1989 the Commission made a revision of the original proposals (influenced by discussions in the Council of Ministers for Economics and Public Finance, the ECOFIN). These revised proposals are more pragmatic and could be interpreted as being more in line with the Danish situation. Instead of the uniform rates of excise duties and the fixed band for the standard VAT rate, minimum rates are proposed. In principle this could allow Denmark to go on with a standard VAT rate of 22 per cent and to make less reductions of excise duties. However, in the practical world the crucial question is still which rates are sustainable, if all customs controls are to be abolished. Denmark might be able to maintain its present standard VAT rate of 22 per cent, but the high Danish excise duties are not sustainable if customs controls are abolished. Furthermore the proposal of a reduced VAT rate for basic necessities within a band of 4—9 per cent is maintained, so this alone would imply a loss of tax revenue (of about 9 billion DKR according to the above mentioned estimate). Another aspect is, however, that a reduced VAT rate for basic necessities would imply a change of the real income distribution in favour of low income groups.

So in any way the loss of tax revenue will be considerable. According to informal statements made by Danish Government officials there is no need for any significant revision of the above mentioned estimate of the loss of tax revenue.

The implications for the Danish economy of fiscal harmonization, and the problems of counteracting measures

The immediate implication of a harmonization – or an approximation – of value added and excise taxes would be a loss of welfare in Danish society. The tax base for a large public sector would be distorted and the Danish Government would not be able to use excise duties as instruments in, for example, health and environmental policies.

The most fundamental economic problem would be that a reduction of value added and excise taxes would cause a **considerable increase in the balance of payments deficit**. Reduced excise taxes would mean lower consumer prices and consequently higher real incomes, and the resulting increase in the demand for commodities would partly be in the form of higher imports.

Consequently **counteracting measures** would be necessary to neutralize this increase in real incomes. In principle a whole range of measures could be appropriate. The most obvious measures would be to introduce compensatory taxes, either through increases of existing taxes or through an introduction of new types of taxes.

Increasing existing taxes would be very difficult due to the current high marginal tax rates. A limitation of deductions (of interest payments in particular) would pose severe problems for new real estate owners. Large-scale user charges on public services would change the distribution of incomes.

In view of the structure of taxation in most EEC countries, it would be natural to consider the introduction of large-scale contributions to social security. However, if these contributions were to be paid by employers, it might adversely affect international competitiveness. Wages are unlikely to adjust immediately and as a result selling prices (exclusive of value added or excise taxes) would increase. Social contributions paid by employees would not alter the marginal tax problem provided that the contributions were proportional to wages, i.e. if the distribution of incomes remained unchanged.

Another type of counteracting measure would be to reduce public expenditure. This might also prove difficult, if the reductions were substantial. As seen in Table 19.1 above, the high level of public expenditure in Denmark compared to other countries is partly due to high interest payments on public debt. Furthermore, a very comprehensive reduction of public expenditures would be needed to counterbalance the deterioration of the balance of payments account arising from tax harmonization.

In conclusion, it would be a very difficult task to counteract the economic consequences of a full-scale tax harmonization, particularly if this had to be done over a very short period of time. The counteracting measures needed have to be very comprehensive, and these economic reforms seem only possible through a gradual introduction.

In view of this the Danish Government – as well as the Danish Council of Economic Advisors – are pleading for a **transitory arrangement** of tax harmonization. This would imply that Danish customs controls were to be maintained over a certain period, in particular where private individuals are concerned. This might apply to a specific number of high tax items. One political argument for such a derogation is that the possibility of transitory arrangements in this area was mentioned explicitly in the White Paper on the internal market. These arrangements should apply to countries where particular problems would arise from a harmonization. Another argument is that a high level of excise duties on alcohol, tobacco and energy products would be in line with health and environmental policies.

The fact that Denmark has so far taken only very minor steps towards a reduction of commodity taxes could be seen as a reflection of a serious belief in these arguments and as a belief in the possibility of transitory arrangements. But if this strategy fails, Denmark runs a great risk. The internal market is planned to be implemented in the very near future and possible transitory arrangements would in any case be temporary. From that viewpoint it is surprising that the present debate about taxation policies in Denmark mostly deals with a reform of the personal income taxation. An important aspect of this is that a reform of personal income taxation might make it necessary to increase other types of taxes or to introduce new ones. This might to some degree mean an erosion of the measures needed to counteract the consequences of a harmonization of value added and excise taxes.

References

Finansministeriet and others, *Redegørelse vedrørende dansk afgiftspolitik og det indre marked*, January 1989.

Økonomiministeriet, Det Økonomiske Sekretariat, *Økonomisk oversigt*, February 1990.

Finansministeriet, Budgetdepartementet, *Finansredegørelse 90*, February 90.

Det Økonomiske Råd (The Danish Council of Economic Advisors) *Dansk Økonomi* (Danish Economy), May 1989.

Chapter 18

Regional policy

Lise Lyck

Acknowledgements are due to Peter Maskell, who kindly let me use his background material to *European Regional Incentives*.

Introduction

In this chapter the main Danish regional goals, considerations and policy are outlined. Secondly, the goals, the instruments and impacts of EC regional policy are described. Finally, the impact of EC regional policy on Danish regional policy is considered and the economic political consequences evaluated.

Danish regional problems and policy

Regional problems are often a result of:

1. Regions being situated far away from the economic centres with difficult natural conditions and low density of population;
2. Regions which have not been directly involved in industrial growth either because they have not wanted it or because they have not had the opportunity;
3. Regions hit by changes of demand with the result that their specialized products and services have become impossible to sell.

The most difficult regional problems are often due to more of the causes being in existence at the same time.

Regional problems typically manifest themselves by a low income level and a high rate of unemployment, but it is also seen that a high level of income goes with high rates of unemployment. This is the case in Denmark and the Netherlands, where in spite of high income levels and very small distances inside the country it is possible to identify areas characterized by high levels of unemployment.

Danish policy has for a long time aimed to diminish income differences between regions. The regional policy has been applied via the Regional Development Act and by other Acts with strong regional impacts.

For the first time since 1958 no earmarked amount for regional policy appears in the Estimates of the Ministry of Finance for the fiscal year 1993. This must be seen as a reflection of the present Government's declared 'hands-off' policy to the effect that still more important parts of the industrial policy cease to exist, ostensibly with a view to general tax reductions. The assets available for the direct Danish regional policy will thus be diminished in 1991.

A new Regional Development Act came into force in Denmark 1988. The Act arose out of proposals contained in a statement on industrial policy submitted to Parliament in October 1986 which suggested a shift away from direct support for individual investment projects and towards improving the technological infrastructure of the Development Regions.

In line with this general shift of policy four specific proposals were made in the October 1986 statement. First it was suggested that, while it should remain possible to support individual investment projects, such support should become more selective and should only be made available to projects introducing some form of new production into the Development Regions (either in the form of new establishments being set up or new production lines being created in existing firms). The aim was to restrict support to projects considered to have a *fundamental* development impact on the area in question. A second proposal was that support be provided for the development of technological infrastructure in the Development Regions. Such support would be directed at the establishment of technical centres, the setting up of centres to assist newly-established firms (such centres to be linked to the technical centres) and the development of consultancy assistance for existing firms. A third proposal envisaged better coordination of administration of regional aid schemes and schemes for technological development and export promotion. Such improved coordination was expected to increase the development impact of the total support given to the Development Regions. Finally, it was the Government's view that any financial support awarded to individual firms should be repaid if the project supported became a commercial success.

Mirroring these proposals, regional incentive support under the new legislation focuses on three specific types of eligible project: first, the setting up of a new manufacturing plant or service firm (either indigenous or involving relocation into the area); second, indigenous local firms beginning a new line of production of some scale; and third, small firms undertaking a first major increase in productive capacity. By and large, the emphasis of the new Act is on indigenous, local firms. Reflecting this, it is now easier for smaller projects (of less than DKr 1 million) to receive assistance than was previously the case – as long as such projects can be viewed as being of special local significance. As a result of the new emphasis, Regional Development Grant applications increased by more than 40 per cent in 1988, though the number and value of grants approved remained much as before.

An interesting feature of the 1988 Regional Development Act is that it contains an article under which the grant may be 'clawed back' if the project is commercially successful (i.e. if it yields a surplus after five years). However, it remains to be seen just how this provision (which is now a standard component of Danish industrial development schemes) will be implemented in practice. One last point to mention about the new Act is that it did not take full effect until June 1988. All applications received by the Ministry before 1 June 1988 were treated in accordance with the rules laid down under the previous legislation.

Although the 1988 Regional Development Act has been the main legislative development in the past year or so, a further important regional policy change has involved the redesignation of the designated problem regions in Denmark. Such redesignation generally takes place every four years in line with changes in the economic situation. However, though originally due to be introduced as from the start of 1987, the latest redesignation exercise did not in fact came into force until 1 January 1988 – and then only with significant transitional provisions under which certain de-designations will not take place until 1990. The delays and the transitional provisions resulted from detailed discussions with the European Commission about the redesignation exercise (see 1989 report). When the redesignation comes fully into force the coverage of the Ordinary Development Regions will have fallen from 24.1 per cent to 19.7 per cent of the national population, while Priority Development Region coverage will have been reduced to 11.1 per cent of the national population (previously 15.7 per cent). At these levels, the population coverage of the designated Danish problem regions is significantly below that found in most other Community countries.

The more indirect regional policy takes place via: 1) state block grants to special areas; 2) by intermunicipality transfers of income and by intercounty transfer of income and 3) by the tax legislation.

The Danish realm includes the Faroe Islands, Greenland and Denmark, which is divided into 275 municipalities and fourteen counties.

State block grants

The Faroe Islands and Greenland are the only regions which are given state block grants.

The Faroe Islands have a population of 48,000 persons. They get a block grant from the Danish state at a level of 100 million ECU a year. The income level is at the same level as in Denmark, but the economy relies almost entirely on fish and fish processing. The Faroe Islands got home rule in 1948 and had thereby the right to decide if they wanted

Table 18.1 Votes for and against EC membership in Greenland 1972 and 1982

	1972	1982
	Percentage of votes	
For EC membership	28.5	46.1
Against EC membership	68.9	52.0

to join the EC together with Denmark in January 1973. They voted against EC membership and have therefore never been a member of the EC, although they are part of the Danish realm.

Greenland had a colony status up to the 1953 Danish Constitution. From 1953 Greenland got status as a Danish county. Greenland has a population of 58,000 persons of whom 18 per cent were born in Denmark. Greenland receives a state block grant at a level of 350 million ECU a year. The average income level is about three-quarters of the Danish. It was a political promise to Greenland that when they got home rule they should have the opportunity of voting on EC membership. In 1972 there was an overwhelming 'no' to EC membership in Greenland. Greenland got home rule in 1979 and one of the consequences was to hold a ballot concerning EC membership.

The poll took place in February 1982. The result was still a majority against EC membership, though less pronounced than in 1972 (see Table 18.1).

After the poll the difficult negotiations concerning Greenland's leaving the EC began and from 1 February 1985 Greenland's membership ceased to exist. The negotiation implied that Greenland became associated to the EC with OLT agreement and OCT (overseas country tariff) status.

Greenland is the only region of the EC which has ever left the EC. To understand Greenland's position it is important to be aware of its old non-European culture and identity. Furthermore, the fact that Greenland was a colony until 1953 and got home rule in 1979 made it historically impossible to have authorities in Denmark exchanged with authorities in Brussels. Finally, Greenland's dependence on fish resources and fish processing and the lack of recognition of overwhelming dependence in the North of the Nordic countries in the EC fishery policy was an important factor in Greenland's attitude to the EC.

Transfers of income

The income transfer among the municipalities and counties takes place via the income tax system and results in income transfer from the capital area to, in particular, North and West Jutland, to the island of Bornholm situated in the Baltic Sea and to the southern island of Lolland.

The municipalities have a high degree of self-determination concerning public expenditure and income, and Denmark can be characterized as the EC member state with the most decentralized public sector.

Tax legislation

Tax instruments are used in order to overcome regional problems by increasing the mobility of the production factors. Worth mentioning are deductions for transportation costs and costs related to compensation for the need of having board and lodging away from home for the purpose of increasing labour mobility. Tax deductions resulting in low cost to plants in regions with low economic development are also part of the regional policy.

Although Denmark has long been aware of regional problems and has tried in its economic policy to overcome the problems by state block grants, by income transfers and a high degree of regional self-determination and by tax incitements, it must be concluded that the regional problems are rather manifest. The more comprehensive problems are normally connected to fishery regulation and fishery policy, especially in the Faroe Islands, Greenland, North and West Jutland and Bornholm. Furthermore, closures of shipyards are causing regional problems in the island of Lolland and in North Jutland.

Denmark has received regional aid from the EC, but apart from aid to Greenland the amounts have been very small and without notable influence on Danish regional problems. It is also questionable whether from an economic point of view it is appropriate to have EC aid to overcome national regional problems in an economy such as the Danish one. Denmark receives less than 0.5 per cent of the European Research Development Fund assistance.

EC regional policy

EC policy has regional impacts of a different character. Some of the impacts are more indirect, as with the agricultural and fishery policy and the creation of the internal market, while other impacts are direct via the EC regional policy. The topic discussed here is solely the direct EC regional policy.

The Treaty of Rome does not deal directly with regional policy. In fact, Article 92, relating to state aid, considered regional policy more as a hindrance for trade than as an appropriate policy to deal with regional disparities. A specific regional policy firstly came into existence with the establishment of the European Regional Development Fund in 1975 after the enlargement of the EC in 1973. The EC regional policy has not been effective due to the small size of funds set aside for this purpose, especially in the 1970s, and due to the distribution of funds being bound to fixed national quotas in order to ensure that all member states receive EC regional aid. Furthermore, the conditions which each project has to fulfil to attain aid were a hindrance.

The enlargement of the EC with Spain and Portugal and the introduction of the internal market policy led to a revision of the Rome Treaty. The objective of reducing disparities between regions became a part of the Treaty (Article 130 A) and Article 130B-E spell out the instruments for this task. The European Regional Development Fund was directly mentioned and structural funds should be increased and made more effective.

The increased weight of regional problems is due to disparities between member states' income level and economic growth rates being considered a danger for the long-term development of the EC. First priority in the regional policy is now given to backward regions in Europe, i.e. mainly to regions in the Southern Europe member states and Ireland, and in the form of coherent structural regional development plans and programmes instead of aid to individual projects.

The second priority is aid for restructuring regions hit by regional problems due to a one-dimensional production structure based on backward industries like shipbuilding, steel-making and textile manufacturing.

Danish regions will not be able to attain much aid according to the above-mentioned priorities. Some Danish regions can perhaps qualify for regional aid related to the development of rural areas in the form of compensation for giving up cultivating agricultural areas of low yield.

The EC regional policy seems to have been of little success in removing regional disparities (Armstrong, 1983, Armstrong, 1978, Robinson, 1987), and even though the policy is given more weight it still counts for less than 0.5 per cent of the GDP of the member states. It can be compared to the development policy towards Third World countries which can be characterized in the same way. Policies of this kind rise a fundamental economic and political question: are supra-national income transfers to backward regions not the way to diminish regional disparities or is the lack of success due to the funds being too small and allocated in an inefficient way?

Conclusion

The Danish realm includes Denmark, the Faroe Islands and Greenland. The Faroe Islands and Greenland suffer regional problems due to being situated far away from the economic centres and due to extreme dependence on natural resources and restraints and by being almost totally dependent on fish and fish products in their international trade exchange. Both regions have decided not to be members of the EC and at the same time call for Danish funds for development as they are part of the Danish realm. Denmark thus has a special regional obligation.

The regional problems in Denmark are concentrated in regions which for a long time have an economic structure basically dependent on fishing activities and on shipbuilding.

Danish regional policy has shown the most progress in diminishing income disparities in relation to the Faroe Islands and Greenland, though it had to be admitted that the regional problems are still comprehensive.

The EC regional policy has, particularly after Greenland leaving the EC in 1985, been without notable influence in the Danish realm. The new criterias for attaining EC regional aid since 1987 have further diminished Danish eligibility for attaining EC regional fund assistance.

Seen from the Danish tax payer's viewpoint the EC regional policy is a costly disadvantage of EC membership. Furthermore, the Danish state – by fulfilling the United Nations recommendation of paying transfer income to less developed countries, by paying state block grants to the Faroe Islands and Greenland and by paying to EC regional policy – pays a larger fraction of the GDP as regional transfer payments than any other EC member state, which is further problematic when the doubt about the effectiveness of the regional policy is taken into account.

Finally, since Denmark became a member of the EC in 1973 Denmark has sunk in the international income ranking and in the same period the unemployment rate has increased from an annual rate of 30,000 full-time unemployed to 300,000 full-time unemployed per year, which – the small size of Denmark taken into consideration – can be interpreted as Denmark itself showing signs of developing into a more backward region.

References

Armstrong, H.W. (1978), Community regional policy: a survey and critique, *Regional Studies, vol. 12*, pp. 511–28.

Armstrong, H.W. (1983), 'The assignment of regional policy process within the EC, in Britain within the European Community': *The Way Forward*, ed. A.M. El-Agraa, pp. 271–99, London: Macmillan Press.

Lyck, L. (1966), *Grønlands økonomi- og relationerne til Danmark*, Copenhagen: Akademisk Forlag.

Maskell, Peter, (1990), *European Regional Incentives*, The European Policies Research Centre, University of Strathclyde, Scotland.

Robinson, P. (1987), *The Economics of International Integration*, 3rd edition, London: Allen and Unwin.

PART IV: CULTURAL, SOCIAL AND EDUCATIONAL POLICIES

Chapter 19

Danish identity: European, Nordic or peasant?

Uffe Østergård

Some reflections on the political culture of the Danish nation state before and after joining the European Community

The very fact that the Danes themselves are hard-working people, good organizers, attentive to detail, systematic and on the job, might incline them to look down on the Irish. But it works the other way. Where a Dutchman has a good stout conceit in himself, fortified by success, by wealth, by a fantastic productivity and an all-round prowess in life and art – think of Rubens – the Dane is one of the least conceited of human beings; he is self-critical and tentative in a world about which he is so informed that he is not rash to judge, and he goes his way quietly and not rambunctiously. For that very reason the salient peoples delight him, and the improvident, the wayward, appeal to that element in him which his own life has perhaps not satisfied. The Irish catch his imagination. Not all the Irish, of course, but there is something disciplined in himself that hails the undisciplined instead of rushing to squelch it and hails it with not the slightest complacency or superiority – no, with a real zest for the liberation he detects in it (Francis Hackett, *I Chose Denmark*, New York 1941 p. 45).

Thus Francis Hackett, American journalist, Irish by birth, and married to a Dane, described his long lasting love affair with traditional Danish society to an Anglo-Saxon audience soon after Hitler's occupation of Denmark and Norway. It may not be true; certainly it is not very precise. But that is the problem with all generalizations about such ephemeral phenomena as national identity, national culture and national mentality. Nobody is able to define them satisfactorily and yet we use them all the time to classify observations out there in the 'real' world. Hackett's characterization has the great merit of conveying an image of a peaceful and tolerant political culture which strikes most observers as fundamental in this little country. It did not succumb to aggressive nationalism in the 1930s when he lived there. On the contrary, it succeeded in implementing a social democratic restructuring of society as an answer to world economic crisis and the threat from fascism and Nazism. On the other hand, if this picture is true, why is it that such a relatively open-minded political culture has gone back on its own professed internationalism and rejected the European project as a grand idea and a challenge? Minor tactical disagreements aside, almost all of the Danish political spectrum agrees on a fundamental mistrust of everything 'big', i.e. transnational and 'European'. The disagreements between left and right are based on different perceptions of the economic benefits they see coming from the Common Market and different evaluations of the necessary adjustments of economic distribution policies. Both sides, however, in matters European basically agree to do as little as possible, as late as possible, as cheaply as possible, and with as little enthusiasm as possible, as has for more than a hundred years been the basic dictum in defence politics.

But is this attitude paradoxical at all? The hard-nosed English weekly *The Economist* in a recent issue published the results of a rather superficial comparison of the commitments of the individual members of the EC to the organization (June 23 1990, p. 32). The chosen measures of Europhilia are each government's enthusiasm for economic and monetary union, perceptions of political reforms, and public attitudes to the community as revealed through the polls published in the Eurobarometer. According to these standards the commitments in the different European countries are surprisingly close. This is because countries that score well on the commitment to the single market, such as Britain and Denmark, tend to win fewer points for enthusiasm about future integration and the European idea. France came out at the top with 39 points out of a possible 60, followed closely by the Netherlands with 38, and Spain, Ireland, and – to the surprise of *The Economist* – Denmark all with 36. Denmark scores so high because of its obedient and efficient implementation of the very measures – preparing for the unified market of 1992 – the majority of the population are so reluctant to accept as a political goal. This is the direct opposite of Italy: so enthusiastic at the level of proclamations but so utterly incapable of translating the rules of the Community into legal practice. Does this mean that Danes are stupid and unknowingly manipulated by clever civil servants infected by 'un-Danish' European values? I don't think so.

Ambivalence has characterized the Danish attitude towards the EC from the very beginning. Reluctantly the majority of the population has let itself be dragged into European cooperation by the arguments of dire economic necessity from political and economic elites. But there has never been any enthusiasm, not even among the intellectuals at the universities and elsewhere who are going to profit from the greater opportunities for intellectual exchange. The socialist left suspects everybody but itself of trying to bring down the supposedly unique welfare state, whereas the political right mistrusts its own ability to compete economically on equal terms without giving up some old sloppy habits and privileges. This defensive attitude may be changing right now, mainly among the young under thirty, but the change of attitude has not yet been translated into significantly different political behaviour.

Why has mistrust of Europe and everything European been the dominant theme in Danish politics and permeated the political culture over the last thirty years? If Hackett's characterization is anywhere close, Danes and their open economy have nothing to fear from Europe – on the contrary. The explanation lies in the experience of a relatively big country with a long history growing ever smaller and more homogeneous: in short, in history.

Another way to summarize Hackett's description of 'Danishness' is to say 'Denmark is a little land'. This Danes do all the time when we want to impress foreigners with how amazingly well we have done. The saying dates back to the prophet of Danish national identity, N.F.S. Grundtvig (1783–1872), who in 1820 produced the ultimate definition of Danishness. It runs like this:

> Far whiter mountains shine splendidly forth
> Than the hills of our native islands,
> But we Danish rejoice in the quiet North
> For our lowlands and rolling highlands.
> No towering peaks thundered over our birth:
> It suits us best to remain on earth.

The song ends on a note of flat hill self-satisfaction;

> Even more of the ore, so white and so red *
> Others may have got mountains in exchange
> For the Dane, however, the daily bread is found
> no less in the hut of the poor man;
> When few have too much and fewer too little
> then truly we have become wealthy.
> (Grundtvig, *Langt højere Bjerge*, 1820, author's translation)

* The colours of the Danish flag.

There is a certain unpretentious, self-ironic note in this version of Danish national discourse. It is hard to detect for foreigners because it is considered bad form to be a nationalist in Denmark, as in most other European countries after 1945. Nevertheless the intrinsic nationalism surfaces immediately foreigners start criticizing anything Danish. We love to criticize everything ourselves but put up the defences as soon as somebody else points out a fault with Danish behaviour or something Danish. Luckily we are not very often confronted with such criticism, as Denmark has had a surprisingly good press in the international community – that is when it is not mixed up with Sweden. This of course is mainly a reflection of the relative lack of importance attributed to this small country in world affairs. But it nevertheless has helped into existence an attitude, for which I with the help of an editor have coined the description 'humble assertiveness'. We know we are the best, therefore we don't have to brag about it. So never mistake the apparent Danish or Scandinavian humbleness for real humbleness. It often conceals a feeling of superiority. Over the last ten to fifteen years this security has been challenged by the arrival of a not very large number of immigrants, some 100,000 foreigners out of a net total population of 5 million, i.e. little more that 2 per cent. Many of these have been uncomfortable with the unspoken Danish way of life and have challenged it in ways never experienced before. That has produced a certain uneasiness among the public. Might the reason why there was no racism earlier on be that there was nobody to discriminate against? An American friend of mine, the sociologist Jonathan Schwartz, who has been living in Denmark for more than twenty years doing research on immigrants, characterizes Danish culture in this way:

> Danish Academic culture, like agriculture, tends to be enclosed, fenced in and hedged. The gård (farm) likewise, is self-contained, and even the house is surrounded by protective trees and bushes. What is Danish in Denmark is so obvious to the foreigner here. Hygge (cosiness), Tryghed (security) and Trivsel (well-being) are the three Graces of Danish culture and socialization. Faces look towards a common gård (yard), or a table with candles and bottles on it. Hygge always has its backs turned on the others. Hygge is for the members, not the strangers. If you want to know what is Danish about Denmark, ask first a Greenlander and then a guestworker . . . . An American asked me the difference between Denmark and America. I ventured an answer. In America there's one politics and fifteen ways to celebrate Christmas. In Denmark there are fifteen political parties and one way to celebrate Christmas . . . .
>
> 'Denmark is a little country'. That's canon number one. A close second is: 'Danish is a difficult language'. How many times have I been chastised for my foreign accent? (Letter to a Danish Historian in *Den Jyske Historiker* 33, 1985 pp. 123–124).

Ultimately this is a rather different way to say the same as most Danes do when we brag about our friendly, small and democratic culture. Of course, Danes tend to see as positive the aspects that irritate the American Schwartz. That only demonstrates how difficult it is to be accepted in such a closely knit national culture. Both positions agree on the importance of the size of the country as an explanation of the specifics of the political culture. For some small is beautiful; for others small means petty, mediocre and tedious. Such differences apart it is important to remember that 'Denmark' was not always small, regardless of how we evaluate size. How and when did Denmark grow small?

From a cultural and historical sociological perspective, the Danish nation state of today represents a rare situation of virtual identity between state, nation and society. But that is a much more recent phenomenon than normally assumed, in Denmark as well as outside. Even though one of the oldest monarchies of Europe with a flag that came 'tumbling down from heaven in 1219' – ironically enough an event which took place in present-day Estonia – the modern Danish national identity is of a much later date. Up to the year 1814 the word 'Denmark' denominated a rather typical, European, pluri- or multinational, absolutist state second only to such powers as France, Great Britain, Austria, Russia and maybe Prussia.

The state had succeeded in reforming itself in a revolution from above in the late eighteenth century and ended up as one of the very few really 'enlightened absolutisms' of the day. It consisted of four main parts and a number of subsidiaries in the North Atlantic Ocean plus some colonies in Western Africa, India and the West Indies. The main parts were the kingdoms of Denmark proper and Norway, plus the duchies of Schleswig and Holstein. How this particular construct came about need not bother us here.

The political catastrophes of the nineteenth century reduced the multinational absolutist monarchy of the late eighteenth century to a tiny nation state. So small was its size that many in the dominating elite wondered whether it would be able to survive as neighbour to the recently united, aggressively dominant, self-confident Germany. On the other side, however, another result of this reduction in size was a very homogeneous population which enabled the rising class of peasant farmers to establish an ideological hegemony over the political culture in the remaining Danish state. That kind of ideological hegemony over all of a nation state is almost unique compared with the rest of Western and Southern Europe. This does not imply that peasant values do not exist in other industrialized societies. Of course they do. But it is a far cry from the existence of some cultural traits to a ideological hegemony over all the other parts of society. And this latter seems to be the case in the Danish society of this century even after the thorough industrialization of the country in the years following World War II.

Contrary to the situation in most other nineteenth-century nation states the very – small that is – size of the amputated state allowed a large class of relatively well-to-do peasants turned independent farmers through the reforms of the late eighteenth century to take over, economically as well as politically. Not without opposition, but gradually throughout the latter part of the nineteenth century, the middle peasant farmers took over from the despairing ruling elites. These latter were recruited from the tiny urban bourgeoisie, the officials of the state trained at German-style universities inside Denmark as well as outside, and the manorial class. They had lost faith in the survival of the state after the debacle of 1864, followed by the subsequent establishment of a strong united Germany next door. Some even played with the thought of joining this neighbouring state which already dominated the culture of the upper classes.

In this situation, however, an outburst of so-called 'popular' energy proclaimed a strategy of 'winning inwards what had been lost to the outside'. This *bon mot* was turned into a literal strategy of retrieving the lost agrarian lands of Western Jutland which had become deserted after the cutting of the forests in the sixteenth and seventeenth centuries. It also took the form of an opening up of the so-called 'Dark Jutland' in an attempt to turn the economy of the peninsula of Jutland away from Hamburg and redirect it towards Copenhagen. This movement is sometimes nowadays somewhat provocatively called 'the exploitation of Jutland', meaning the exploitation of Jutland by its capital Copenhagen, situated on the far eastern brim of the country as a leftover from the former empire, much like Vienna in present-day Austria. This battle is not yet over, as demonstrated in the heated controversies over whether or not to build a bridge between the islands of Fyn and Sjælland or connect Sweden and Copenhagen directly with Germany over the Fehmern Sund. The attempt to keep the Danish nation state together and Jutland away from Hamburg won, as the bridge between the islands is now being built. However, it was decided on a very narrow margin and the decision will probably turn out to be economically unwise.

What is more important, though, is the cultural, economic and political awakening of the middle peasants who became farmers precisely during this period. The reason for their success lies in the relative weakness of the Danish bourgeoisie and the late industrialization. The take-off happened only in the 1890s and the final breakthrough as late as the 1950s. The middle peasants developed a consciousness of themselves as a class and understood themselves to be the real backbone of society. Their ideology supported free trade, which is of no surprise as they were beginning to rely heavily on the export of food to the rapidly developing British market. This was the case to such a degree that Denmark, economically speaking, must be considered part of the British empire from the mid-nineteenth to the mid-twentieth century. What is more surprising is the fact that their ideology also contained strong libertarian elements because of their struggle with the existing urban and academic elites. The peasant movement won out basically because it succeeded in establishing an independent culture with educational institutions of its own. This again was possible because of the unique organizational device applied in the organization of the agrarian industries, the cooperative.

The basic agrarian production was still pretty much a typical individualistic production on independent farms, albeit of an average size somewhat larger than usual in a European context. However, the processing of these products into exportable products took place in local farm industries run on a cooperative basis. As they put it themselves: 'the vote was cast by heads instead of heads of cattle' (i.e. one man, one vote). This pun (in Danish 'hoveder' and 'høveder') is less true when one starts investigating the realities of the cooperatives. Yet the myth stuck and produced a sense of community which through means of various political traditions has been transformed into a hegemony that has lasted so long that it today has become an unspoken common mentality. Such a mentality is hard to define as it is precisely what makes it possible for members of a community to communicate by means of words, symbols, and actions. Humour and understatements thrive on a common understanding that precedes the spoken words.

The libertarian values, however, were not originally meant to include the other segments of the population. The agrarian system was based on a crass exploitation of the agricultural labourers by the farmers. These were, together with the urban elites, often not even considered part of 'the people' by the peasants. However, in an interesting and surprisingly original ideological manoeuvre, the rising Social Democracy adapted its ideology to the unique agrarian-industrial conditions in Denmark and developed a strategy very different from the Marxist orthodoxy of the German mother party. The Danish Social Democracy even agreed to the establishing of a class of very small farmers called 'husmænd'. They thus fulfilled the expectations of their landless members among the agricultural workers but at the same time undermined the possibility of ever obtaining an absolute majority in the parliament as did their sister parties in Sweden and Norway.

This apparently suicidal strategy, in addition to later compromises in housing policy, ruled out any position of virtual Social Democratic monopoly of power, as became the case in Norway and Sweden. Yet as far as we can judge today they did it knowingly and on purpose. In the course of World War I it became clear to the Social Democratic leadership that the party would never be able to achieve absolute political majority. Under Thorvald Stauning's thirty-two years of charismatic leadership (1910–1942), the party restructured its line from a class-based to a more popular one. The popular line was first openly formulated in 1923, and later on adopted in slogans such as 'the people's cooperating rule' and, somewhat less clumsily, 'Denmark for the people' (1934). The platform resulted in a stable governing coalition, from 1929 to 1943, of the radical liberals ('Det Radikale Venstre') and the Social Democratic Party. The Social Democratic leaders apparently accepted the ultimate check on the influence of their own movement in the interests of the society at large. Or maybe they did not distinguish between the two. Many things might have turned out differently in Germany had the Social Democracy in that country in the 1920s adopted a policy directed towards the people as a whole and not just the working class in the Marxist sense.

The German socialist theoretician Karl Kautsky (1854–1938) never really understood the role of agriculture in modern societies. He saw it as something of the pre-capitalist past which would be better run according to the principles of mass industrialization. The Danish Social Democrats had a better understanding of agriculture in their practical policies. They failed, however, to turn this understanding into coherent theory. At the level of doctrine the party stuck to the formulations in the 1913 programme. These formulations reflected the international debates in the Second International rather than the Danish reality and the practical policy of the party. The very fact that the programme of 1913 remained unchanged until 1961 testifies to the lack of importance attributed to theory in this, the most pragmatic of all reformist Socialist parties. The Danish Social Democracy never was strong on theory, but the labour movement has produced an impressive number of capable administrators and politicians, at least until recently.

This lack of explicit strategy enabled remnants of the libertarian peasant ideology to take root early on, in the party and in the labour movement as such. The Social Democrats embarked upon a policy for the people, and not just for the working class, as early as 1914. This testifies to the importance of the liberal-popular ideological hegemony dating back to the last third of the nineteenth century. It is also proof that the leaders realized that they would never gain power on their own. The farmers proper only constituted a fragment of the population as a whole, but small-scale production permeated the whole society then as it still does today. Ironically, the Marxist who understood Denmark the best was Lenin. In his 1907 discussion 'The Agrarian Programme of the Social Democracy' he has a long section on the Danish cooperatives which he had studied on the spot (in the Royal Library in Copenhagen, that is). He turns out to be rather positive towards such a self-reliant strategy but refuses to endorse it for Russia because of any number of reasons. Maybe he should have done so.

That a strategy directed towards the majority of the people would turn out more rewarding seems pretty obvious from today's point of view. Yet such a sophisticated socialist party as the German Social Democrats only embarked on the strategy as late as 1959 in Bad Godesberg; the British Labour and the French Socialist Party even today do not seem to have made up their minds; and what is going to happen in Eastern Europe remains to be seen. The main reason why a libertarian ideology of solidarity ended up dominating a whole nation-state was the small size of this particular state.

It has been hotly debated among Danish historians and sociologists as to whether the peasant ideological hegemony resulted from a particular class structure dating back to the 1780s or even further back to the early sixteenth century, when the number of farms was frozen by law, or whether it was this ideology that created the particular class-structure of the Danish nineteenth century society. Put in such terms the discussion is almost impossible to solve as both of the protagonists' positions reveal some part of the truth. I tend to explain the outcome in terms of the existence of a particular ideology of populism or 'popularity' (folkelighed) stressing the importance of consensus among people. It was first and most coherently formulated by the important but virtually untranslated and untranslatable philosopher, historian, priest, and poet

Nikolaj Frederik Grundtvig who lived from 1783 to 1872. Grundtvig was a contemporary of Kierkegaard but has attracted much less attention outside Denmark. In Denmark, on the contrary, his influence is much greater than that of Kierkegaard. He wrote more than 1,500 songs, and his psalms take up almost half of the present book of psalms. He is more than any other single person responsible for the Danish church. Grundtvig's public opponent, Christian Kold, is the single person who is responsible for Folk High School, the other peculiar institution in Denmark. The Lutheran church in Denmark is not a state church and does not have an official constitution; yet more than 90 per cent of the population are members. Although very few actively attend service nowadays, and everybody hates paying taxes, more than 90 per cent have decided not to leave this institution and keep paying an extra one per cent in taxes even though tax evasions and tax protests are the most current themes in the Danish political debate.

This is as surprising as is the prevalence of an overall liberal economic policy in a country with a huge public sector. Such apparently contradictory behaviour in a political culture which is dominated by libertarian and solidarian attitudes, and where the Conservative Party is more socialist than most socialist parties in Europe, are examples of the particular Danish national identity or mentality. It also helps explain the apparent paradoxes in the popular attitudes toward Europe and the Common Market. The frequent invocation of particular democratic Nordic values may to the foreigner seem nationalistic, narrow minded and egotistic and yet at the time by the proponents to be somewhat naively taken at face value. In a now classic account of Danishness, Robert Molesworth (1656–1725) British ambassador to the King of Denmark, subscribed to the former position. Molesworth hated everything Danish, their petty peasant slyness and short-sighted scheming. He apparently loathed every minute he had spent in the country. The conclusion runs as follows:

> To conclude; I never knew any Country where the Minds of the People were more of one calibre and pitch than here; you shall meet with none of extraordinary Parts of Qualifications, or excellent in particular Studies and Trades; you see no Enthusiasts, Mad-men, Natural Fools, or fanciful Folks; but a certain equality of Understanding reigns among them: every one keeps the ordinary beaten road of Sence, which in this Country is neither the fairest nor the foulest, without deviating to the right or left: yet I will add this one Remark to their praise. That the Common People do generally write and read. (Molesworth, *An Account of Denmark as It was in the Year 1692*, London 1694 p. 257).

The book was presented to the audience as a travel account but the actual intention was to warn the English aristocracy, who had recently expelled James II, of the dangers of absolutism. Denmark had been proclaimed an absolutist regime in 1660 after the disastrous defeat in the wars with Sweden. One might say that on principle it was the most absolutist regime in all of Europe, as its absolutism was actually put into writing in 1665 ('The King's Law', Lex Regia). This never happened in the France of Louis XIV, the very country where absolutism was invented. As warning against this ominous fate was the intention of Molesworth, one probably should not pay more attention to his descriptions than to those of his friend and contemporary Jonathan Swift when describing the countries of Lilliput or Brobdingnag. Yet his characterizations remind us of any number of subsequent descriptions by Danes as well as foreigners. What varies is the valuation of mediocrity and mundaneness in a society; some see this as the utmost boredom, others as the egalitarian haven on earth.

Another way to look at this ideology of mediocrity is to accept it as the prerequisite of popular consensus. If laws and reforms are to work they have to be based on general acceptance among people. And this has more often than not been the case in Denmark. At a time when the overwhelming majority of intellectuals in a Europe of rising nation states talked of the necessary 'nationalization of the masses' or the necessity of transforming peasants into citizens through policies from the top down, Grundtvig developed an ideology centered on the concept of 'folkelighed' denominating a common feeling in the population.

According to him the feeling only originates in a historically developed national community and is manifested in actions of solidarity. At the level of ideological discourse at least, Grundtvig succeeded in transforming the traditional amorphous peasant feelings of community and solidarity into symbols and words with relevance for a modern industrialized imagined community. It remains to be seen whether the resulting mentality can survive the transplantation to entities larger than the Danish nation state. Maybe it cannot. However, at one time it was capable of influencing the majority of an industrial working class and establishing a welfare state. By means of easily remembered lyrics and *bon mots* such as 'Freedom for Loke as well as for Thor' (1832) Grundtvig succeeded in influencing the mentality of a whole nation. Danes learned those concepts by heart at school and at home until the late 1960s. Whether people live by them or not is of course another question. Yet, at the level of discourse, i.e. in the political culture, they have had great impact by determining what can be expressed and what not, what does not have to be expressed at all, and which values are considered worthy of pursuit.

These are the 'peasant roots of Danish modernity' or the 'peculiarity of the Danes'. They help explain many of the apparently paradoxical features of Danish political and social life, down to the anarchistic party structure. Real values are at stake and many Danes fear they will disappear when society, nation and state are not any longer identical as has been the case for more than a hundred years. This is why they have been reluctant to participate wholeheartedly in 'the construction of Europe'. What they have failed to realize is the fact that the former situation will change anyway and that the only choice involved is whether we want to have a political say or not. This naivete has been shared by the overwhelming majority in the generations older than thirty-five, i.e. those too old for the Inter Rail experience. This attitude is now rapidly changing and many more Danes are becoming involved in Europe at a real level. Maybe the day is not far away when Denmark will stop acting as a reluctant periphery disguising its petty peasant meanness as 'Nordicness' and begin to act out their positive values at a real level in confronting different values. That is my hope for the future, but it has to be admitted that such a prediction is as yet far from being based on hard facts.[1]

Note

1 The latest poll, though, reported in the *Eurobarometer 33*, June 1990 reveals what might amount to a significant change in the attitude of Danes towards the EC. Fifty-one per cent now think it a good thing, whereas only half a year ago the percentage was 44. Compared with the other members of the EC, however, this is still a fairly low percentage. The European average in favour is 71 per cent. The percentage of those against the EC has fallen from 31 to 27 per cent. Thirty-eight per cent would feel very anxious if the EC were abolished compared to 31 per cent half a year ago. Sixty-eight per cent think that the eighteen years of membership have been economically advantageous for the country. They seem to think, however, that these advantages may vanish with the introduction of the unified market. The percentage of those who are anxious for the future market has risen to 42 per cent; yet there is still a majority of 57 per cent who look at the future with confidence and optimism. These rather more favourable percentages, however, do not invalidate my analysis of the contradictory and economistic nature of the attitude of Danes towards the EC. If it were possible only to subscribe to the economic benefits and keep all the national institutional arrangements unaltered the majority would feel less uneasy. Unfortunately this seems no longer to be possible. Therefore most Danes are in favour of continuing to block common health, social educational, and media policies. Narrow majorities or very substantial minorities, though, do accept common foreign, environmental and development aid policies.

Chapter 20

Cultural politics in the light of the EC

Peter Duelund

Influences, possibilities, and limitations

In these years Danish culture and cultural politics face challenges which call for well deliberated efforts and new ways of thinking, both nationally and internationally.

Internationally the world has grown smaller. To an increasing extent, Danish culture is part of a cultural dialogue which knows no national borders. The economic, social, and political development since World War II has changed the conditions of Denmark's taking part in international cultural exchanges.

Many things imply that cultural exchange solely on a Nordic level is insufficient, in spite of common cultural and democratic traditions. The cultural exchange efforts in the Council of Europe have been a vehicle for a significant exchange of ideas and experiences concerning goals and measures of cultural policies, but they have lacked sufficient thrust to accomplish such goals (Duelund, 1988).

UNESCO is still an important forum for global cultural exchanges, not least as a forum for the dialogue between industrial and developing countries. However, there is a considerable risk that these exchanges will drown in abstraction. At the same time, great efforts have been made made in the EC to include cultural questions in EC policies, although cultural matters are not included in the Treaty of Rome. The European Commission has, since 1975, commissioned more than forty 'Studies in the Cultural Sector', some of which are also available as regular book publications.

Of most relevance to the discussion of culture in relation to the Internal Market and the future of culture in Europe are the discussions papers 'Community action in the cultural sectors' (1976), 'Stronger Community action in the cultural sector' (1982) and 'A Fresh Boost for Culture in the European Community' (1987). In the first two publications the

Commission advocated the strengthening and harmonization of copyright and allied rights.

The 'Boost' is of most interest at present, because it was intended by the Commission to be a cultural framework for initiatives which the Commission wished to advance in 1988–92, i.e. the last five years before the establishment of the Internal Market. Also, it is stressed in the introduction that this report should form a basis for an actual political plan of action concerning cultural exchange within the EC. Since then, a number of initiatives concerning cultural exchanges have been taken within the EC, to be executed either by the Commission or via a coordinated voluntary effort among the member states. This concerns most of the traditional cultural spheres, the media (the television directive and the MEDIA programme), and the technological area, where a number of development programmes have affinity to cultural questions (EUREKA, HDTV, ESPRIT, DELTA, BRITE, ORA, etc).

Similarly, in accordance with a Council decision, the Commission has established a number of sub-committees and working groups on administrative levels and among people directly involved in cultural activities. An example is the decision by the Council and the European Ministers of Culture to advance the talks about the principles of cultural exchange in the 'Cultural Committee' and in the 'Committee of Cultural Consultants' (CCC), both formed in 1988.

The status of Culture in Europe – pluralism or assimilation?

The EC policies in recent years have thus to an increasing extent been marked by a large number of political and concrete initiatives in the cultural area. The changed market situation after 1992 with the establishment of the internal market will further stimulate this trend. This has generated a need for a thorough discussion of the role and function of culture in the EC and the Europe of the future.

Should the European countries and nations move towards a unified culture, or should they move towards cultural diversity, taking inspiration from the many cultural forms and traditions which have marked Europe?

Should culture serve as a legitimation and tool of political, economic and technological interests, or should it exist in its own right?

How can EC cultural politics be shaped in such a way that they promote goals set out by the individual member states? What hindrances exist? What initiatives should be taken? How will the future EC cultural politics look in the light of the new developments in Eastern Europe and the wish to strengthen the CSCE?

The issue – pluralism or assimilation – is about whether Europe in a period of intensification of economic, technological, social and political cooperation should continue to be multi-cultural. It is also about whether a development of a multi-cultural competence within a nation is seen as a strength, or whether an assimilation over time is desired – i.e. a unified culture, where national, regional and ethnic diversity is reduced to names in a telephone directory. In this Europe, there are no longer authentic differences in patterns of life, values and outlook. Cultural sociology contains a number of theory formations about this issue, which has not yet unfolded in the present European integration process. It would be to go too far in the present context to expound integration and assimilation theories and their relevance for European culture and cultural policies, or to discuss the political and cultural consequences of the establishment of the internal market and a economic/monetary and political union in Europe. But it is certain that the establishment of the internal market, the closer economic and political cooperation in the EC and the changes in Eastern Europe will force cultural questions onto the political agenda – as we have seen happen in the EC in recent years.

Besides the need to develop a general theory about the relations between economic/political integration and culture and the possibility of stimulating cultural diversity and pluralism in an integrated economic and political Community, it is important to conceive of theoretical models which can describe and analyse whether the integration process is heading one way or the other. This presents a great challenge to social theory of culture.

In a research project 'Denmark in the International Cultural Cooperation With Special Reference to the EEC' (Duelund, 1989b), we have tentatively chosen the following operational criteria to determine whether legal or treaty decisions tend to promote a development in the EC towards a unified culture or towards cultural pluralism. Some rules and subsidy principles pointing towards assimilation, i.e. a unified culture, can be arbitrarily mentioned:

- EC rules making definite demands and setting fixed quotas about contents, involvements of Member States, etc. (e.g. the television directive).
- EC rules which block independent national, regional and local legislation and initiatives concerning cultural issues (e.g. the rules in the Treaty of Rome concerning state subsidies and discrimination).
- Criteria in EC subsidy arrangements, which formulate fixed demands concerning contents, but not concerning representation of working artists or cultural workers, national participation, decision-making structures, etc.
- Provisions in national cultural legislation and subsidies which tend to imply multinational participation from one or more member states and restrict initiatives on a solely national basis, etc. (e.g. concerning Cinema).
- Other circumstances (e.g. reduction in national cultural subsidies with reference to EC subsidy arrangements, national subsidy arrangements

which require international co-financing, indirect supernational stimulations in the form of expectations of future benefits, etc.).

Up till now, these questions have only rarely been asked in connection with the concrete political and economic integration process which is currently taking place in the EC.

What political means exist to promote the desired balance between cultural unity and cultural diversity? Which are at present the most important constitutional and institutional challenges/obstacles for such a development?

I shall briefly throw some light on these questions from a Danish point of view, using the results of an investigation 'Det indre marked og kulturen' ('The Internal Market and the Culture'), which I conducted for the Danish Ministry of Culture (Duelund, 1989).

Danish culture and the EC

For political and cultural life in Denmark, cultural exchange in the EC contains a number of paradoxes on several levels, which demand initiative and action on each level in order to turn drawbacks into benefits. The five principal paradoxes which from a Danish cultural policy point of view mark the EC and its common practices are:

1. Cultural politics in principle fall outside the Treaty of Rome. Nevertheless, for many years initiatives concerning cultural issues have been taken at an increasing rate, and the European Ministers of Culture meet regularly both formally and informally. This confuses matters somewhat and the resulting ambiguities and double standards of political morals erode respect for the democracy as well as the belief in the possibility of individual nations having democratic governments based on formal constitutions.

As an argument for officially incorporating cultural politics into the EC, it is held that historically it has proved impossible as well as undesirable to separate economic and cultural development and exchange. This tends to lead to an economic and cultural determinism with unfortunate cultural consequences, leaving political decisions too often to economists and technical experts.

As an argument against involving culture officially in EC politics, it is emphasized by many that the present Single European Act concerning the internal market counteracts the possibility of cultural diversity, because it can be used to restrain independent national cultural legislation and subsidies. This has happened in several member states – including Denmark. Therefore, there is now a need for an amendment to the Treaty which will prevent such use of the rules, if the incorporation of Culture and an official part of the areas of exchange covered by the Treaty is not to become a bad bargain for cultural life in Europe.

2. The Commission mentions several general programmatic declarations, concerning among others the different funds used for structural interventions, the Citizens' Europe, the importance of culture to democracy and social development, the development of a common European identity and value basis. However, the Commission in its motivation for launching these programmes reduces culture to an instrument for economic and technological growth and the development of a political union. The artist and the cultural worker are cast as raw material in this process.

For instance, in the 'Boost' (1987) the television directive was motivated as follows: 'The aim is to give direct support to the Community's cultural industries by requiring member states to ensure that television companies reserve a percentage of total broadcasting time for programmes of Community origin'.

About the extensive MEDIA programme it is said: 'It is hoped that the programme will act as a catalyst, creating a trans-national dimension required to make the European audio-visual industry competitive on the world market. This is to be achieved by improving the production and distribution of programmes in response to the demand created by technological innovation'.

From a Danish cultural point of view, this is a confusion of means and ends which will become a vehicle for the cultural industrialization tendency which is making itself felt globally and in all European countries. An important goal in Danish cultural politics is exactly to counteract that trend to unidirectionality and stereotyping which is currently strong in the cultural industries. This is emphasized in the national cultural political aims as well as in the goals of the Nordic cultural cooperation. Most recently, this has been expressed in the plan of action for Nordic cultural cooperation in the nineties, adopted by the Nordic Council of Ministers in 1988 (Duelund, 1988).

3. On one hand, the Commission points out the importance of giving special attention to small language areas and regional cultures, in order to promote cultural identity in Europe. This has been declared in the scheme for the translation of literature which came into effect in 1989, as well as in the subsidy scheme for low-budget films which is being tried in the MEDIA programme. On the other hand, however, the Commission makes decentralization and cultural diversity very difficult through its enforcement of rules concerning state subsidies, discrimination and labour forces, thus impeding national and regional cultural development.

The rules about state subsidies can be found in articles 92 and 93 of the Treaty, concerning measures that restrain free competition:

Article 92,1: 'Save as otherwise provided in this Treaty, any aid granted by a member state or through state resources in any form whatsoever which distorts or threatens to distort competition by favouring certain undertakings or the production of certain goods shall, in so far as it affects trade between member states, be incompatible with the common market'.

Article 93,1: 'The Commission shall, in cooperation with member states, keep under constant review all systems of aids existing in the states. It shall propose to the latter any appropriate measures required by the progressive development or by the functioning of the common market'.

The basis of the rules against discriminations of nationalities or of persons are found in article 7 of the Treaty, where it is stated:

> Within the scope of application of this Treaty and without prejudice to any special provisions contained therein, any discrimination on grounds of nationality shall be prohibited. The Council may, on a proposal from the Commission and after consulting the Assembly, adopt, by a qualified majority, rules designed to prohibit such discrimination.

The rules concerning discrimination are most often used in close relation to the rules about the free movement of labour (Article 48) and the free movement of independent businessmen (Article 52) – rules that look upon discrimination in relation to the individual worker.

4. The Commission stresses the importance of cultural freedom and local cultural competence in decision-making concerning granting economic support to culture, but it has up till now been inclined to appoint supernational committees and working groups, without the national cultural bodies, organizations and authorities having had any influence. For example, this has happened concerning several of the MEDIA programme's working groups, and the Committee of Cultural Consultants (CCC) which was charged with the drafting of the EC's first report and actually the culture of the Community, 'Culture for the European Citizen of the Year 2000'.

4. The Commission draws up goals for the Citizens' Europe and European democracy, but fails to take as its starting point the national and regional conditions. It is thus unable to create that educational basis and information level which is a precondition for any democratic influence and cultural participation of citizens.

The lack of sufficient education and information has contributed to the undermining of the democratic tradition which marks Danish government, in which public information as a basis for public discussion has been a cornerstone of the democracy and the forming of public opinion. This is the reason for the decision of the Danish Parliament in June 1990 to ease public access to EC documents.

The lack of information and the secrecy about initiatives concerning cultural issues has for many years made it difficult for Danish cultural life and Danish citizens to take an active part in a democratic cultural development in Europe.

Only when the Danish Minister of Culture in 1989 took the initiative of holding the so-called 'Brandbjergkonference' at a folk high school in Central Jutland and also initiated the investigation 'The Internal Market and Culture', was a debate launched. Still, however, there exists a lack of knowledge concerning cultural and cultural political activities in the other European countries and on the European administrative levels.

Rules concerning state subsidies and discrimination.

The paradoxes mentioned above constitute the main issues for Danish cultural life in the light of the internal market.

The most important political discussion in Danish cultural life at present with regard to the internal market concerns the question of whether the rules regulating state subsidies and discrimination will apply to cultural matters in the future. For one thing, these rules may – as we have seen – restrict that real development towards cultural diversity in Europe which is a concern of Denmark – as of most other member states.

Also, the rules create a number of specific problems, not least for Denmark which is the smallest language area in the Community, because the Danish market, with few exceptions, is too small to maintain quality culture on a free market basis.

Finally, the effect of these rules in Denmark is stronger, because cultural subsidies to a larger extent than in other member states are regulated by legislation.

These rules will also be effective against regions in EC member states which already administer their own cultural policies or are struggling for increased regional and local democratisation of cultural matters. It is explicit in the comments to the present Treaty of Rome that the rules about state subsidies and discrimination also apply to regional and local cultural products, working artists and cultural services.

That the rules thus also constitute a problem in other member states can be seen be looking at Germany. The German states which have the authority in cultural questions adopted a resolution in May 1990 at an all-state meeting, warning against unifying cultural tendencies and tendencies to centralization in the EC. It was therefore proposed that cultural exchange should be integrated into the Treaty, but in a form that ensures that cultural decentralization and autonomy are maintained. In all European countries we can currently see regional and local struggles for increased cultural autonomy and pluralism.

The question of whether the rules about state subsidies and discrimination should apply to cultural matters therefore has a great importance for a large part of European cultural life.

The need for an amendment to the Treaty of Rome

The rules about state subsidies and discrimination will have their greatest effect on Danish culture politics in areas where cultural legislation is developed: subsidy arrangements and grants form the State Art Fund, subsidies to music, to the theatre, to museums and to film.

The Commission has enforced these rules primarily within the audio/visual area (film/TV/video), firstly because this area covers a large part of the transnational cultural trade, secondly because the Commission views the film industry and broadcasting as unambiguously coming under the provisions in the Treaty about exchanges of goods and services.

This linkage of Treaty provisions was, for instance, effective when the Danish film legislation was revised in 1988, when the Commission claimed that the new film legislation conflicted with article 48 concerning the free movement of labour, article 7 concerning discrimination of persons, and article 52 concerning regulations of state subsidies. The Commission did not believe that Denmark had obtained the right balance between market considerations and artistic considerations, though the Commission did not dispute that the latter falls outside the provisions of the Treaty.

Concerning literature, the rules are also relevant in relation to the subsidy arrangements – for instance, the subsidizing of public libraries' acquisition of volumes by Danish authors. This could also mean that public libraries' acquisition of volumes by foreign authors should be subsidized. This would produce a lot of economic problems for the libraries and the authors.

For the reasons mentioned above, one can in Denmark detect great apprehension about whether EC subsidy rules will apply to Danish cultural legislation and, if they do, to what extent this will effect cultural subsidies.

An attack on Denmark's future ability to implement independent cultural legislation will lead to a serious deterioration of the possibility of Danish cultural life being able to compete on equal terms with the larger EC member states.

The main conclusion in 'Det indre marked og kulturen' is therefore that an amendment should be made to the Treaty of Rome which once and for all puts an end to the application of the above-mentioned rules – concerning state subsidy regulation and concerning discrimination – to cultural matters which are very important to the individual member states and regions in Europe.

The Committee of Cultural Consultants (CCC) in November 1989 reached the same conclusion in its final report. Such an amendment has also been proposed by the international artists' organizations, FIA and FISTAV, as well as by a number of Danish and other national artists' organizations in Europe.

Other cultural political needs

Regarding the other paradoxes in the EC outlined above, I will mention some conclusions and suggestions which the investigation into the Internal Market and Culture (Duelund 1989) have given rise to:

- In the cultural political cooperation in the EC, an effort should be made on both political and administrative levels to use 'Nordic models' as a starting point in the shaping of concrete cultural exchange, subsidy arrangements, committees, working groups, etc. – i.e. it should be recognized that cultural professionals, appointed by national governments and cultural organizations, should have decisive influence on cultural political decisions and the practical application of these decisions in concrete cultural exchange.

At the same time, it should be ensured that other European countries – including Eastern European and Scandinavian countries – will have a possibility of participating according to some accepted guidelines.

- The national cultural policies in Denmark, as well as in the other member states, should be adjusted and supplemented with the intention of encouraging cultural diversity in Europe. It should also be an aim to accommodate present and future needs that may develop in relation to the intensification of European cultural exchange and the development of an international culture, without losing national and regional cultural identity and background.

In 'Det indre marked og kulturen' I have mentioned a number of proposals which could help in adapting the contents and administration of national cultural politics in relation to the new common European challenges, e.g.:

- defending copyright and other rights of primary importance to artists – not least in relation to the new distribution techniques and the expansion of electronic media;
- increasing the efforts to provide good conditions for the development of teachers and pupils, artists and cultural workers at national and regional cultural training facilities and institutions. Such efforts comprise increased possibilities of obtaining personal grants, more flexible residence permits, mutual acceptance of degrees and informal systems of merit;
- stimulating cultural activities to assert the regional cultures and the cultural minorities in the European countries. In a time when the integrated approach to regional problems has fully prevailed in the EC, the incorporation of a cultural dimension into integrated programmes of regional and urban rehabilitation would be a very

important step. No regions or minorities should be deprived of an effective right to cultural development;

- initiating national and regional initiatives in different cultural areas, thus aiding cultural life actively to take advantage of the increasing European political and economic integration and strengthening a culturally diverse Europe;
- making an active effort to secure bilateral exchange, non-European countries' participation, and an opening in relation to other international initiatives (the Council of Europe, UNESCO, the Nordic Council);
- establishing cultural information and service offices in the individual EC member states, aiming to advance national, regional and local cultural life's ability to face the challenges; to improve information about cultural exchange in the EC; and to increase cultural debate on both national and European levels.

A cultural charter

The different areas of Danish cultural life which were investigated generally agree that it would be a bad bargain if Denmark and the other member states should sell their independent possibilities of formulating national cultural policies by accepting cultural exchange as an official part of the EC. In contrast, there is a constructive will to expand cultural exchange within the EC through concrete initiatives that may promote both national and international cultural exchange.

It is the main conclusion in the investigation 'Det indre marked og kulturen' and in the debate which has taken place among cultural professionals and politicians since 1989 that the above-mentioned initiatives would promote cultural diversity in Europe and make it a challenge for Denmark and the other member states to participate in the development of a democratic form of cultural exchange within the EC.

In the most recent programmes and initiatives which have been launched in the EC, a change in focus has taken place. More emphasis is now placed on diversity and cultural pluralism, consideration of cultural identity and the interests of artists, and finally – as regards the organizational aspect – on networks and voluntary participation.

This applies to, for example, the objectives and adaptation of the translation subsidies and various exchange initiatives within the MEDIA 92 (MEDIA 1989) and EUREKA programmes (Assises Européennes de l'Audiovisuel 1989). Compared to the 'Fresh Boost' of 1987 greater emphasis is placed in these programmes on voluntary professional networks and on a decentralized decision-making process.

From a democratic point of view on culture, however, the main problem continues to be that the Commission – in spite of the democratization which has taken place in concrete programmes – with its subsidy regulations, discrimination rules, and other provisions may in effect prevent or obstruct national cultural legislation and politics.

In the long run, this will not make for a fruitful balance between unity and cultural diversity in the European cultural exchange, as the economic and political integration process picks up speed. Therefore, an amendment to the Treaty of Rome, guaranteeing the free expression and development of cultural life, is essential.

References

'A Fresh Boost for Culture in the European Community' (1988), *Bulletin of the European Communities, Supplement* 4/87, Luxembourg, Office for Official Publications of the European Communities.

Assises Européennes de l'Audivisuel – *Project EUREKA Audivisuel* 1989: Paris, Ministère des Affaires Etrangères République Française.

Blue Book – Europe in Education and Culture (1987), Paris, Ministère des Affaires Etrangères République Française.

Committee of Cultural Consultants (1989), Culture for the European Citizen of the Year 2000, Final Report, Brussels.

Community action in the cultural sector (1976), Luxembourg, Office for Official Publications of the European Communities.

Duelund, Peter (1988), Det almenkulturelle samarbejde i: Nordisk Ministerrad: *Handlingsplan for nordisk kulturelt samarbejde*, 217379 (The Cultural Cooperation in: Plan of Action for the Nordic Cultural Cooperation, Copenhagen, Nordisk Ministerråd (The Nordic Council of Ministers).

Duelund, Peter (1989a), *Det indre marked og kulturen – en undersøgelse af konsekvenser* (The Internal Market and The Culture – a Research of the Consequences, Copenhagen: Danish Ministry of Culture.

Duelund, Peter (1989b), *Danmark i det internationale kultursamarbejde med hovedvægten på samarbejdet i EFprojektbeskrivelse* (Denmark in the International Cultural Cooperation With special reference to the ECC – Description of the Project), paper, The Institute of Cultural Sociology, University of Copenhagen.

Media 92 (1989), 3rd Edition, Brussels, Direction Générale de l'Information, de la Communication et de la Culture.

Enzensberger, Hans Magnus (1987), Ach Europa, Frankfurt am Main: Suhrkamp Verlag.

Europe under Transformation: *The Cultural Challenge Culture – Technology, Økonomi* (1987), Luxembourg: Office for Official Publications of the European Communities.

Europe without Frontiers – The Purpose of The Internal Market (1988), Luxembourg, Office for Official Publications of the European Communities.

Morin, Edgar (1987), Penser l'Europe, Paris: Editions Gallimard.

Stronger Community action in the cultural sector (1982), Luxembourg: Office for Official Publications of the European Communities.

Chapter 21

Manpower: structural problems of the labour market

Per Vejrup Hansen

In recent years there has been a strong belief that a substantial increase in employment in the future will imply 'mis-match' problems for the labour market. In other words, the demand for persons with specific educational attainments and qualifications will not be met by a corresponding supply of labour.

The belief in the existence of such underlying bottlenecks originates from the experiences of the 1983–86 period in Denmark. During that period there was a substantial increase in employment in the private sector, while employment within public services stagnated. The overall figures are shown in Table 21.1. From 1983 to 1986 the total increase in employment was 7 per cent, while in the manufacturing industries the increase was 13 per cent and 18 per cent in the building industries.

Firms within these industries reported that they were faced with vacant jobs, which were hard to fill. Shortages of skills were also reported by the local labour market authorities. These skills included certain types of skilled workers (mechanics, electricians), some semi-skilled workers (e.g. welders), and technicians, engineers, etc.

These shortages of skills developed in spite of a high overall level of unemployment. According to Table 23.1 the rate of unemployment was 10.5 per cent in 1983, and as high as 7.9 per cent at the end of the period of economic recovery in 1986. This paradox seemed to indicate a general lack of specific skills among the unemployed.

It should be noted that the issue of vacant jobs is complicated as regards conceptualization, as well as the measurement of vacancies. Furthermore, the economic recovery of the 1983–86 period was characterized by a structural change of the economy as the expansion only took place within the private sector, while there was no growth in the public sector. As the composition of skills in the manufacturing and building industries is different from that in the public sector, there might easily emerge problems of occupational or educational adjustment if a sudden change of structure should occur.

Table 21.1 Employment and unemployment in Denmark, 1980–89

	Number of employed persons[1] 1980 = 100	Unemployment rate (%)[2]
1980	100	7.0
1981	99	9.2
1982	99	9.8
1983	99	10.5
1984	101	10.1
1985	104	9.1
1986	106	7.9
1987	107	8.0
1988	107	8.7
1989	n.a.	9.4

1. National account figures
2. Registered unemployed persons in percentage of the total labour force

Source: Danmarks Statistik: Statistik Tiårsoversigt 1989, and Statistiske Efterretninger, Arbejdsmarked, 1990: 4.

Even so, the events of the 1983–86 period left a clear impression of the existence of structural problems in the labour market. The skills demanded were not matched by the skills among the unemployed. This is also illustrated by the fact that among persons without any education at secondary level the rate of unemployment is more than double the rate among persons with a vocational or a higher education. In 1986 the rate of unemployment was nearly 11 per cent among the first group (the unskilled), but only around 5 per cent among persons with a vocational education and 2–4 per cent among persons with a higher education (according to the register-based labour force statistics).

These figures clearly illustrate that an economic recovery followed by a general rise of employment could easily lead to shortages of manpower with vocational or higher education. In the initial situation the unemployment rate is already quite low among these groups. This is labelled a 'growth-trap'. The problem of possible future shortages of labour will be further aggravated as the growth of the overall labour force is expected to slow down. According to forecasts the growth of the labour force will stop in the mid-90s. The reasons for this are low birth rate and a stagnating rate of female participation (as in Denmark the female participation is already very high). Also factors on the demand-side could aggravate the mis-match problems of the future: for example, a tendency towards a somewhat higher demand for labour with vocational or higher education. The historical evidence seems to point in that direction (Andersen and Buch, 1989). One might also consider the impact of the EEC internal market on Danish industries. In view of Denmark having a small number of big or medium-sized companies, it seems unlikely that Danish companies can compete in large-scale mass production. The competitive strength of Danish industry seems to be in flexible and innovative small-scale production, in which, probably, the proportion of employees with vocational or technical education is higher.

The direct answers to these structural problems of the labour market would be to expand vocational education and, in particular, to develop more extensive retraining programmes among the labour force. How this should be organized has been debated during recent years. One important issue is how such training programmes should be financed. Another and related issue is how to improve the incentives among employees to choose vocational training and retraining. The issue also involves the question of how companies make use of manpower planning and educational planning. Recently an investigation of the occurence and nature of human resource planning in Danish companies has been undertaken by researchers at the University of Aalborg (Jørgensen *et al.*, 1990). This study shows that, in general, planning of human resources is very short-sighted and oriented towards acute problems of recruitment.

In addition to the issue of structural mis-match problems of the labour market, a reform of the financing of the unemployment insurance system is under discussion. The main purpose of a reform is to abandon the present system of financing through general taxes, and instead to finance the system by contributions from the employees and employers. The participants would thus become more responsible for increases in the level of unemployment and consequently, it is hoped, be more favourably disposed towards reducing the level of wage increases (see next section).

These issues have lately been extensively investigated by the Danish Council of Economic Advisors (in Dansk Økonomi, June 1988) and by several ministries in a white paper on the structural problems of the labour market (Hvidbog om arbejdsmarkedets strukturproblemer, May 1989). A similar study on the Danish labour market is the OECD Economic Survey on Denmark in 1990 (OECD, 1990).

Labour Market Programmes and the Unemployment Insurance System

Looking at labour market programmes it is usual to make a distinction between active and passive measures. Active measures aim at reducing structural problems by employment and training programmes, while passive measures are income support for the unemployed and for those withdrawing from the labour force.

In principle there is a widespread consensus that more emphasis should be placed on active measures in Denmark. It is very common to compare the distribution between active and passive measures in Denmark with that in Sweden. In Sweden the proportion of active measures is much

Table 21.2 Public spending on labour market programmes in the OECD, Denmark and Sweden, 1988: percentage of GDP

	OECD[1]	Denmark	Sweden
1. Active measures, total of which:	0.72	1.19	1.79
– employment services and administration	0.11	0.11	0.20
– training programmes for adults	0.20	0.51	0.51
– special youth measures	0.13	0.24	0.13
– direct job creation	0.15	0.03	0.20
– measures for the disabled	0.13	0.30	0.75
2. Passive measures, total of which:	1.40	4.34	0.80
– unemployment compensation	1.08	3.04	0.70
– early retirement scheme	0.31	1.30	0.10
All measures	2.12	5.53	2.59

1. Simple average of OECD countries

Source: OECD (1990), p. 82, and Finansredegørelse 90 (1990), p. 83.

larger than in Denmark, but this is not the case when comparing Denmark with many other countries. Table 21.2 shows the average level of active and passive public spending on labour market programmes in OECD countries, Denmark and Sweden. Actually, the level of public spending on active measures is fairly high in Denmark (1.19 per cent of GDP) compared with the average in OECD countries (0.72 per cent of GDP). Also compared to other EEC countries Denmark is placed at the upper level regarding active measures.

Of course one should make reservations on such figures. First, the figures only include public spending and not private spending (e.g. on training). Secondly, the statistics only show summary figures. Obviously, it would be necessary to have a detailed look at the actual nature of the programmes. Take for instance 'training programmes for adults' which can include employment programmes for the unemployed as well as training programmes.

As to programmes for unemployed in Denmark the main emphasis was on 'job offers', and not on training and education as such. The system of job offers provides temporary employment for the long-term unemployed. If a person is unemployed again for a certain period (1–2 years) after a job offer, a new job offer can be received. However, the job offer system was recently changed to a 'job and education offer' system. This means that in certain spells a long-term unemployed person is offered an education instead of a temporary job. This change is viewed as a shift towards more active measures in relation to the structural problems of the labour market.

Concerning passive measures the level of spending is very high in Denmark (see Table 21.2). This is partly caused by the Danish early retirement scheme. All persons above the age of sixty are entitled to receive an early retirement payment until the age of sixty-seven, provided that they are members of an unemployment insurance fund.

But the high level of spending in Denmark also applies to unemployment benefit. The Danish rules for receiving unemployment benefit are considered to be generous. Unemployment benefit is obtainable after having paid contributions for twelve months to an unemployment insurance fund and having been employed for two months in the same period. Entitlement can also be obtained via the job and education offer programme, or after finishing vocational or higher education. Unemployed people can receive unemployment benefits from the second day of unemployment, the first day being paid by the employer. The maximum length of time for receiving unemployment benefit is two and a half years. Compared to other countries the level of unemployment benefits is high for low income groups, but not for high income groups. These generous rules – and only one day paid by the employer – are often seen as the price to be paid for the virtual absence of legal rules for job security, i.e. lack of restrictions on lay-offs in Denmark.

When comparing the overall levels of unemployment benefit in different countries one should also look at the figures with reservations. Such figures are influenced not only by differences in the level of unemployment, but also by the classification of spending, e.g. between unemployment benefit and social security programmes. Furthermore, the figures in Table 21.2 only include public spending.

This leads us to the question of the financing of the unemployment insurance system in Denmark. As mentioned earlier, the system is financed through general taxes to a large extent. Around a third of the spending is payed by employers and employees, but the contribution is a fixed amount. The result is that marginal spending rests on the government budget, i.e. the cost of a rise in the number of unemployed is payed by the government.

The aim of a financial reform would be to impose the cost of marginal spending on the employees, i.e. the insured, by raising contributions. By this incentive wage moderation is thought to be encouraged. The new means of financing unemployment benefits could be through block grants from the government to the unemployment insurance funds or by a special tax on wage earners. Block grants would be a fixed amount, which means that the cost of a higher level of unemployment would be paid by members of unemployment insurance funds.

Block grants could apply to individual unemployment insurance funds or to all funds taken together. If the cost of a rise in unemployment is imposed on individual funds, this might result in economic hardship for specific groups. Furthermore, the reason for a large increase in the level of unemployment among members of certain unemployment funds need not be large wage increases. Also, this could possibly be due to structural and cyclical changes, implying different charges in the level of unemployment within individual funds. The consequence could be withdrawals from certain unemployment insurance funds or from the unemployment insurance system in general. Such problems do point to a more joint arrangement, e.g. applying to all funds. On the other hand, this might weaken the incentives to wage moderation.

Financing by employers has also been considered. The considerations also contain a proposal that employers should finance unemployment benefit for the casual unemployed. A considerable proportion of the total number of unemployment spells consists of temporary lay-offs, i.e. the employees return to the same employer after a short period of unemployment. The proposal is that employers should pay the benefit for one or two weeks instead of just one day as they do now.

Summing up, the structural problems of the Danish labour market concern the measures of labour market policies as well as the functioning of the labour market.

References

Andersen, Lars and Ingerlise Buch (1989), *Tilpasningsproblemer frem mod år* 2000, Arbejdsnotat nr. 1 til Specialarbejderforbundets beskæftigelsesudvalg, 1989.

Det økonomiske Råd (The Danish Council of Economic Advisors) (June 1988), *Dansk økonomi* (Danish Economy).

Finansministeriet, Budgetdepartementet (February 1990), *Finansredegørelse 90*.

Hvidbog om arbejdsmarkedets strukturproblemer (White Paper on the Structural Problems of the Labour Market) (May 1989), by six ministries.

Jørgensen, Henning *et al.* (1990), *Personale, planlægning og politik*, ATA-rapport nr. 23, Aalborg.

OECD (1990), *OECD Economic Surveys*, Denmark, Paris: OECD.

Chapter 22

Labour mobility

Gert Nørgaard

Introduction

A number of the proposals for directives the EEC Commission has put forward in the white paper (The European Act) have a direct or indirect influence on labour mobility in the EEC. In this chapter we will pick up some of the most important items related to Danish policy and examine their importance for Denmark. The Commission previously had a social policy for the EEC, but the initiatives in the labour market field and the effect of the initiatives were rather modest until the white paper was put forward.

Labour mobility in EEC terms is often understood as being confined to labour movement across borders, but the opportunity for mobility between companies, industrial sectors, etc., at a national, as well as an international, level, made possible by flexible skills and mobility-increasing education and training programmes, is probably of greater importance. Proposals for training programme opportunities (graduate, post-graduate and on the job training) and equal treatment of men and women, to mention but a few, also have the effect of increasing mobility. In addition to this, working out and administrating the Structure Funds may increase mobility.

EEC – goals and means

Including the mobility-increasing proposals put forward in the white paper, thus making mobility a subject for political treatment, might be seen as a contradiction of other parts of the social policy, that rather late, and after a strong political pressure has been included in the Commissions political initiatives according to 'the social dimension'.

The proposals from the Commission might be seen as an attempt to break down the barriers between the national labour markets in the EEC, leading to increased competition in the labour market, but they might also be viewed in a more positive way as allowing the populations of the EEC countries greater job opportunities and the freedom to become established in other EEC countries.

The Commission has particularly stressed the latter purpose. But the context in which the proposals are put forward, and the more modest pace at which the Commission has progressed compared with other proposals on the labour market, suggest that the white paper proposals rather aim to create the largest possible competition inside the EEC, not only among plants and professionals, but also among employees and unemployed workers, including wage and price competition. This should among other things take place – as proclaimed by the Commission – through minimizing the risk for labour market bottlenecks. These would otherwise be an inevitable consequence of the structural changes made by the increased competition among enterprises in the EEC. This is obviously one of the means to achieve the full completion of the economic policy the Commission's white paper prescribes.

At the same time, however, the policy tries to remove some of the worst employment problems: to ensure a sufficient future supply of labour, in possession of the necessary qualifications; to ensure a development in the less developed parts of the EEC (especially parts of the southern countries); and to ensure a more appropriate dispersion of the social costs between the regions.

Proposals directly aiming at liberalizing the rules of geographic mobility include among others, proposals to guarantee labour permits in other EEC countries; foreign labour rights to be employed in public enterprises and in government administration, equal to those of the national citizens; and proposals ensuring the right to achieve unemployment subsidies and early pensions in another EEC country. The proposals would also ensure a person's free right to become established in another member country. This would be achieved by mutual recognition of diplomas and by exchange programmes.

Another group of proposals, more indirectly promoting the labour mobility, and which aim to adjust the labour force as a consequence of the structural changes that follow from the formation of the internal market, include proposals for labour rights of post-graduate education and leave for education and adult education programmes in the enterprises. They also include proposals for education and job integration of young people and for the equal treatment of men and women and programmes for incorporating long-term unemployed and other marginal labour groups into the labour market.

Theory of labour mobility

It is also relevant at this point to distinguish between mobility across borders and structurally determined mobility. In the following sections we will in particular deal with geographic mobility, partly because of the limited space, but first of all because it has proved very difficult to obtain information about structurally determined mobility.

Most literature dealing with labour mobility forming a common market is indeed inspired by theories of commodity trade movements by forming free trade areas, custom unions, etc., as discussed by Straubhaar (1987). In general increased commodity factor movements are expected, when customs barriers and other obstacles are removed. An increased intra-EEC commodity trade movement has in fact emerged, and has been more significant in the last few years.

The question is, however, whether one might expect the same theories to work when dealing with movements of the labour force, by removing the barriers that exist between the national labour markets. As Straubhaar shows, with the EEC as an example, the formation of the Common Market has not significantly stimulated labour migration among the EEC countries.

The EEC case showed that the elasticity of commodity trade patterns is much higher than the elasticity of labour migration, according to a number of very complex mechanisms. This might, among other things, be caused by non-economic barriers, such as differences in culture and family relations, and other more qualitative relations which modify mobility factors, such as differences in wage levels and high unemployment rates between the potential migration countries.

Denmark has for many years had an agreement with the other Nordic countries concerning the rights of free mobility across borders for Nordic citizens. In many ways the deal looks like the directives that are now agreed on in the EEC. This has been possible, without problems, because of a high extent of similarities in social policy and regulation of the labour market in the Nordic countries. In all the Nordic countries, a large part of the social insurance is payed for by public taxes and duties, and all the countries have a well-extended employment service and – related to the EEC – a rate of unionization (though the unionization is somewhat lower in the other Nordic countries), making deals between the labour market parties well regulated. Even with a large difference in the unemployment rate, where Denmark in latter years has had about 10 per cent unemployment and its neighbour country Sweden has had an unemployment level of about 1–2 per cent of the labour force, and in spite of a common cultural and social basis between Denmark and Sweden, the amount of Danish labour moving to Sweden has been very modest, though it is rising. Migration between Denmark and the other Nordic countries is at an annual level of 12,000 to 14,000 migrants, in each direction, and makes no significant changes in the size of the population, as mentioned by the Danish Labour Department (1988).

Danish labour mobility policy

The Danish social system departs markedly from the systems of the other EEC countries. Denmark has a high collective financing of the social expenses and unemployment insurance, among others through the tax system by law, while the financing of expenses with such a purpose in other EEC countries depends on the individual and on the employers, through contributions and by negotiations.

The Danish financing system makes the maintenance allowance higher and the contributions paid by each ensured person are relatively lower. The system has a special advantage for low-payed groups in society and fields and professions with a high rate of unemployment.

At the same time, differences also occur in the training system, and in the employment service system, in which an unemployed person is guaranteed the right of re-education and in-service training. This is of special advantage for the potentially long-term unemployed. The policy potentially increases structural mobility, and the policy is – to some extent – adopted in the Commission's social policy.

Though it has been a common understanding that the Danish policy has a large importance for geographic as well as for the structural mobility inside the country, we will not here go into the technical details in depth. These are described by Per Veirup Hansen and Sven Bislev elsewhere in this volume. It should be mentioned, however, that the collective social insurance (partly via taxes and duties) has for instance made possible a higher average economic covering of maintenance allowance, longer payed maternity leave for both parents and partially government payed employment offers for the long-term unemployed, to a higher extent than is the case in other EEC countries. However, we have still not reached the level of Sweden, which has a more offensive labour market policy.

Denmark has had a fear of losing these arrangements as a consequence of the immigration to the Danish welfare of poor and unemployed people from other parts of the Community, if the barriers for labour mobility in the EEC are further liberalized as the Commission has proposed. A large immigration of foreign labour would reduce the possibility of the maintenance of these favourable arrangements, as well as having a downward pressure of the wage level, not to speak of a pressure on the high level of unionization, which has been feared for by the trade unions.

Apart from this, the Danish policy on labour mobility has had a strong national emphasis. The policy has been organized partly to increase labour mobility among regions inside the national borders, and partly to increase mobility between the skills and social groups of the society. The latter is achieved mainly through education and training programmes. For example, unemployed people previously had the possibility of getting migration expenses covered by the government, if there were no other unemployed people available in the area to fill the job. This rule is now replaced by more general initiatives (especially information campaigns). Even national mobility is very difficult to promote, with the Danish social system and Danish family patterns. The Danish social system and living expenses have since the 1960s been based on an income from both parts of the family, which makes migration very difficult (you have to get two jobs in the new area, you have to get the children into kindergartens, of which there is often a shortage, etc.). In a number of other EEC countries the family might still be able to exist with the income from the one part of the family. If this were the case in Denmark, the social insurance system would collapse. In 1987, 78 per cent of the male population and 67 per cent of the female, aged between 15 and 74, participated in the labour force.

In the Danish labour unions, among politicians and in the population, there has been a fear that immigration of labour from the new member states in southern Europe would be so high that the Danish social system and the labour market system would break down, so the relatively high standard of unionization, wage level, maintenance allowance, maternity leave and the high extent of tax financing of the social system would be reduced markedly.

Labour mobility development

Like a number of other EEC countries, Denmark had a high immigration of foreign labour at the end of the 1960s, and in Denmark this continued until 1973/74, where an economic crises reduced the immigration markedly.

The reason for allowing a relatively high rate of immigration was the very low unemployment rates, down to 1.2 per cent of the registered labour force, which threatens to be an invisible barrier to industrial production.

The immigrant labour did not come from the EEC countries, nor from the south European countries that were not yet members of the Community. The labour migrated from Turkey, Yugoslavia and Pakistan. Further, the stay in Denmark to some extent had a temporary character, since some of the former immigrants have returned to their country of origin.

Several EEC countries have seen the same patterns. The immigration from countries outside the EEC to the Federal Republic of Germany was double the size of the immigration from other EEC countries, in spite of a large immigration of, in particular, Italians. To France, The Netherlands and the UK, the immigration from countries outside the EEC was of the size of the immigration from other parts of the EEC (for these countries their former colonies abroad might be of importance). In the other countries the migration pattern has been more limited.

The intra-EEC migration has mainly been:

Table 22.1 Foreign part of the population in Denmark, 1979–89

Year	Total	Foreign part of total pop. (%)	Nordic (%)	EEC[1] (%)	Third World[2] (%)
1979	5,112,000	1.92	0.44	0.49	0.99
1983	5,116,000	2.01	0.43	0.46	1.12
1985	5,112,000	2.11	0.44	0.48	1.19
1987	5,125,000	2.50	0.46	0.52	1.53
1989	5,130,000	2.77	0.45	0.52	1.80

1. From 1981 also Greece. From 1986 also Portugal and Spain.
2. Apart from Nordic Citizens.

Source: Danish National Statistical Department.

To Germany: migrants from Greece, Italy, and then Spain. *To France*: migrants from Spain and Portugal. *To the UK*: Irish. *To Luxembourg*: French and Portuguese. Apart from this, intra-EEC migration has not been of significance to the local/national labour markets.

These trends show migration of labour inside the EEC first of all taking place between neighbour countries and nearby countries, while migration over longer distances is very modest, and hardly has an effect in the receiving countries.

According to the above position, the Danish geographic position on the periphery should limit immigration from other EEC countries, apart from, potentially, Germany. A factor of uncertainty, however, is whether labour will be drawn to Denmark by further liberalization of the rules of migration and residence, and whether, if the high unemployment rates in the south European countries are not brought down (among other things by the rather considerable amounts from the Structure Funds poured into the south European countries).

Another factor that might prevent high migration rates is the relatively high unemployment in Denmark of about 10 per cent of the workforce (300,000 workers).

The share of foreign citizens with residence in Denmark rose in the 1980s (see Table 22.1). From a population of approximately 5 million people in 1979, 98,000 foreign citizens had their residence in Denmark, and in 1989 the number was 142,000 foreign citizens, a rise from 1.9 per cent to 2.8 per cent of the total population, while the total population has been relatively constant during the years. This has partly been caused by a falling birth rate. Though there has been a marked rise, the number of foreign citizens with residence in Denmark is still modest compared with most other EEC countries.

The proportion of citizens from other parts of the European Community has been rising, and a little higher than that coming from the other Nordic countries, but, Table 24.1 shows, the real rise is due to

Table 22.2 Net migration pattern, 1977–87

Year	Net migration[1]	Danish citizens	Foreign citizens
1977	5,834	1,553	4,281
1979	5,452	– 1,263	6,715
1981	– 1,845	– 4,137	2,292
1983	1,719	– 891	2,610
1985	9,493	– 1,649	11,148
1987	6,173	– 3,742	9,915

1. Positive values are net migration, negative are net immigration.

Source: Danish National Statistical Department.

immigration of persons from the 'old' immigration countries (Turkey, Yugoslavia and Pakistan), and partly – and specially – refugees from countries at war and civil war (those previously came from Vietnam, and from Chile and other South American countries. In later years they come from Ethiopia, Sri Lanka, Iran, Lebanon and Poland). The number of these immigrants has varied quite a lot over time, depending on national relations, and until 1989, where the immigration rules for the refugees, and the rules of family-conciliation, were tightened markedly. Now Denmark almost only accepts refugees in the amount we are obligated to by the UN convention.

In recent years, a net emigration of Danish citizens (see Table 22.2) has taken place. The migration pattern primarily has been intra-Nordic and to the FRG and the UK, which are the countries with whom Denmark has had the major trade connections.

In contradiction to this, there has been a net immigration of foreign citizens, rising, through with large fluctuations, and especially coming from the refugee patterns as pointed out above. It would be interesting to see from what social layers and with which educational background the main migration takes place, but such information has not been possible to obtain.

There have been suggestions of an exodus of taxpayers and of 'brain drain', as the primary explanation for the larger emigration of Danish citizens, but such suggestions might possibly be rejected. Among other studies, a research project of Danish emigration to the UK shows, that the migration mainly takes the form of unemployed people seeking jobs in another country. The UK is one of the countries in the EEC where Danes would have the fewest problems with the language and with the culture. The UK would rather be expected to be a residential country for the exodus of taxpayers.

For some years, it has been possible for unemployed Danes to receive maintenance allowance for three months when staying and looking for a job in another EEC country, but the possibility has hardly been used.

Conclusion

The main purpose of the EEC policy on labour mobility is to break down the barriers of free competition, and so also competition among labour for employment, wages and living conditions. The political initiatives aim at avoiding labour market bottlenecks, which might prevent enterprises an unlimited access to a sufficient amount of labour with the necessary qualifications. To at least an equal extent, the EEC policy deals with structural mobility as it deals with geographic mobility.

From a Danish point of view, it has been feared that the proposals for directives, would break down the effective and high-level social field, through allowing the unlimited access of foreign labour to force wages downwards and to obtain maintenance allowance financed by the Danish tax payers, via the social system and the employment insurance system.

However, statistics of the migration patterns show a very modest intra-EEC migration with a character of relatively regional moving. At the same time, the immigration of labour from the Third World to the EEC countries has been higher than the intra-EEC migration. Nor, over time, has there been significant change in the intra-EEC migration pattern.

The Danish fear of massive immigration from other EEC countries breaking down the social system seems to be groundless, though one could expect a slight rise in migration, especially among younger EEC citizens who do not have family commitments. This will follow the economic integration. The mobility might rather have more indirect causes, due to structural changes, education programmes across borders and a rising intra EEC-commodity trade. These items have, probably to a high extent, caused the Danish emigration in more recent years.

The mobility that results from the structural changes and the economic integration might also prove to be migration across borders, but there will be few major changes in the short run.

The favourable agreements between Denmark and the other Nordic countries need not be affected by a more open access to Denmark from other EEC countries.

We will now sum up some of the most distinct gains and losses that might be the consequences of the EEC migration policy for Danish citizens:

Gains:

a) It has been easier for Danish citizens to become established in other EEC countries with a private enterprise or profession, through labour work and for education.
b) The EEC policy has contributed to a more international orientation of the Danish population, especially the young.

Losses:

a) The possibility, at a national level, to decide limitations for immigration is limited.
b) If the planned proposals for extending the right of migration, in such a way that an EEC citizen gets free access without time limits or other limitations, and gets free access to obtain social contribution according to rules of the country he has migrated to, no matter whether he is unemployed and with no prospect of getting a job, the liberalization might mean a cost increase, and in an extreme case a weakening of the Danish social system.
c) Denmark might be forced to privatize a major part of the social insurance expenses and other social expenses. This would inevitably mean larger differences in the size of maintenance allowance and other social contributions, and it would hit the low-payed, the marginal labour groups, and single parents.

References

Danish Labour Department (1988), *Rapport om konsekvenserne for arbejdsministeriet af gennemførelsen af det indre marked i EF.*

Danish Statistic Department, *Yearbooks.*

Cornett, Andreas P., 'Regionalpolitik i Danmark after 1992? – Muligheder og perspektiver', in *Politica* no. 4/1989.

Straubhaar, Thomas (1987), 'Freedom of Movement of Labour in a Common Market', *EFTA Bulletin* 4/87.

Chapter 23

Industrial relations

Gert Nørgaard

Introduction

For some years now, it has been discussed whether or not the process of internationalization which has taken place during the last 45–50 years also results in a higher institutionalization of industrial relations in Europe.

As Due (1990) describes, two understandings of forming institutions in the labour market field, which might be able to explain the development in the EEC, have been stressed in recent years. Due describes the forming of the institutions as being: 'establishing of rules and procedures in order to solve conflicts in the labour market' (1990, 3).

The one understanding, first expressed by John Dunlop (1958) says that external factors which unify the industrial relations in the single national states lead to a rising institutionalization. According to Dunlop, the external factors are primarily composed of market conditions, importance of the development of technology for industrial structural development, and working conditions and the division of power within the society.

During recent years, research has questioned this understanding, as stressed by Michael Poole (1984, 1986). The research still shows large differences in the national forms of regulating the labour market, in spite of the fact that a long range of economic-structural relations have progressively become more alike. The other theoretical understanding thus emphasizes the probability of continuous large national differences in industrial relations. In this sense, the economic and social conditions make a framework in which factors of the labour market are able to act. Internal factors, such as the level of action, are put forward as an important explanation of the possible development.

The establishing of the internal market might become the factor that shows in which direction the forming of institutions might go. Industrial relations and labour relations have for many years only peripherally been brought into the debate about the economic and political development in the EEC. But after forming the programme for the internal market, and in time with the fulfilment of the proposals for directives, the European Council and the EEC Commission have, to a still larger extent, seen that the internal market can not be carried to its full extension without including the social dimension. This requires that employers' and employees' organizations – at an EEC level – participate in the process of forming the internal market. This has most recently been expressed in the fifth report from the Commission to the Council of Ministers and the European Parliament: 'The European Council has . . . found that the social aspects should be given the same importance during the formation of the European Single Market as the economic aspects, and that there should therefore be balance between them' (KOM (90), 10).

In this chapter, we will describe the EEC initiatives in the field, and the industrial relations policy in Denmark, in order to clarify the advantages and disadvantages of the EEC policy for Danish society.

The EEC policy

In the field of commodity goods, an extensive process of internationalization, that breaks down the national barriers, is taking place. This is to some extent in opposition to the labour market field. Here, we see a variety of industrial institutional actors. The EEC is divided into a number of labour markets, mainly with a national and intranational-regional setting of agreements between employers and employees.

In opposition to this, there is great similarity between the EEC policy in the field of commodity goods and the labour market field, concerning the policy of liberalization. In essence the Commission want a removal of barriers between the national labour markets, in order also here to optimize the 'laws of competition'. This we can see clearly from the proposals for directives in the European Single Act. In the Act, the Commission has included proposals for directives that increase labour mobility and ensure free rights of establishment within the EEC, but other proposals also show the Commission's intentions for an increased liberalization.

On the other hand, the Commission has been attentive to the fact that a dialogue between the agents in the labour market field might stabilize the labour market. This appears partly from an extension to the EEC treaty in 1987, article 118B, stating that: 'The Commission endeavours to develop a dialogue between the parties of the labour market at a European level, since this dialogue, if the parties find it desirable, may lead to connections of agreements' (European Single Act, 1986). It can also be seen from the Commission's latest attempts to institutionalize three-party negotiations at an EEC level, for instance during the Val Duchesse meetings in 1985 and during the frequent meetings in the board of occupation.

Through the Economic and Social Committee, consisting of 189 members, the Commission has already included a number of actors in the social field for assembled negotiations and exchange of views about the labour market policy. The committee has as yet mainly confined its work to dealing with environmental problems, especially concerning the establishing of minimum levels for health and security at the workplace and social political arrangements, including equal rights for men and women and the situation of unemployment. The committee has not yet put the bargaining system into the negotiations, though the organizational framework makes it possible.

In spite of the latest attempts by the Commission to further common European labour market agreements, we have not yet seen any actual breakthrough. This is also illustrated by the very few and rather late initiatives of importance from the Commission. The policy of the Commission is most clearly illustrated in the Social Charter, which was put forward and agreed upon in the Council of Ministers in Strasbourg as late as December 1989, after a proposal from the Economic and Social Committee, put forward in February 1989 and after tight bargaining during the year. The main content of the Social Charter (Europæisk Dokumentation, 1990) is:

- The right of free movement and establishing the rights of occupation and wage;
- demarcation of flexible forms of employment contracts and atypical work (for instance part-time work and time-limited work) and procedures for collective dismissals;
- the right to be socially safe (securing a minimum income and the right of being covered by social insurance);
- the right to be covered by a collective agreement;
- the right to obtain on-the-job training and further education;
- equal treatment of men and women;
- the right of the employees to be informed and heard, when major changes in the plant have an influence on occupation or on working conditions;
- protection of health and security at the work place;
- protection of children and young people (minimum age for admission to the labour market and obtaining a minimum wage);
- aging persons' right to obtain pensions;
- rights for handicapped persons.

A proposal for the bargaining right across borders for employees in international firms has not been carried through (after pressure from employers' organizations and multinational companies).

Beside this, the Commission has dealt with less comprehensive proposals, such as:

- abolishment of double taxation in border regions;
- workers' rights to move maintenance allowance, pension and other social benefits obtained in one country to another country, when staying there;
- information on job possibilities in other EEC countries.

The Social Charter only put forward the main guidelines in a program for basic social rights in the EEC. Since some of the proposals in the charter go further than the EEC treaty, the Commission has no authority to carry through the charter, as it has with the Single Act. The single member states may decide to what extent they wish to carry out the Social Charter. Single nations, especially the UK, have been reluctant to contribute to the carrying out of basic social rights according to the labour market. Apart from the above standing initiatives, the actual work of the Commission has been the effectuation of investigations of the social problems.

In general, the trade unions, represented by the ETUC (European Trade Union Corporation) have tried to attain EEC-wide agreements in a number of fundamental fields, while the employers' associations have rejected such agreements, and they have among other things obtained that the Commission has withdrawn its proposal for the rights of bargaining, when amalgamating companies across borders.

The Danish labour market system and policy

The institutionalization of the Danish labour market has a long tradition. Early after industrialization, the trade unions as well as the employers' organizations obtained a high level of organizing people, and the first Danish main agreement ('Hovedaftalen'), which was agreed upon in about 1900, is, with later adjustments of course, still the basic foundation for bargaining agreements in the labour market field. Ever since, the government, the trade unions and the employers' associations have agreed upon maintaining a high level of regulation in the labour market.

An important tool for observing the 'Hovedaftalen' is the institutionalization of a Court of Arbitration agreed upon by the labour market organizations. Disagreements about or violation of the treaty might be put before the Court of Arbitration, which in practice is similar to the civil law. The Court of Arbitration consists of a number of arbitrators, appointed by the main labour market associations.

Trade unions and employers' associations are organized in larger cartels. The largest and most important cartels are 'Landsorganisationen' (LO), consisting of white collar and blue collar trade unions and 'Dansk Arbejdsgiverforening' (DA), which consists of a number of employer's associations, among others from the manufacturing industry. These organizations have agreed upon the 'Hovedaftalen', and traditionally, have formed the framework for Danish labour market agreements.

At the beginning of the 1980s, the Danish government began to involve the labour market organizations in negotiations concerning the national economic situation, the so called three-parties negotiations. The discussions have on several occasions resulted in agreements, traditionally comprising agreements upon limiting the increase of wage levels and governmental initiatives in the labour market field, for instance a rise of the maintenance allowance and initiatives in order to reduce the unemployment level. Later on, there have been great difficulties in obtaining results by the three-parties negotiations, especially when talking about major disagreements, as for example the forming of education funds and general agreements about the labour market retirement pension (that is supposed to supplement the national financed pension). However, such negotiations have for some time led to an improved connection between development in the labour market field and the national economic policy.

Compared with a number of other EEC countries, another field with a high degree of institutionalization in the Danish labour market is that of working conditions, including laying down minimum levels for health and security at the work place. A well-known example is commodity labelling and rules for protection against health-damaging substances at the workplace, such as organic solvents and substances containing asbestos. In this field, the Danish policy has in general been more restrictive than the EEC policy. The trade unions, especially, but also to some extent politicians and employers, have feared that lower EEC standards may force a lowering of the Danish standards, consequently followed by a worsening of the working conditions and reduction of the competition abilities for Danish companies which have invested in machines and equipment that are more expensive, but also less dangerous.

Denmark is the EEC country with the highest public financing of social insurance expenditures (see Table 23.1). In all other EEC countries, the social expenses are, to a much higher degree, financed by contributions from the employers' and/or by the workers' personal insurance. The high public financing in Denmark has contributed to the highest pressure of taxation in the community, as well as a wide range of duties contributing to the financing (though a number of the duties also have the purpose of bringing down the use of alcohol, tobacco, energy etc.).

The duties in Denmark are much higher than in most other EEC countries in a number of fields, such as duty on motor vehicles depending on weight, on beer, wine and spirits, on tobacco and on energy. As well as these duties' contribution to financing a high insurance level in the social field, they also spread the expenditure over a larger part of the population.

The attempts by the Commission to harmonize these duties, among others, might to some extent force through a changed financing of social expenditures, in fact an individualization. This development appears gradually more clearly in the policy of the Danish government.

Table 23.1 The financing of social insurance in the EEC in 1984, divided into income sources

Nation	(1)	(2)	(3)	(4)
Italy	53.1	14.5	30.1	2.1
France	52.8	23.6	20.5	3.1
Portugal	52.1	18.5	25.8	3.0
Belgium	41.3	19.1	33.8	5.1
Germany	40.5	29.8	26.3	3.4
Luxembourg	34.7	25.8	32.2	8.3
Holland	31.7	35.8	18.1	13.2
UK	31.3	16.8	42.6	9.7
Ireland	21.6	13.2	64.2	1.0
Denmark	10.0	3.8	79.2	7.0

(1) Contribution from employer.
(2) Contribution from employee/tradesman.
(3) Public contribution.
(4) Contribution from other sources.

Remarks: There is a lack of information from Spain and Greece. The numbers for Portugal are from 1980, for Holland from 1983.

Source: Eurostat (1989), here from Due (1990).

The differentiating of the social security contributions, led by the individualization of the contributions, forces through a further differentiation and a general reduction of the unemployment relief and other labour market benefits.

The great differences between the national labour markets in their process of institutionalization also makes a further internationalization of the industrial relations difficult. In some countries e.g. (the UK), bargaining activities between the labour market organizations are to a large extent taking place at a plant level, while in other countries (Denmark) bargaining traditionally takes place at a higher organizational level, to determine the general agreements and then, more de-centrally, to fill in the details. In some countries in the Community, the bargaining takes place at a sectorial level, or regional (FRG), or with a great difference from sector to sector. To some extent, the bargaining level depends on how, and to what extent, the employers and the labour are organized.

We also see great differences in how the national states stand in relation to the bargaining system. In Denmark, there is a long tradition of taking part actively in labour market agreements, while in other countries, there is no tradition for governmental participation (Social Europe, 1988).

Another relation of importance is the difference in the level of labour organizing. At the top, about 80 per cent of the workforce are organized in Denmark, at the bottom Portugal and France organize about 20 per cent of the work force.

A high level of organizing means that a larger part of the labour force is involved in the collective bargaining system, which gives employees as well as employers fairly homogeneous frames for action. This means that policies of the nation state for the development of the labour market might be determined from more safe assumptions. Together with the above conditions, the differences make it difficult to extend the cooperation from the national level to the EEC level. The existing conditions are of great importance for the Danish society.

To a large extent, a fear of impairing these conditions has made Danish political parties, and especially the Danish trade unions (and to some extent employers), demand that the criterion of unanimity is upheld in the Council of Ministers as regards the social dimension. The political effort of the Commission to increase economic integration through liberalizing the field of commodity goods seems to have incurred some costs in the social fields which the Danish trade unions are, in particular, not prepared to pay for.

The feelings about the criterion of unanimity have, however, during the last 1–2 years turned around, in favour of majority voting. This is partly because of the changed attitude to the importance of the social dimension shown by the Council of Ministers and especially by the Commission. This is due to the fact that a number of EEC countries now stress the importance of the social dimension as being equal to the economic dimension. The Danish trade unions have also seen the absurdity of the fact that a single member country is able to slow down progress in the social field. The unilateral UK rejection of determining even minimal basic rules in the labour market field, and at an EEC level (the Social Charter), to guarantee basic rights for the labour, has been one reason for the change in the Danish attitude. Also of importance has been the EEC court decision that a nation may decide whether or not national bargaining agreements and rules in the labour market field must also apply to foreign enterprises operating in a country. By this decision the Court has removed the threat of social dumping from enterprises using lower-paid labour from other EEC countries.

Two key notions influencing the Danish trade unions' former rejection of first EEC membership in any form, and later of the European Single Act, have been the fear of 1) unpredictable geographic changes in the industrial structure (moving of workplaces away from Denmark), and 2) social dumping, which,according to Social Europe (1988, 66) might not quite be rejected. The concept includes labour mobility (as described in Chapter 22) and 'the consequences of differences in, and eventual harmonization of, collective agreements and bargaining systems and national labour market policy and regulations' (Lind, 1989, 10).

The fear of social dumping, connected to a low level of trade union organizing, a high difference in wages (Table 23.3), and the Single Act

Table 23.2 The share of the labour force belonging to a trade union in the first half of the 1980s

70–80%	Belgium, Denmark
60–70%	Luxembourg
50–60%	Ireland, Italy, UK
40–50%	FRG
30–40%	The Netherlands, Greece
15–30%	France, Spain, Portugal

Source: ILO, *World Labour* no. 2, 89.

Table 23.3 Gross wage costs (direct wage, inclusive of social contributions) in 1987

Nation	(1)
FRG	100.0
The Netherlands	84.4
Denmark	83.3
Belgium + (Lux)	80.4
Italy	74.3
France	68.6
Ireland	54.2
UK	54.1
Spain	51.0
Greece	25.0
Portugal	16.3

(1) Gross wage costs.

Source: Institut der Deutche Wirtschaft, 1987, here from Due (1990), and Économie européene, here from Social Europe (1988, 67).

proposals for ensuring free labour mobility, have made the Danish trade unions and almost half the population fear a further integration of the European Community. The high level of labour organizing in Denmark is probably to some extent connected to the administration of the unemployment funds, which are administered by the trade unions. Membership of an unemployment fund is closely connected to skill. To be a member of the skilled metal worker unemployment fund, you have to be a skilled metal worker. The trade unions fear a reduction in the number of unionized labour, and weakening of bargaining situations, if the administrations of the unemployment funds are amalgamated into larger funds, and no longer administered by the single trade unions.

This fear has not been completely unrealistic, not so much with regard to migration, but more to workplace environment (working conditions) and social costs, while it is still uncertain as to what extent the process of integration – in the longer term – might change the geographic localization of industry, eventually from high-wage countries to countries with less wage costs. This is the well known and well described north-south problem.

The more positive attitude from the Danish labour movement to the integration thus regards the view of more political unity (at an EEC level), regarding the importance of a further institutionalization of the social field, consequently to involve the trade unions in decision making.

Conclusion

Besides the field of commodity goods, the EEC policy also involves the labour market development into the process of liberalization through forming the Single Market. This is a difficult process, since, besides the industrial structural differences, there are also differences in the level of institutionalization, the level of regulation and differences in the bargaining system from one EEC country to another.

Only in the last few years, in forming the Single Market, the policy concerning regulation of the labour market field has been given almost the same weight as the process of liberalizing the field of commodity goods. But still no real breakthrough on common European bargaining agreements has emerged.

This makes the EEC labour market policy look rather poor, as some of the most important initiatives have concerned minimum rules for security and health, equal opportunities for men and women, the right to be included in a collective agreement and the right to be a member of a social fund.

The trade unions have tried to push through bargaining agreements at an EEC level, but so far the employers' associations have been able to reject such agreements.

The Danish level of regulation and institutionalization is higher than in most EEC countries, and there is close collaboration between the government and the organizations in the labour market field. The labour market is regulated through a main agreement ('Hovedaftalen') and a Court of Arbitration, but other fields of the labour market are also highly regulated, such as health and security, labour training, fighting unemployment and social funds.

Apart from Ireland, Denmark is the country in the EEC with the highest public financing of the social costs and, in reality, with a uniformity of the level of social benefits. The EEC Commission proposals for harmonizing taxes and duties might force Denmark to move the financing of the social expenditures from the tax and duties financing to be financed directly by employers and employees, and thus not only change the Danish tax and duty policy and system, but also individualize the financing of the social welfare benefits. This would probably polarize and in general reduce the social benefits.

The Danish trade unions have feared that the rather low level of regulation in the EEC might lead to social dumping in Denmark by removal of the barriers for migration and of minimum health and security levels at the workplace. There has in particular been a fear of a downwards pressure on wages, for instance by migration from low-wage countries or by (the threat of) moving Danish enterprises to the low-wage countries. Earlier this attitude caused Danish opposition to majority decisions on the social dimension. The Danish attitude to majority decisions is now positive, however, among other reasons following the negotiations about the Machinery Directive and the decision from the EEC Court, which stated that a country may decide that national bargaining agreements must also apply to foreign plants and labour operating in the country.

This leads to a summary of the major advantages and disadvantages for Denmark of EEC membership in the field of industrial relations.

Advantages

The labour market is to a higher extent regulated at an EEC level, which might prove to be a long-term advantage.

Higher common standards might strengthen the competitive position for the minor Danish enterprises, because for a number of years, the Danish labour market standards have been more progressive.

The trade unions are now more motivated to collaborate internationally.

Disadvantages

The process of liberalization might reduce the level of, and further polarize, the Danish social benefits, if an individualization of the financing of the social funds is forced through.

Harmonization has reduced the Danish level of standards in the field of health and security in some areas, for instance when using organic solvents or asbestos.

The EEC membership might lead to a less progressive level of standardization in the labour market field, considered the Danish tradition. This would in particular be the consequence if a higher level of regulation in the EEC can not be agreed on.

References

Due (1990): in Due, Jesper, Madsen, J.S., Jensen, C.S., *På vej mod internationale industrielle relationer i Europa* University of Copenhagen, January 1990.

Dunlop, John T. (1958), *Industrial Relations System*, Harvard.

Poole, Michael (1984), 'A Framework for Analysis and an Appraisal of main Developments', in Poole, M. *et al.*, *Industrial Relations in the Future Trends and Possibilities in Britain over the next Decade*, London.

Poole, Michael (1986), *Industrial Relations Origins and Patterns of National Diversity*, NY.

KOM (90) 90 endelig udg. (March 1990), *Femte rapport fra Kommissionen til Rådet og Europaparlementet – om gennemførelsen af Kommissionens Hvidbog om virkeliggørelse af Det Indre Marked*, Bruxelles.

Eurostat, *Eurostat – statistiske basisoplysninger om fællesskabet*, 1989, 3.35.

Molle, Willem (1990), *The Economics of European Integration*, Dartmouth, Aldershot.

Social Europe: *EF-socialt set. Den sociale dimension af det indre marked.* Særnummer. Luxembourg: EF-kommissionen 1988.

Europæisk Dokumentation (1990), Europas Sociale dimension, Periodisk 2/1990, Bruxelles.

Chapter 24

Social security and health

Sven Bislev

Outline of the field

The field of social security and health (SS&H) comprises public and publicly supported measures of two kinds, namely:

- services to protect and aid people who are sick, or who have too little private income
- financial arrangements to compensate for loss of income.

These definitions comprise two large programmes: social pensions and health services. And a host of smaller programmes, i.e. sickness benefits, unemployment and maternity benefits, family benefits, social assistance, assistance and services to the disabled, etc. These programmes are often called 'social insurance', but they do not always have insurance form. They have different sizes and institutional forms in the different countries, and the extent of public involvement varies widely. The variations are so great that even common definitions are hard to establish. In this chapter the pattern of variations will be described, in order to characterize the Danish situation.

Danish SS&H institutions are specific, due to historical and geographical reasons: Denmark is part of the Scandinavian region, and the Danish economy has been dominated by small-scale agriculture. Industry came late, and there has been no large, heavy industry. For that reason, the Danish welfare state has been a compromise between industrial and agricultural interests; in this context, the important results of this are that: 1) Danish SS&H institutions are strongly integrated into the social fabric, being part of a large, politically important public sector; 2) they function in a relatively efficient and egalitarian way, cover a large part of the population and swallow almost half the national income – creating a political ambivalence, clearly visible in public debate.

Danish SS&H institutions are difficult to compare directly with institutions in the other EC countries, and their national political importance is larger. The Danish welfare state, and the means to develop and maintain it, are important to the Danes and therefore important in Danish attitudes towards the EC. The deep-seated ambiguity in the EC towards social questions, compounded by the ambivalence in Danish politics, has against this background created a very difficult political situation and a very complex political debate in Denmark.

The SS&H initiatives of the EC

The EC, being above all an economic organization, has formulated a much less explicit welfare goal for its activity (Article 2 in the Treaty) than usual for *national* economic regulations and institutions. The MacDougall report of 1977 (EC Commission, 1977) characterized social and labour policies as being one of the areas where a common effort was less suitable for the Community, because of the heterogeneity of national arrangements and the absence of benefits of scale.

Various initiatives in the field (Teague, 1989) have shown that a political interest exists, nonetheless, in the EC, for producing welfare improvements for wage earners and their dependents. But there is nothing approaching a consensus on the matter. Debate and disagreement run along two lines:

First, the classic left-right dimension is visible in the schism between the neo-liberals, who wish to extend liberalization from foreign trade to domestic policies, and the social reformists, who regard the size of the growing community as an opportunity to raise living standards in the poorer areas and segments of Europe.

Secondly, there are different approaches to creating EC initiatives: harmonization of national policies versus EC programmes – and for Community programmes: targeted, *ad hoc* funds versus permanent institutions. Some nations favour harmonization of national policies with no direct involvement from Brussels, others want EC initiatives with a lean administration. A third group wish for accountable, permanent bureaucracies with broader functions, to cooperate with national administrations.

The history of EC social policies shows conflict avoidance, oscillation among/between the different approaches and evolving compromise.

One way of avoiding conflict has been to attach initiatives very closely to the main goals of the EC: to the operation of business and specifically the transnational operation of business. Therefore, what is called the 'social dimension' is very narrowly a labour market dimension, concerned with welfare questions for wage earners. And the only 'social' area, where the difficult process of harmonization is still alive, is in the – still very limited – field of migrant labour, where efforts to harmonize the granting of social rights have been intense and partially successful.

The evolving compromise is seen most clearly in the case of the social funds, which were initially relatively small, to fund locally decided projects. They are now being expanded and reorganized, integrated in a more comprehensive regional policy, but are still of a limited size.

The 'social charter' being fought about at the present represents perhaps an instance of the oscillation process: French socialists and British conservatives have pressed initiatives in opposite directions, and the attempt to find a compromise, expressing concern for the welfare of ordinary people without expanding the activities of the EC unduly, has proven very difficult.

To sum up, all that exists in the area of social security and health is

- a coordination of policies towards the social rights of migrant workers,
- funds to finance labour market and infrastructural projects in underdeveloped regions, and
- a declaration of intent, concerning the welfare of workers.

From a Danish point of view, this is practically nothing. Although the European Court of Justice hears more cases in the social area than in any other, this hardly ever affects Denmark. In countries with a social security system built upon the insurance principle, the rights of migrant workers are very important to define and uphold. The Danish SS&H system is founded not upon employment and the payment of membership fees, but upon residence. Anybody who legally lives in Denmark has a right to Danish social benefits – pensions, health care and some of the smaller schemes.

Therefore, the question of social rights practically never crops up in a Danish context, and EC initiatives have been largely irrelevant. What has been relevant, and remains so, is the overall impact of the integration process on the Danish economy, especially on the public sector, through which the ample welfare state is financed.

Danish social security and health programmes

The major programmes of Danish SS&H are universal and tax-financed: every resident above the age of 66 has a right to a full public *pension*, paid for through general taxation. *Health* care is free at the general practitioner and in public hospitals. Public pensions are low, compensating only around 30–35 per cent of average net income, and additional private pensions abound. Private hospitals are recent and few in number.

The minor schemes of social insurance are generally characterized by: a high coverage of the population, heavy public involvement and benefits that compensate for between 60 and 90 per cent of the income loss.

Danish municipalities are involved in the administration of all social security and health schemes (except unemployment benefits and some minor ones), in an attempt to create an integrated centre of responsibility for the welfare of citizens. This is one of the reasons for the high degree of integration of the welfare state into the daily lives and political/social concerns of people.

In Denmark, social security is not only for wage earners, but all the minor schemes are aimed at the economically active. And Denmark has a higher proportion of economically active people than any other country in the EC: 67 per cent of the relevant age cohorts were active in the labour market, against an EC average of 53 per cent in 1986. The reason was that 60 per cent of Danish women were working or seeking work, while the average of the EC was around 41 per cent (Eurostat, 1986). Many of these working women are employed in social welfare institutions (Denmark also has a high proportion of social expenses devoted to services instead of cash benefits). This 'socialization of care' gives added importance to the SS&H institutions in a Danish context.

Any attempt at harmonizing Danish social and health policies with the predominant EC system of industrial welfare states would shake the foundations of Danish culture and society. On the other hand, the foundations are perhaps cracking already. The Danish welfare state has been caught in a fiscal crisis since the middle of the seventies.

Danish social policies were built on Social Democratic initiative throughout the post-war period, with an intensive build-up during the sixties and early seventies: benefits were raised, eligibility broadened, new schemes were added and new services instituted. The resulting growth of the public sector was accepted by everybody, as long as inflation and sustained economic growth appeared to be footing the bill.

The oil-shock of the mid-seventies put a sudden halt to the possibilities of expansion, but the actual stopping has been a painful and protracted process: few of the schemes were self-limiting, many had an inbuilt expansionary tendency, and the failure to restrict unemployment in Denmark (whereas Norway and Sweden have consistently kept unemployment below 5 per cent), meant that the fiscal pressure has been acute for fifteen years.

The current retrenchment involves limiting benefits and attempts at privatizing parts of the SS&H apparatus. These are initiatives that are independent of any direct EC influence on social policies; whether the more indirect influence of the EC upon the national economy and public revenues has eased or tightened the fiscal squeeze is another matter.

Costs and benefits of EC membership

The one great social concern of the EC has been migration: a political goal of supporting migration by securing migrant workers the same rights as resident nationals – and, on the other hand, a concern to prevent exploitation of national systems by guarding against double payment of benefits. Apart from the very limited scope of migration, this is a major concern for the insurance systems, but of little importance for Denmark, where most benefits are earned by mere residence.

The negative concern in Denmark has been a fear that nationals from other member countries would take advantage of the relatively generous benefits in the Danish SS&H system, and move to reside here. In one instance, around 1980, some 2,000 foreign-born British citizens moved to Denmark, to exploit the 100 per cent difference between social benefits in the two countries.

But there has only been this one major instance of 'social tourism', and later changes of the rights of movement and residence in the EC have imposed limits on the freedom of movement of people without jobs.

The fear of 'social dumping' nonetheless persists, for which reason the Danish Centre-Right government, in line with socialists in other countries, strongly supports an active 'social dimension' in the EC (Weekendavisen, 3 August 1990). Denmark supports, for strategic reasons, social *convergence* and administrative *coordination*, but is strongly against *harmonization*, unless it is strictly an 'upward' trend, lifting the socially low countries to the high level of Denmark. So far convergence is going very slowly and is largely unaffected by the EC, and Denmark has had nothing to fear from any harmonization initiative. Coordination is uncontroversial.

References

EC Commission (1977), *The Role of Public Finance in the European Communities*, Brussels.

Teague, P. (1989), *The European Community: The Social Dimension*, London: Kogan Page.

Eurostat (1986), *Employment and Unemployment*.

Weekendavisen, Copenhagen 3 August 1990.

Chapter 25

Consumer policy

Hans Rask Jensen

Introduction

Although the preamble to the Treaty of Rome among its essential objectives lists the constant improvement of the living conditions within the member states, it makes no express provision for the defence or adjustment of consumer interests. However, the very logic of the Treaty provisions as worked out in practical measures and in the jurisprudence of the European Court has led to Community involvement in consumer policy, and this involvement has been given enhanced status by increased awareness of governments of consumer issues *per se*. Still, the scope of consumer policy is mainly economic. Consumer action is justified only in terms of the effectiveness of the single market which in turn is justified by the need to improve the living conditions for all.

In this chapter consumer policy within the single market will be highlighted. Because the Community's scope for consumer action is mainly economic, a broader social approach will be used as the general framework. Within this approach consumer problems and consumer policy will be characterized, and three paradigms describing the social and political influence of consumers will be discussed as guidelines for consumer action. In the light of this analysis some consequences concerning consumer policy at Community level and in Denmark will be outlined.

A social system approach to analyzing consumer policy

Analysis of consumer policy can take its point of departure in different social circumstances. This chapter will primarily reflect the sociological fact that households do not themselves, to the same degree as earlier, produce the goods and services which are used to satisfy needs, even if self-sufficiency and barter economy in the member states and to some extent enjoying a renaissance. The economic development since World

War II has increased the physical and psychological distance between consumers and producers. Consequently, the single market can be characterized by the existence of three social systems related to each other by interaction (Jensen, 1986).

In the production system all activities are directly or indirectly connected with manufacturing and marketing of goods and services. Seen from the point of view of the actors within this sub-system of the EC – the producers – the satisfaction of consumer needs is a means of reaching other goals typically related to economic growth, employment, or the earning of incomes. In the consumption system all activities are directly or indirectly connected with utilization of the output from the production system. Seen from the point of view of the actors within this sub-system of the EC – the consumers – satisfaction of needs is the main objective. Products and services from the private and public sectors are means of achieving this goal. In the political system all activities are directly or indirectly connected with the process of social regulation.

Seen from the point of view of the actors within this sub-system of the EC – the politicians – consumers should be informed, educated, protected, represented, and heard in order to get their physical, psychological and social needs satisfied in a way that is desirable seen from a general European point of view.

It is, of course, both possible and desirable for producers to take care of the consumers' interests. Within the single market suppliers will even be forced to adjust their production and marketing activities to consumer demand. The needs and wants of consumers can, however, not be understood if seen in isolation from the manner in which they are actually satisfied. The supply of goods and services from private and public sectors in itself plays a decisive role in fostering the consumers' needs, wants and interests.

A typology of consumer problems and consumer policy within a social system approach

As the various goods within the single market will reflect a number of considerations other than regard for the consumers, we have to take for granted the existence of some consumer problems which are not necessarily identified and solved by producers. Such problems, perceived by consumers as barriers to need satisfaction in the pre-purchase, purchase, or post-purchase process, can be characterized as functional or structural (Jensen, 1986).

Functional problems are mainly caused by lack of information, education, advice or a defective communication process between consumers and producers. They can, however, also be caused by practices of individual firms that do not follow good marketing standards, thus preventing consumers from adopting as expected to existing market structures. Such problems can be solved by consumer-centred consumer action directed at individuals, smaller or larger groups of consumers, e.g. by means of personal or mass communication. They can also be solved by producer-centred consumer action, e.g. small claims, directed at individual firms and/or individual salesmen.

Structural problems are caused by the conditions to which consumers have to adjust in the short run. In contrast to functional problems they are always more of less general. Such problems might be determined by market conditions that prevent the satisfaction of consumer needs, either by influencing the buying process directly, or by predisposing the decisions and behaviour of sellers in the process of competition. Consumer problems caused by market structures do not stem from some unique behavioural incidents within specific industries or trades. On the contrary, they reflect more or less normal market conditions which are generally viewed differently by consumers and producers. Structural problems might also concern the general societal framework within which consumers function. Consequently, they might be political by nature. Such problems can be solved either by producer-centred consumer action directed at, for example, industries, producer and labour organizations, or by society-centred consumer action directed at, for example, actors within the political systems at national or Community level, extra-parliamentary groups, lobbyists and the mass media.

Seen from the consumers' point of view it is important that functional problems are identified and solved. Fortunately this is also desirable from many other points of view, since solutions of such problems are a prerequisite for a well-functioning single market. If the consumers are not informed and educated to some extent, and if industries and firms are not behaving according to accepted rules of conduct, resources are not expected to be used in the most efficient way. For consumers, however, it is perhaps even more important that structural problems are identified and solved as they decisively predispose both the extent and the nature of those functional problems which consumers will meet in the future. Consumer decision-making and problem-solving in the single market take place within a social context, where consumer and producer interests do not always coincide, and where social, political and ideological resources are unequally distributed between producers and consumers. Certain consumer problems in the EC would simply not exist if such resources were more equally distributed. However, to solve structural consumer problems is not necessarily perceived as desirable seen from other points of view than that of the consumers'.

Three paradigms describing the social and political influence of consumers

To what degree one finds it essential to solve functional and structural consumer problems by means of consumer action depends among other things on the observer's frame of reference. Basically economic and social literature offers three different interpretations of the interrelationship between consumers and producers, and, consequently, of the social and political reality of consumers. As these interpretations typically are regarded as self-evident and a matter of unquestionable validity within the context where they normally appear, they might be called paradigms describing the relative social and political influence of consumers and producers (Jensen, 1986).

If you believe in consumer sovereignty, the supply of goods and services is supposed to reflect consumer needs. The immediate instructions of consumers are supposed to control all activities in the market of goods and services as well as in the market of production factors. According to this paradigm the needs of consumers are supposed to be the proper cause of production and marketing. The consumer is the king of the single market. Consumers are supposed to reveal their fundamental needs when they demand goods and services. Consequently, one can hardly expect consumers to have any problems. This paradigm can, therefore, hardly justify consumer policy. A *laissez-faire* economy is the best solution to consumer problems, because in the long run the interaction between producers and consumers is supposed to result in a macro-economic equilibrium, where needs are satisfied and production factors used in the best possible way. Through the demand of goods and services it is up to the individual consumer to decide how consumer-adapted the single market shall be.

If you believe in interdependence between consumers and producers, the supply of goods and services does not reflect only consumer needs. On the one hand, by means of their marketing mix, producers are capable of influencing consumers, but fundamental human characteristics prevent the latter from being manipulated. On the other hand, by means of their demand, consumers set limits to possible producer action. Consumers and producers are, so to say, in the same boat. They keep each other in check. According to this paradigm it is the business of firms to find, stimulate or derive needs in order to satisfy them – when profitable. One cannot say that consumer needs are determined by the activities of producers at variance with consumer interests. Certainly, producers do not satisfy all consumer needs, but the needs which actually become satisfied are supposed to be derived from original needs reflecting fundamental human characteristics – a notion often used to legitimize marketing activity. This does not mean that consumers always get what they want even in cases where it is profitable for firms to supply goods and services. On the one hand, non-competitive markets, for instance, deprive the producers of their capacity to satisfy consumer needs. On the other hand, consumers are not always capable of assessing accurately either their needs and wants or the supply of goods and services in heterogeneous markets. A *laissez-faire* economy is therefore insufficient to secure a solution of consumer problems. Consequently, this paradigm provides some *raison d'être* for a consumer policy which aims at overcoming the information gap between consumers and producers, as well as purging markets of undesirable elements. As the single market seen within this framework most probably will be characterized mainly by congruent interests and equality between producers and consumers, one in primarily predisposed to perceive and attack functional problems. Structural problems will be solved only if it is in the interest of both consumers and producers to do so.

If you believe in producer sovereignty, the demand of production resources, as well as the main conditions for the demand of goods and services, are determined by producers. According to this paradigm identified consumer needs are still a necessary prerequisite for an output from the production system. These needs reflect, however, more the influence from firms than some fundamental human characteristics. Consequently, the paradigm allows a critical investigation of different methods applied by producers to influence consumers. One can claim, for example, that in the long run consumer needs are determined by producers, perhaps in conflict with consumer interests. Marketing can be characterized as a process which contributes to the development of wants and needs which are not necessarily in the best interest of consumers. Perceived within the framework of this paradigm markets cannot always be characterized by a congruence of interests between producers and consumers. Consumers are not necessarily aware of possible conflicts of interests, among other reasons because marketing activity might veil this. Functional problems still exist, reflecting short-term difficulties of choice. Structural problems, however, are especially highlighted, because the conditions under which consumers make decisions and solve problems might not necessarily be adequate, since they reflect primarily the interests of producers. This can be true even when consumer choice is based on information, advice and education made available through consumer action inspired by the paradigm of interdependence between consumers and producers. The paradigm of producer sovereignty therefore contains a particular justification for solving those structural consumer problems within the EC which producers and their organizations do not necessarily want to solve.

Within the single market firms will most certainly attend more to knowledge about consumer behaviour because of intensified competition. However, consumer behaviour as characterized through market research reflects, in addition to needs and wants, the influence that individual firms direct at consumers as well as the influence of the single market and a more coherent Europe at large. Consequently, because consumers do not determine production the paradigm of consumer sovereignty should at most be regarded as interesting within a theoretical context. Consumer action within the EC is due to the fact that *laissez-faire* is not sufficient for the solution of consumer problems. Both the paradigm of interdependence between consumers and producers and the paradigm of producer sovereignty should be considered as relevant guidelines for future consumer action at Community level. They should not be perceived as mutually exclusive, but as supplementary to each other, because they are highlighting different problems and policies that should all be attended to in practice.

Some consequences of the single market to consumer policy at community level

Functional consumer problems have been especially highlighted in the process of creating the single market, and consumer policy at Community level has as an element of this process been guided primarily by the paradigm of interdependence between producers and consumers. According to Lawlor (1989, p. 8) the producer-user relationship within the single market is supposed to be equally founded on a common aim: the satisfaction of consumer needs. The appropriate and most effective way of increasing the influence of the individual user in the European economy is according to Lawlor (ibid. p. 47) by providing objective information related to questions of consumer choice. Information is also supposed to be the real key to problems related to physical and economic safety (ibid., p. 59), and it is supposed to be the most obvious way to combat abuses of power accumulated by suppliers within the single market (ibid. p. 41). To know what one is buying, is, however, not only considered to be the most essential right of the individual consumer. It is also considered to be the most important precondition for an efficient single market characterized in the longer run by consumer sovereignty, as purchasers according to Lawlor should exercise the discipline which only they can enforce: that of rejecting inefficient production and encouraging efficiency. However, a consumer sovereign single market is also considered to be an important prerequisite of the evolution of democratic institutions within the EC (Lawlor, 1989).

Even if consumer interests within the single market are supposed to be best safeguarded by individual consumers' own influence, legal measures are to some extent required, but only in order to eliminate abuses which deprive consumers of their right to choose and reject. The most important consequences of the single market to consumer policy at Community level will therefore probably be reflected by activities related to removal of internal barriers to trade, promotion of general technical standards, stimulation of consumer research in order to monitor the consequences of the general safety directive, evaluation of national procedures taken to protect consumers against claimed dangerous products, and mobilization of consumer power partly by informing and educating individual consumers, and partly by creating more effective consumer representation within the EC. Consumer action inspired by the paradigm of producer sovereignty will probably not be possible, because the framework provided for consumer policy by the philosophy of the single market is mainly economic, and within such an approach to consumer policy structural consumer problems can only be identified and solved if it is in the interest of both consumers and producers to do so.

Some consequences of the single market for Danish consumer policy

In a policy-delphi study published in 1980 it was demonstrated that the Danish consumer movement in the 1970s did identify and solve both functional and structural problems (Damgaard, 1980).

According to the conception particularly prevalent in one of the clusters identified by Damgaard, the consumer's social role was primarily characterized by acts of demanding goods and services. Consumer problems were related especially to the activities of buying and using supplied goods. For the members of this Cluster 2, consumer policy should primarily aim at improving the use of production within a given context. Neutral information about goods and services and the acquisition of knowledge about behavioural aspects of consumer demand were considered to be the main strategies of consumer policy. In the opinion of this cluster, a well-informed and educated consumer was considered to be able to adapt rationally to given circumstances in the market and in society at large. Damgaard concluded that this conception demonstrated the existence of a paradigm according to which society could be characterized by congruent interests and equality between consumers and producers.

According to the conception particularly prevalent in another cluster identified by Damgaard, Cluster 1, the consumer's social role was not considered to be related solely to the buying and using of goods and services. Because supply was considered to reflect first and foremost the interests of the producers, the situation of consumers was perceived to be dependent upon the possibilities of influencing this supply. Within this cluster, consumer policy would still comprise activities which aim at improving the use of goods and services. Seen from the point of view of this cluster, however, consumer policy should to an even larger extent increase consumers' influence on production. Damgaard concluded that the conception of Cluster 1 demonstrated the existence of a paradigm according to which society could be characterized by conflicting interests and inequality between consumers and producers.

In an interview-study published in 1986 it was demonstrated to what extent and to what relative degree the two clusters formed by Damgaard did represent fundamental conceptions of consumer problems and consumer policy within the Danish consumer movement before the present European context represented by the single market (Jensen, 1986). He concluded that resources within the Danish consumer movement were then used predominantly to identify and solve functional problems guided by the paradigm of interdependence between consumers and producers. This situation was perfectly congruent with the official Danish consumer policy in the 1970s, even if the four reports from the Government Consumer Commission (1971–77) showed a changing perception of the balance of power and influence between consumers and producers. Only the Consumer Council, Danish Local Consumer Groups, and the Danish National Tenants' Association attached at that time particular importance to the solution of structural problems, but this orientation was in fact officially supported, because it was then generally accepted that it should be just as legitimate to pay attention to the consumers' interests as to the interests of producers and the general socio-economic situation in Denmark (Securing the Future, 1988).

However, the mere concept of consumer policy as well as its general acceptance as an important political tool was linked to a period in which the public sector in Denmark did interfere in the market mechanism to a large extent. Given the present political will in Denmark to reduce public spending and the new European context represented by the efforts to create a single market, consumer policy is doomed to be perceived as less important than earlier, irrespective of the real conditions to which consumers are exposed. This situation is reflected by a report from the Danish Ministry of Industry (Securing the Future, 1988) according to which resources to public and semi-public institutions established mainly in the 1970s to inform and protect consumers should not only be generally reduced, but also reallocated so that the supply of neutral information and advice based on, e.g., comparative testing of products should be promoted at the expense of, e.g., consumer policy information which might highlight structural consumer problems (Securing the Future, 1988, pp. 114–125). Apparently the paradigm of producer sovereignty is perceived as an irrelevant guideline for consumer action by the present political majority in Denmark.

After all, this is not surprising. Also politicians behave within a social framework where the existing consumer and producer roles primarily reflect the interests of the actors in the production system. By producer-controlled socialization we are all continuously brought up to function as consumers in a way which first of all is intended to facilitate goal achievement in our producer roles. Generally speaking, our human identity is related to producer values to a much larger extent than to consumer values. This sociological matter of fact, however, is not especially compatible with the assumption of the single market that it is in the social role of consumer that the citizen in Europe should reject inefficient production and encourage efficiency to the benefit of all.

References

Cecchini, P. (1988), Europa 92 – Realiseringen af det indre marked, (Europe 92 – Realization of the Single Market), København: Børsens Forlag.

Damgaard, J. (1980), 'Forskellige forestillinger om mål og midler i dansk forbrugerarbejde' (Different Visions of Goals and Means Among Danish Consumer Activists), B. Dahl and F. Hansen (eds), *Forbrugerforskning i Danmark*, pp. 35–57, København: Samfundslitteratur.

Fremtidssikringsudvalget, 1988, *Fremtidssikring* (Securing the Future), Rapport fra Industriministeriets fremtidssikringsudvalg, København: Stougaard Jensen.

Jensen, Hans Rask (1986), 'The Relevance of Alternative Paradigms as Guidelines for Consumer Policy and Organized Consumer Action', *Journal of Consumer Policy*, 9, pp. 389–405.

Lawlor, Eamonn (1989), *Individual Choice and Higher Growth*, The Aim of Consumer Policy in the Single Market, Luxembourg: Office for Official Publications of the European Communities.

Petith, H. (1987), European Integration and the Terms of Trade, *Economic Journal*, vol. 87, pp. 262–272.

Wallberg, Knud (1989), Forbrugerbeskyttelsen i EF's indre marked, (Consumer Protection within the Single Market). *Retfærd* nr. 44, 12. årgang 1989, pp. 82–98.

Winters, A. (1988), Completing the European Internal Market: Some Notes on Trade Policy, *European Economic Review*, vol. 32, pp. 1477–1501.

Chapter 26

Education policy

Lise Lyck

Introduction

In this chapter Danish education and research are first discussed. Secondly, the EC education and research goals and policies are outlined and the increased EC weight on this area explained. Finally, the Danish and the EC development of the education research area are compared and evaluated from a Danish perspective. The Danish tradition and position of education is outlined and the changes in goals and policies described. Furthermore, the structure of the educational system is analysed. The Danish research structure and system are also described and related to the educational system.

The Danish educational system

The educational tradition

Education has for many years had an important position in the Danish society and has been considered both as a quality factor and as a right related to being a Dane and as a basic element in production. As early as 1814 Denmark passed its first education law introducing a general right to free education for all children, and this right is a part of the Danish Constitution of 1849 (Article 76). It is worth stressing that it is a right but not a constraint to a special school or educational system.

During the latter half of the nineteenth century education played a very visible role for the development of Danish society and in this way established a basic position of relevance and utility in social development. The visible development was connected especially to the handling of two problems: the change in agriculture from corn production to animal production of first quality and the intensive efforts to cultivate the moors, especially in Jutland after the loss of the south of Jutland from the river Kongeåen to Eideren as a consequence of the wars with Prussia in

1848–50 and 1864. Denmark lost about 30 per cent of its territory but managed to keep up production under the slogan 'what you lose to the outside world you have to regain inside'. (After a poll in 1920 Denmark regained half of the territory, from Kongeåen to the present border with Germany).

A labour force of a high educational level has since been considered as a must to secure competiveness of Danish production and it has been considered a public task and responsibility to secure the quality of education. The educational system has been centrally governed and also governed at a very detailed level. In fact the education system is part of the infrastructure and the state obligation is both to preserve Danish identity and culture and at the same time to safeguard production aspects.

Education is considered a lifelong process so educational policy is not only related to children and young persons but to all ages.

Changes in education policy

For the last ten years Denmark has had a Conservative-led minority government consisting of more than one political party but with the same Minister for Education and Research from the Liberals. During the 1980s comprehensive changes in the education system have taken place, especially concerning the economic guiding principles and the established organizational power relations of the education institutions.

The old system in which the state decided most of the activities in detail has been substituted by a more decentralized system, in which the state sets the main purpose and framework but the institutions and the users of the institutions decide their implementation in detail.

Appropriations have been directly related to the number of students and to the number of students passing their examinations. This has made it possible to move students and money among different educations and education institutions in a flexible way. At the same time more people have passed examinations due to a more effective system but also to a degree because of a lower level of quality.

Locally the single education institutions have boards which means that the users of the education system have much more influence on the institutions, both economically and concerning the content of the education. Also the leaders of the single education institution have much more power, having both the administrative and the pedagogical management and responsibility for the education institution.

Education flexibility has been increased by increased free choice of education and by breaking the education up into packages which can be combined more individually. Also the Open-Education Reform from 1990 has increased this flexibility. It is based on the Danish tradition that adults in Denmark go for further education at different times of life. The new reform makes it possible to choose among packages of different kinds and from different institutions and combine them into a complete education.

The internationalization of education has been increased. Danes already had more education in foreign languages than the other EC member states, but in spite of this education in foreign languages has been further increased. A bachelor degree has been implemented at the tertiary level, and the foreign exchange of students and professors and the economic possibilities for these activities has been increased.

It has also been a characteristic of the educational system that the number of students has been larger than the number of education opportunities, resulting in waiting lists and dissatisfaction. The strict state regulation of the number of students allowed into nearly all kinds of education has been debated for over ten years. It was introduced in order to ensure that students did not end up unemployed owing to a surplus of graduates in particular subjects. In fact it has resulted in fewer students of human and medical sciences and more students studying science, technology and social science, but many educated students still do not find jobs after graduation.

The structure of Danish education

Children normally go to a one-year introductory school when they are six years old and start in the basic school when they are seven. About 10 per cent of a particular year (double in the capital area and few in the countryside) go to private schools. Private schools are mainly paid by the state but there is a student fee. The public schools (Folkiskolen) are free. The basic school includes nine years' compulsory education and an extra year for those who want it.

From the basic school it is possible to continue in high schools of five different types and carry on to graduate after three years or to continue to social and health education or to agricultural and industrial education, normally for three years. Only about 10 per cent leave the education system after basic school. Students who have graduated can apply for a higher education of normally five years' duration but since 1977 there is no free admittance. In 1990 48,700 applied for higher education and 14,000 (28.7 per cent) were not allocated places. Furthermore, 20—50 per cent dependent on the type of higher education never pass their final examinations.

The number of persons in the education system is about 1.1 million, of whom about 700,000 are in basic schools or private schools. Seventy thousand are in high schools, 200,000 are in agricultural, industrial or social and health education and 110,000 in higher education.

Research

The change in the education system has to a large extent also influenced research. Public research and development amount to the same relative level as in other member states, but private research and development is much smaller mainly due to the firm structure in Denmark with many firms of small size, and due to research traditionally being considered to be a public task. Research and development amounts to 1.5 per cent of GDP.

The education of researchers has been improved. The Research Academy was established in 1980 with the purpose of attaining a level of 400–500 Ph.D. final examinations every year.

Public research money has been given to specific research areas to a much higher degree than earlier, e.g. the material-technological research and development programme (495 million DKr), the biotechnological research and development programme (875 million DKr), the programme for research in foods (525 million DKr) and the information-technology programme (180 million DKr). The programme resources have increased relatively more than the basic research resources to the universities.

The internationalization has changed quality, norms and standards. Participation in international research programmes has also increased. Danish expenses to international research projects will be increased from 1990–93 by 15 per cent to 300 million DKr in 1993. Most is spent on ESA (space research), CERN (nuclear research) and EUREKA. Also some of the membership fee in the EC and the Nordic Council is spent on research and development programmes. Denmark has on average 3.5 per cent of EC research resources and has contributed about 2 per cent to the EC research budget. Up to 1990 EC research funds have financed 2 per cent of the total Danish research and development projects and it is expected that this will increase to 4 per cent.

Danish research and development economy

Public expenses given to research and development amounted in 1989 to 58 billion DKr. Thirty million DKr was financed by the municipalities and 28 billion DKr by the state. Table 26.1 shows the expenses on the main activities. The 58 billion DKr is also 7.6 per cent of GDP and this level for education and research is among the highest in the world.

EC research and development

Education and research as an EC matter was of marginal influence when the Rome Treaty was signed in 1954, and the kind of education being dealt with directly was vocational training. It had its roots in the European Coal and Steel Community Treaty of 1951 where openings of

Table 26.1 Public expenses given to education and research, 1989

	Total expenses (billion DKr)
Basic school, private school and high schools	24.054
Agricultural, health and industrial educations	11.653
Higher educations	8.692
Research	5.294
Other activities	5.591
Adult education	2.171
Education outside Denmark (mainly the Faroe Islands)	668
TOTAL	58.123

markets were forseen to provoke unemployment among miners and steel workers, creating a need for retraining. In the Treaty of Rome the same viewpoint was represented in Articles 123–128 together with a provision for establishment of a European Social Fund.

Though the national ministers for education have met regularly since 1971 education has been an area of primarily national concern, and only to a small extent an EC matter up to the mid-eighties. Vocational training was long considered the most important area for common activities, as it was seen as a prerequisite for a market-oriented economic development already in the Euratom Treaty. In this context it is important to be aware of the widening of the concept of vocational training, see the Gravier judgement of 1985 (No 293/83), according to which vocational training embraces all sorts of school and out-of-school education and training, higher education included, if it is to prepare the student for working life. It implies that EC students may not be charged higher tuition fees than national students and that EC students should have the same conditions as national students concerning financial support, regulation, etc.

General education and the higher priority given to all sorts of education and training is a consequence of the need to develop a European 'identity and culture' and thereby the greater weight on structural societal elements, especially after the presentation of the EC internal market agenda. Furthermore, there is a close relationship between vocational and university education and the general system of primary and secondary schools. In 1985 the European Council announced that it should be an EC education policy to strengthen the European dimension in the national school systems, and in 1988 the Council proposed to implement a European dimension in general curricula, to improve the teaching of foreign languages, to prepare the young for the European future and to organize multicultural education.

The main objectives for education can be outlined as follows:

1. Free movement of persons among the EC member states – achieved by:
   a) encouragement of foreign language learning;
   b) weight on the European dimension in education;
   c) equal recognization of diplomas and certificates by all member states;
   d) same structure in education;
   e) equal educational opportunities for men and women.
2. High productivity and quality in production in order to be competitive to US and Japan – achieved by:
   a) EC research and development programmes;
   b) intensified links between educational systems and the business community;
   c) technology intensive education;
   d) increased cooperation in research, development and education.

The means to achieve the objectives have been EC programmes and changes in national laws. Among the EC programmes the following are to be mentioned: ERASMUS (87) 327/EEC is a source for increasing mobility of students and professors and to support projects including cross-national cooperation in research and education. COMETT (86) 365/EEC and its more research-oriented sister programmes ESPRIT (885) 479/EEC, BRITE/EURAM (88)/108/EEC, SCIENCE (88)/419/EEC and DELTA (88)/417/EEC support research and cooperation among EC member states between higher education institutions and new technology enterprises. Youth for Europe (88)/348/EEC is created to increase exchange of young peoples. LINGUA (88)/841 finally promotes foreign language instruction.

Conclusion

The Danish education and research system has been strongly influenced and changed by the formulation of EC policy objectives and by EC membership side-effects being transformed into a national education and research policy. The impact has been internationalization, flexibility in education, more coherent education systems and research support to special areas and more programme financing than institutional financing. The Danish education and research system has in this way become very much like the system in most of the EC member states. Specific Danish culture, language and history have had a lesser role in education and research than earlier, i.e. the Danish identity-creating disciplines have had less room than earlier. Instead technical disciplines, science and social science have had an increased number of students and research has been related to the core production industries.

It is difficult to evaluate whether the development has been an advantage for Denmark because of problems related to monitoring. If related to employment, it is seen that the attempts to regulate education and students have resulted in increased weight on technical and economic educations but that the regulation has not been effective in avoiding unemployment if measured from unemployment data. The market principle in the form of free choice of education has been overruled by regulation and has been in contrast to the industrial policy. The increased weight on European topics has been a demand or an explicit wish from the users of the school system and has sometimes been considered as an artificial appendix to the school system, mainly due to most Danes not having an active pro-European attitude.

However, the possibility that internationalization in education can turn out to be an advantage exists, as well as the common and combined research activities implying increased possibilities for participitation in research activities in which Denmark would not otherwise have been active due to economic restraints.

Postscript

Denmark and the Maastricht agreement – perspectives for Denmark, EC and Europe

Lise Lyck

The discussion before the Maastricht agreement

The decision on the Single Market was taken in 1986 and though the implementation of the directives in national laws was initially slow in the member states, there was a great deal of discussion of the next step and the direction of integration and further EC development among EC bureaucrats, employees and politicians: Should the next step be primarily a widening or a deepening of the EC? Or should it be both at the same time?

The unforseen developments in the former Soviet Union and in Eastern Europe were looked upon with great surprise. The so-called 'iron wall' between East and West weakened and then came down altogether in the space of a few months. This revealed the enormous discrepancy between the imagined situation and reality in the East and West. The first concrete problem to be solved was the question of East Germany . Should there be a German reunification? And should this happen at once or as the result of a slow process? Events in the East had happened so fast that there was little basis for a slow process. At the same time, a new super Germany that would be larger than any of the other member states gave rise to a widespread fear among its neighbour states, especially France. The wish to include and involve Germany in a coherent EC development became pronounced in France, the Netherlands, Belgium and among the Southern European member states. This wish was often combined with the idea of the EC as the basis of a United States of Europe. This development, which favoured expanding the role of the EC, was not what was wanted in the UK and Denmark, countries who have always favoured European co-operation among nations/states which retain a high degree of sovereignty.

In Denmark the Danish Parliament was aware of this development and put forward a negotiating position regarding what should be included and excluded in a new agreement. Although the UK and Denmark did not consent to signing the whole Maastricht agreement but got special protocols, the reality was that areas the Danish Parliament had required in her memorandum should be excluded were in fact included in the Maastricht agreement (e.g. the military question); as well as this, other factors which had been found to be very important had been excluded, e.g. instruments to deal with the democratic deficit, the lack of openness in administration, decentralization. The subsidiarity principle in its loose form was compared to the fairytale by the Danish poet H. C. Andersen, *The Emperor's New Clothes*, in which a little boy looking at the Emperor cries 'Oh, he has nothing on'.

Already when the Maastricht agreement was negotiated in December 1991, it was evident that many Danes' who wanted a widening of the EC to include the other Nordic countries and the new East European democracies as members or close cooperation partners, felt cheated by the fact that some of the Danish ministers and politicians seemed to be more concerned with their EC negotiations and their own wishes regarding the European development than in listening to the Danish people and presenting their points of view. Immediately after the Maastricht agreement was published, the Danish people founded new associations working on disseminating information about the agreement and about voting for or against it. The associations included both persons who were and were not members of political parties; the political parties whose members were involved were mainly those arguing for a yes to the Maastricht agreement.

The Danish discussion of the Maastricht agreement

All the Danish parliamentary political parties except the left party 'SF', the right party 'Fremskridtspartiet' and a very small party 'Kristeligt Folkeparti', argued in favour of the Maastricht agreement, but in the other political parties there were large minorities, maybe even majorities, wanting and arguing for a no to the agreement. How could this happen? During recent years only a small proportion of the population has joined political parties and many politicians have not been good at knowing and listening to people's opinions and wishes, and thus, naturally, has bred mistrust.

In the debate the Danish Prime Minister Poul Schlüter, who back in 1986 stated: 'If you vote yes to the internal market, the idea of a European Union will be stone dead', now stated: 'If you vote yes to the Maastricht agreement, the European Union will be even more stone dead than in 1986'. The Danish people, however, saw the Maastricht agreement as a relinquishing of sovereignty, a centralization and the beginning of a federal European Union.

The Danish foreign minister, Uffe Elleman Jensen, argued that while sovereignty is given up, 'you' will gain influence over the whole EC. Many Danes understood 'you' as having two meanings in this argument, i.e. 'you' as a democrat give up influence and hand it over to a technocratic 'you', and in this way place certain areas outside democratic responsibility – e.g. as in the case of the national central bank versus the European central bank. Jens Peter Bonde, head of 'Union, No Thanks' stated: 'Why not say that Denmark gets 3 out of 76 votes on the EC and most of its own matters. I prefer not having this influence but instead influence on our own matters.'

The debate was widespread. The Maastricht agreement was translated into Danish and more than 500,000 copies were read by a Danish population numbering only five million! Many Danes read and studied the agreement and asked questions on the radio, on television, in papers and in local discussions. Many foreign journalists came to Denmark and were astounded at the extremely high information level of the Danish population.

In the preceding weeks up to less than a fortnight before the referendum was to take place, there had been a balance between 'yes' and 'no' votes. In this situation unemployment became a major question in the debate. The Danish central bank director, together with a few economists, had long argued that the referendum was primarily a political question not an economic decision, but now EC Commissioner Henning Christophersen stated: 'A no will result in 200,000 more unemployed'. (Unemployment in Denmark today stands at 300,000 full-time unemployed a year.) And some days later, another 'expert', Ørstrøm Møller, doubled the increase to 400,000. This campaign increased the yes votes and the pre-referendum polls, which had indicated a too-close-to-call outcome, changed to a yes outcome; the mainstream politicians, the establishment and Denmark's partners in the EC relaxed and felt sure that a yes to the agreement would be the outcome. See Table 27.1 for the development of the voting in the pre-referendum polls. Also, many EC employees contributed to the debate through the threat of their plans to diminish the influence of the minor member states and the papers on that topic strengthened the no campaign, though Jacques Delors was 'forced' by the Danish Foreign Minister, Uffe Elleman Jensen, to deny the plans would be realized. Table 27.1 and Figure 27.1 give an overview of the pre-referendum polls.

The referendum

Twice before, Danes had voted 'yes' in referenda on European issues: first, in 1972, on joining the community; then, in 1986, on approving the blueprint for the internal market, but the 'yes' majority had decreased drastically over the years. In contrast to 1986, however, the Social

Table 27.1 Danish voting preferences in the period leading up to voting in the referendum on Maastricht

Date (1992)	NO	YES	Do not know/ will not vote	NO per cent (without do not know)
1–4 March	25	34	33	42
8–11 March	27	31	38	53
15–18 March	28	32	36	53
22–25 March	31	32	32	51
29 March–1 April	32	36	27	53
5–8 April	36	35	25	49
12–15 April	37	32	27	46
19–22 April	39	32	25	45
26–29 April	38	32	26	46
3–6 May	37	40	19	52
10–13 May	36	38	21	51
14–18 May	38	36	26	51
15–18 May	41	39	20/3	51
17–21 May	40	39	21/3	51
19–23 May	41	39	20/3	51
21–25 May	39	41	20/5	49
22–26 May	37	43	20/3	46
23–27 May	37	43	20	46
24–28 May	35	43	22/4	45
25–29 May	35	44	17/4	44
1 June			12/2	47
2 June			17.1	50.7

Democrats, the largest political party, voted 'yes' for the first time, together with the Liberals and the Conservatives.

At 10 pm on 2 June 1992 the outcome was that 50.7 per cent of the votes were 'no' and that the Danes had said no to the ratification of the Maastricht agreement. Most of the establishment in Denmark was shocked, while many Danes joyfully went out on to the streets celebrating the no to the European Union as a yes to self-reliance, self-government and democracy. Table 27.2 presents the results of the referendum in 1972, 1986 and 1992. Table 27.3 gives the 1992 referendum split up geographically.

While the nation at the earlier referendum was split up with the capital area being the most sceptical about the EC and Jutland the most EC-minded, the referendum this time showed a much more homogeneous picture for all Denmark, a result – besides the resistance to an extending of the EC – of fishermen having lost their trust in EC fishing policy and the farmers having become more dissatisfied with the EC agricultural policy. The EC agricultural policy of letting the most fertile

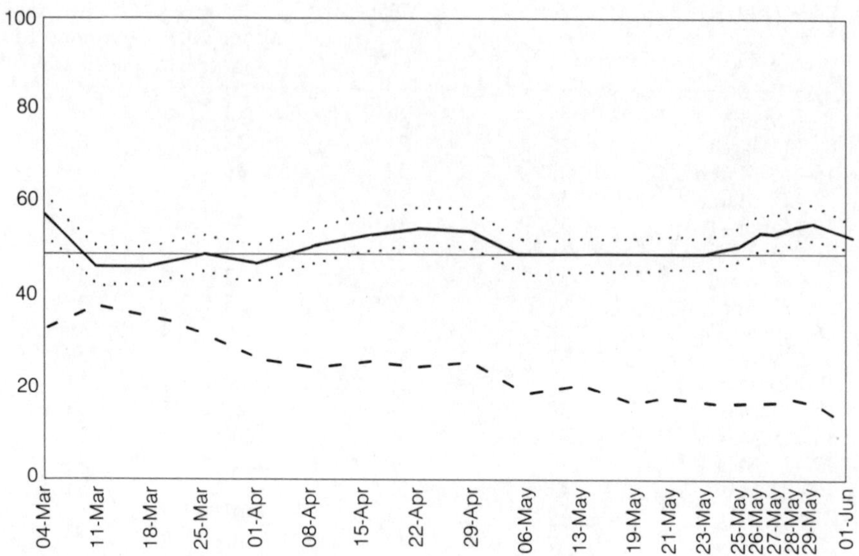

Figure 27.1 Gallup Institute information on the pre-referendum polls in Denmark (4 March to 1 June 1992). The relation between yes and no votes

Note: The thick line shows the yes per cent, the dotted lines show the 95 per cent confidence limits. The thin line is the result of the 2 June referendum. The dashed line shows the per cent not knowing what to vote among all those interviewed. (Results are based on 5-day averages of 1000 interviews, and on 1 June on 1600 interviews.)

Table 27.2 EC referendums in 1972, 1986 and 1992

	Votes placed (per cent)	
	Yes	No
1972 EC membership	63.4	36.6
1986 The Internal Market	56.2	43.8
1992 The European Union	49.3	50.7

Table 27.3 The 1992 referendum split up geographically

	Yes votes	No votes	Yes per cent	No per cent	Voting per cent
Denmark, total	1,606,730	1,652,999	40.6	41.7	82.3
Capital, downtown	372,256	221,710	30.9	49.9	80.8
The Islands	706,286	716,103	41.6	42.2	83.8
Jutland	772,092	722,812	42.3	39.6	81.8

Table 27.4 The referendums of 1972, 1986 and 1992 split up geographically

	1972		1986		1992	
	Votes given percentage					
	Yes	No	Yes	No	Yes	No
Capital, downtown	52.8	47.2	36.3	63.7	38.2	61.8
The Islands	67.5	32.5	54.9	45.1	49.7	50.3
Jutland	68.6	31.4	62.5	37.5	51.6	48.4
Denmark, total	63.4	36.6	56.2	43.8	49.3	50.7

fields lie fallow is totally against Danish ethics and morality. Table 27.4 illustrates the still stronger homogeneity of the Danish attitude to the EC.

Why did the Danes vote no to the Maastricht agreement?

Denmark is a very decentralised nation. About 50 per cent of all public expenditure and income is decided upon at the municipality level, and Greenland and the Faroe Islands have home rule. Danes are very anti-centralistic and in general find it hard to accept that people and minorities must fight over several generations for freedom and self-government without result in so many EC member states; problems such as the Basques in Spain, Northern Ireland, Sardinia, Corsica, Macedonia etc. are seen from the Danish point of view as being dealt with extremely badly by centralistic nations.

Furthermore, when Danes look at the borders that were drawn up centrally after the First World War, establishing countries such as Yugoslavia and Czechoslovakia, they become even more determined to retain their own democracy and find it unacceptable to give up sovereignty and their own Constitution to a European Union if it is not decided upon by referendums, i.e. if it is not the choice and wish of the *peoples* of Europe.

Also, the way decisions are taken in the EC, that the Community legislates behind closed doors, is viewed as riding roughshod over democracy from the Danish standpoint.

Another point that most Danes are against is the EC developing into a *political* superpower, having its own army and intervening militarily in other states. Further to this, European Union citizenship and European money are not wanted by many Danes and are considered to be unnecessary for economic cooperation.

The finance policy, including the fact that the public deficit was only allowed to amount to a maximum 3 per cent of gross national product, was also considered to be too restrictive and to split the member states up into A and B members (according to whether or not they were able to fulfill these conditions), and at the same time as being a real hindrance for increasing economic cooperation, especially with the new Eastern European democracies.

The EC has also in some cases forced Denmark to lower its ecological standards and to approve laws that Danes do not approve of.

The view of most Danes is that the EC should concentrate on economic matters, should engage in having the internal market realized in all members states, should be more democratic and less bureaucratic and centralistic, and should concern itself with extending economic cooperation to the rest of Europe.

The Danish voting no to the Maastricht agreement was neither an accident nor a mistake. A poll at the end of June 1992 showed that about two-thirds of the population would vote no if they should vote again.

Perspectives of the Danish voting no to the Maastricht agreement

The ratification procedure presented in the Maastricht agreement cannot be executed after the Danish no and Denmark is, and still wants to be, an EC member state based on the Rome Treaty and the Single Market Amendment. From a juridical point of view the Maastricht agreement cannot be realized, but of course political negotiations can loosen the juridical knot.

The interesting perspectives are the development and reactions caused by the Danish no. The EC meeting in Oslo stated that negotiation of the agreement cannot take place. However, it is clear to all that this is not the case; rather, it depends on the reactions, attitudes and decisions of the member states.

In the UK there is increased resistance to the agreement both among Conservative and Labour MP's and a pronounced wish for a referendum.

In Germany, more than 60 professors of economics, among these the former minister Karl Schiller, have warned against the ratification of the agreement. Also the German Länder are against giving up autonomy and sovereignty, and people do not want to replace the Deutschmark with the ECU (Esperanto money, as it often is called in Germany). The paper *Der Stern* conducted a poll and found that the majority of the German population was in favour of a referendum. Count Otto von Lamsdorff, the leader of FDP, has also argued recently for renegotiation.

In France, it has been decided that a referendum will take place in September 1992. In Luxembourg the majority of the population is against European Union citizenship. Also in the other member states debate on the subject has begun.

The Irish referendum in June 1992 did, as expected give a yes result to the Maastricht agreement. Participation in the referendum was low. Jacques Delors participated actively in the debate, threatening the Irish people with isolation even in the UN, with the withdrawal of investments, poverty and other miseries, and promising heavy capital injection and money transfer from the EC if the agreement was accepted by the Irish. This took place in a situation in which the member states, which are supposed to finance the 30 per cent increase of the EC budget, have refused to contribute to such a large increase. When the Danish people listen to such statements many feel proud of Danish democracy and reassured that a 'no' was the only right answer.

Finally, the Danish 'no' has started a process which nobody today knows the end-result of, but I think that I can speak for all Danes when I say that I hope it will provide support for a democracy of the *peoples* of Europe and for widespread and open economic cooperation in Europe.

Index